Prime Ministers an
A Book of Rer

CW01064633

George William Erskine Russell

Alpha Editions

This edition published in 2024

ISBN 9789362092700

Design and Setting By

Alpha Editions

www.alphaedis.com

Email - info@alphaedis.com

Contents

I
PRIME MINISTERS

I

LORD PALMERSTON

I remember ten Prime Ministers, and I know an eleventh. Some have passed beyond earshot of our criticism; but some remain, pale and ineffectual ghosts of former greatness, yet still touched by that human infirmity which prefers praise to blame. It will behove me to walk warily when I reach the present day; but, in dealing with figures which are already historical, one's judgments may be comparatively untrammelled.

I trace my paternal ancestry direct to a Russell who entered the House of Commons at the General Election of 1441, and since 1538 some of us have always sat in one or other of the two Houses of Parliament; so I may be fairly said to have the Parliamentary tradition in my blood. But I cannot profess to have taken any intelligent interest in political persons or doings before I was six years old; my retrospect, therefore, shall begin with Lord Palmerston, whom I can recall in his last Administration, 1859-1865.

I must confess that I chiefly remember his outward characteristics—his large, dyed, carefully brushed whiskers; his broad-shouldered figure, which always seemed struggling to be upright; his huge and rather distorted feet— "each foot, to describe it mathematically, was a four-sided irregular figure"—his strong and comfortable seat on the old white hack which carried him daily to the House of Commons. Lord Granville described him to a nicety: "I saw him the other night looking very well, but old, and wearing a green shade, which he afterwards concealed. He looked like a retired old croupier from Baden."

Having frequented the Gallery of the House of Commons, or the more privileged seats "under the Gallery," from my days of knickerbockers, I often heard Palmerston speak. I remember his abrupt, jerky, rather "bow-wow"-like style, full of "hums" and "hahs"; and the sort of good-tempered but unyielding banter with which he fobbed off an inconvenient enquiry, or repressed the simple-minded ardour of a Radical supporter.

Of course, a boy's attention was attracted rather by appearance and manner than by the substance of a speech; so, for a frank estimate of Palmerston's policy at the period which I am discussing, I turn to Bishop Wilberforce (whom he had just refused to make Archbishop of York).

"That wretched Pam seems to me to get worse and worse. There is not a particle of veracity or noble feeling that I have ever been able to trace in him. He manages the House of Commons by debauching it, making all parties laugh at one another; the Tories at the Liberals, by his defeating all

Liberal measures; the Liberals at the Tories, by their consciousness of getting everything that is to be got in Church and State; and all at one another, by substituting low ribaldry for argument, bad jokes for principle, and an openly avowed, vainglorious, imbecile vanity as a panoply to guard himself from the attacks of all thoughtful men."

But what I remember even more clearly than Palmers ton is appearance or manner—perhaps because it did not end with his death—is the estimation in which he was held by that "Sacred Circle of the Great-Grandmotherhood" to which I myself belong.

In the first place, it was always asserted, with emphasis and even with acrimony, that he was not a Whig. Gladstone, who did not much like Whiggery, though he often used Whigs, laid it down that "to be a Whig a man must be a born Whig," and I believe that the doctrine is absolutely sound. But Palmerston was born and bred a Tory, and from 1807 to 1830 held office in Tory Administrations. The remaining thirty-five years of his life he spent, for the most part, in Whig Administrations, but a Whig he was not. The one thing in the world which he loved supremely was power, and, as long as this was secured, he did not trouble himself much about the political complexion of his associates. "Palmerston does not care how much dirt he eats, so long as it is gilded dirt;" and, if gilded dirt be the right description of office procured by flexible politics, Palmerston ate, in his long career, an extraordinary amount of it.

Then, again, I remember that the Whigs thought Palmerston very vulgar. The newspapers always spoke of him as an aristocrat, but the Whigs knew better. He had been, in all senses of the word, a man of fashion; he had won the nickname of "Cupid," and had figured, far beyond the term of youth, in a raffish kind of smart society which the Whigs regarded with a mixture of contempt and horror. His bearing towards the Queen, who abhorred him—not without good reason—was considered to be lamentably lacking in that ceremonious respect for the Crown which the Whigs always maintained even when they were dethroning Kings. Disraeli likened his manner to that of "a favourite footman on easy terms with his mistress," and one who was in official relations with him wrote: "He left on my recollection the impression of a strong character, with an intellect with a coarse vein in it, verging sometimes on brutality, and of a mind little exercised on subjects of thought beyond the immediate interests of public and private life, little cultivated, and drawing its stores, not from reading but from experience, and long and varied intercourse with men and women."

Having come rather late in life to the chief place in politics, Palmerston kept it to the end. He was an indomitable fighter, and had extraordinary health. At the opening of the Session of 1865 he gave the customary Full-Dress Dinner, and Mr. Speaker Denison,[*] who sat beside him, made this curious memorandum of his performance at table: "He ate two plates of turtle soup; he was then served very amply to cod and oyster sauce; he then took a *pacirc;té*; afterwards he was helped to two very greasy-looking entrées; he then despatched a plate of roast mutton; there then appeared before him the largest, and to my mind the hardest, slice of ham that ever figured on the table of a nobleman, yet it disappeared just in time to answer the enquiry of the butler, 'Snipe or pheasant, my lord?' He instantly replied, 'Pheasant,' thus completing his ninth dish of meat at that meal." A few weeks later the Speaker, in conversation with Palmerston, expressed a hope that he was taking care of his health, to which the octogenarian Premier replied: "Oh yes—indeed I am. I very often take a cab at night, and if you have both windows open it is almost as good as walking home." "Almost as good!" exclaimed the valetudinarian Speaker. "A through draught and a north-east wind! And in a hack cab! What a combination for health!"

[Footnote *: Afterwards Lord Ossington.]

Palmerston fought and won his last election in July, 1865, being then in his eighty-first year, and he died on the 15th of October next ensuing. On the 19th the Queen wrote as follows to the statesman who, as Lord John Russell, had been her Prime Minister twenty years before, and who, as Earl Russell, had been for the last six years Foreign Secretary in Palmerston's Administration: "The Queen can turn to no other than Lord Russell, an old and tried friend of hers, to undertake the arduous duties of Prime Minister and to carry on the Government."

It is sometimes said of my good friend Sir George Trevelyan that his most responsible task in life has been to "live up to the position of being his uncle's nephew." He has made a much better job of his task than I have made of mine; and yet I have never been indifferent to the fact that I was related by so close a tie to the author of the first Reform Bill, and the chief promoter—as regards this country—of Italian unity and freedom.

II

LORD RUSSELL

Lord John Russell was born in 1792, and became Prime Minister for the first time in 1846. Soon after, Queen Victoria, naturally interested in the oncoming generation of statesmen, said to the Premier, "Pray tell me, Lord John, whom do you consider the most promising young man in your party?" After due consideration Lord John replied, "George Byng, ma'am," signifying thereby a youth who eventually became the third Earl of Strafford.

In 1865 Lord John, who in the meantime had been created Earl Russell, became, after many vicissitudes in office and opposition, Prime Minister for the second time. The Queen, apparently hard put to it for conversation, asked him whom he now considered the most promising young man in the Liberal party. He replied, without hesitation, "George Byng, ma'am," thereby eliciting the very natural rejoinder, "But that's what you told me twenty years ago!"

This fragment of anecdotage, whether true or false, is eminently characteristic of Lord Russell. In principles, beliefs, opinions, even in tastes and habits, he was singularly unchanging. He lived to be close on eighty-six; he spent more than half a century in active politics; and it would be difficult to detect in all those years a single deviation from the creed which he professed when, being not yet twenty-one, he was returned as M.P. for his father's pocket-borough of Tavistock.

From first to last he was the staunch and unwavering champion of freedom—civil, intellectual, and religious. At the very outset of his Parliamentary career he said, "We talk much—and think a great deal too much—of the wisdom of our ancestors. I wish we could imitate the courage of our ancestors. They were not ready to lay their liberties at the foot of the Crown upon every vain or imaginary alarm." At the close of life he referred to England as "the country whose freedom I have worshipped, and whose liberties and prosperity I am not ashamed to say we owe to the providence of Almighty God."

This faith Lord Russell was prepared to maintain at all times, in all places, and amid surroundings which have been known to test the moral fibre of more boisterous politicians. Though profoundly attached to the Throne and to the Hanoverian succession, he was no courtier. The year 1688 was his sacred date, and he had a habit of applying the principles of our English Revolution to the issues of modern politics.

Actuated, probably, by some playful desire to probe the heart of Whiggery by putting an extreme case, Queen Victoria once said: "Is it true, Lord John, that you hold that a subject is justified, under certain circumstances, in disobeying his Sovereign?" "Well, ma'am, speaking to a Sovereign of the House of Hanover, I can only say that I suppose it is!"

When Italy was struggling towards unity and freedom, the Queen was extremely anxious that Lord John, then Foreign Secretary, should not encourage the revolutionary party. He promptly referred Her Majesty to "the doctrines of the Revolution of 1688," and informed her that, "according to those doctrines, all power held by Sovereigns may be forfeited by misconduct, and each nation is the judge of its own internal government."

The love of justice was as strongly marked in Lord John Russell as the love of freedom. He could make no terms with what he thought one-sided or oppressive. When the starving labourers of Dorset combined in an association which they did not know to be illegal, he urged that incendiaries in high places, such as the Duke of Cumberland and Lord Wynford, were "far more guilty than the labourers, but the law does not reach them, I fear."

When a necessary reform of the Judicature resisted on the ground of expense, he said:

"If you cannot afford to do justice speedily and well, you may as well shut up the Exchequer and confess that you have no right to raise taxes for the protection of the subject, for justice is the first and primary end of all government."

Those are the echoes of a remote past. My own recollections of my uncle begin when he was Foreign Secretary in Lord Palmerston's Government, and I can see him now, walled round with despatch-boxes, in his pleasant library looking out on the lawn of Pembroke Lodge—the prettiest villa in Richmond Park. In appearance he was very much what *Punch* always represented him—very short, with a head and shoulders which might have belonged to a much larger frame. When sitting he might have been taken for a man of average height, and it was only when he rose to his feet that his diminutive stature became apparent.

One of his most characteristic traits was his voice, which had what, in the satirical writings of the last century, used to be called "an aristocratic drawl," and his pronunciation was archaic. Like other high-bred people of his time, he talked of "cowcumbers" and "laylocks"; called a woman an "oo'man," and was much "obleeged" where a degenerate race is content to be "obliged."

The frigidity of his address and the seeming stiffness of his manner were really due to an innate and incurable shyness, but they produced, even among people who ought to have known him better, a totally erroneous impression of his character and temperament.

In the small social arts, which are so valuable an equipment for a political leader, he was indeed deficient. He had no memory for faces, and was painfully apt to ignore his political supporters when he met them outside the walls of Parliament; and this inability to remember faces was allied with a curious artlessness which made it impossible for him to feign a cordiality he did not feel. In his last illness he said: "I have seemed cold to my friends, but it was not in my heart." The friends needed no such assurance, for in private life he was not only gentle, affectionate, and tender to an unusual degree, but full of fun and playfulness, a genial host and an admirable talker. The great Lord Dufferin, a consummate judge of such matters, said: "His conversation was too delightful, full of anecdote; but then his anecdotes were not like those told by the ordinary raconteur, and were simply reminiscences of his own personal experience and intercourse with other distinguished men."

When Lord Palmerston died, *The Times* was in its zenith, and its editor, J. T. Delane, had long been used to "shape the whispers" of Downing Street. Lord Russell resented journalistic dictation. "I know," he said, "that Mr. Delane is very angry because I did not kiss his hand instead of the Queen's" *The Times* became hostile, and a competent critic remarked:"

"There have been Ministers who knew the springs of that public opinion which is delivered ready digested to the nation every morning, and who have not scrupled to work them for their own diurnal glorification, even although the recoil might injure their colleagues. But Lord Russell has never bowed the knee to the potentates of the Press; he has offered no sacrifice of invitations to social editors; and social editors have accordingly failed to discover the merits of a statesman who so little appreciated them, until they have almost made the nation forget the services that Lord Russell has so faithfully and courageously rendered."

Of Lord Russell's political consistency I have already spoken; and it was most conspicuously displayed in his lifelong zeal for the extension of the suffrage. He had begun his political activities by a successful attack on the rottenest of rotten boroughs; the enfranchisement of the Middle Class was the triumph of his middle life. As years advanced his zeal showed no abatement; again and again he returned to the charge, though amidst the most discouraging circumstances; and when, in his old age, he became

Prime Minister for the second time, the first task to which he set his hand was so to extend the suffrage as to include "the best of the working classes."

In spite of this generous aspiration, it must be confessed that the Reform Bill of 1866 was not a very exciting measure. It lowered the qualification for the county franchise to £14 and that for the boroughs to £7; and this, together with the enfranchisement of lodgers, was expected to add 400,000 new voters to the list.

The Bill fell flat. It was not sweeping enough to arouse enthusiasm. Liberals accepted it as an instalment; but Whigs thought it revolutionary, and made common cause with the Tories to defeat it. As it was introduced into the House of Commons, Lord Russell had no chance of speaking on it; but Gladstone's speeches for it and Lowe's against it remain to this day among the masterpieces of political oratory, and eventually it was lost, on an amendment moved in committee, by a majority of eleven. Lord Russell of course resigned. The Queen received his decision with regret. It was evident that Prussia and Austria were on the brink of war, and Her Majesty considered it a most unfortunate moment for a change in her Government. She thought that the Ministry had better accept the amendment and go on with the Bill. But Lord Russell stood his ground, and that ground was the highest. "He considers that vacillation on such a question weakens the authority of the Crown, promotes distrust of public men, and inflames the animosity of parties."

On the 26th of June, 1866, it was announced in Parliament that the Ministers had resigned, and that the Queen had sent for Lord Derby. Lord Russell retained the Liberal leadership till Christmas, 1867, and then definitely retired from public life, though his interest in political events continued unabated to the end.

Of course, I am old enough to remember very well the tumults and commotions which attended the defeat of the Reform Bill of 1866. They contrasted strangely with the apathy and indifference which had prevailed while the Bill was in progress; but the fact was that a new force had appeared.

The Liberal party had discovered Gladstone; and were eagerly awaiting the much more democratic measure which they thought he was destined to carry in the very near future. That it was really carried by Disraeli is one of the ironies of our political history.

During the years of my uncle's retirement was much more in his company than had been possible when I was a schoolboy and he was Foreign Secretary or Prime Minister. Pembroke Lodge became to me a second home; and I have no happier memory than of hours spent there by the side of one who had played bat, trap and ball with Charles Fox; had been the travelling companion of Lord Holland; had corresponded with Tom Moore, debated with Francis Jeffrey, and dined with Dr. Parr; had visited Melrose Abbey in the company of Sir Walter Scott, and criticized the acting of Mrs. Siddons; had conversed with Napoleon in his seclusion at Elba, and had ridden with the Duke of Wellington along the lines of Torres Vedras. It was not without reason that Lord Russell, when reviewing his career, epitomized it in Dryden couplet:

"Not heaven itself upon the past has power,
But what has been has been, and I have had my hour."

III

LORD DERBY

My opportunities of observing Lord Derby at close quarters, were comparatively scanty. When, in June, 1866, he kissed hands as Prime Minister for the third time, I was a boy of thirteen, and I was only sixteen when he died. I had known Lord Palmerston in the House of Commons and Lord Russell in private life; but my infant footsteps were seldom guided towards the House of Lords, and it was only there that "the Rupert of debate" could at that time be heard.

The Whigs, among whom I was reared, detested Derby with the peculiar detestation which partisans always feel for a renegade. In 1836 Charles Dickens, in his capacity of Parliamentary reporter, had conversed with an ancient M.P. who allowed that Lord Stanley—who became Lord Derby in 1851—might do something one of these days, but "he's too young, sir—too young." The active politicians of the sixties did not forget that this too-young Stanley, heir of a great Whig house, had flung himself with ardour into the popular cause, and, when the Lords threw out the first Reform Bill, had jumped on to the table at Brooks's and had proclaimed the great constitutional truth—reaffirmed over the Parliament Bill in 1911—that "His Majesty can clap coronets on the heads of a whole company of his Foot Guards."

The question of the influences which had changed Stanley from a Whig to a Tory lies outside the purview of a sketch like this. For my present purpose it must suffice to say that, as he had absolutely nothing to gain by the change, we may fairly assume that it was due to conviction. But whether it was due to conviction, or to ambition, or to temper, or to anything else, it made the Whigs who remained Whigs, very sore. Lord Clarendon, a typical Whig placeman, said that Stanley was "a great aristocrat, proud of family and wealth, but had no generosity for friend or foe, and never acknowledged help." Some allowance must be made for the ruffled feelings of a party which sees its most brilliant recruit absorbed into the opposing ranks, and certainly Stanley was such a recruit as any party would have been thankful to claim.

He was the future head of one of the few English families which the exacting genealogists of the Continent recognize as noble. To pedigree he added great possessions, and wealth which the industrial development of Lancashire was increasing every day. He was a graceful and tasteful scholar, who won the Chanceller's prize for Latin verse at Oxford, and translated the Iliad into fluent hexameters. Good as a scholar, he was, as became the grandson of the founder of "The Derby," even better as a sportsman; and in private life he was the best companion in the world, playful and reckless, as a schoolboy, and never letting prudence or propriety stand between him and his jest. "Oh, Johnny, what fun we shall have!" was his characteristic greeting to Lord John Russell, when that ancient rival entered the House of Lords.

Furthermore, Stanley had, in richest abundance, the great natural gift of oratory, with an audacity in debate which won him the nickname of "Rupert," and a voice which would have stirred his hearers if he had only been reciting Bradshaw. For a brilliant sketch of his social aspect we may consult Lord Beaumaris in Lord Beaconsfield's *Endymion*; and of what he was in Parliament we have the same great man's account, reported by Matthew Arnold: "Full of nerve, dash, fire, and resource, he carried the House irresistibly along with him."

In the Parliament of 1859-1865 (with which my political recollections begin) Lord Palmerston was Prime Minister and Lord Derby Leader of the Opposition, with Disraeli as his lieutenant in the House of Commons. If, as Lord Randolph Churchill said in later years, the business of an Opposition is to oppose, it must be admitted that Derby and Disraeli were extremely remiss. It was suspected at the time, and has since been made known through Lord Malmesbury's *Memoirs*, that there was something like an "understanding" between Palmerston and Derby. As long as Palmerston kept his Liberal colleagues in order, and chaffed his Radical supporters out of all the reforms on which their hearts were set, Derby was not to turn him out of office, though the Conservative minority in the House of Commons was very large, and there were frequent openings for harassing attack.

Palmerston's death, of course, dissolved this compact; and, though the General Election of 1865 had again yielded a Liberal majority, the change in the Premiership had transformed the aspect of political affairs. The new Prime Minister was in the House of Lords, seventy-three years old, and not a strong man for his age. His lieutenant in the House of Commons was Gladstone, fifty-five years old, and in the fullest vigour of body and mind. Had any difference of opinion arisen between the two men, it was obvious that Gladstone was in a position to make his will prevail; but on the immediate business of the new Parliament they were absolutely at one, and that business was exactly what Palmerston had for the last six years successfully opposed—the extension of the franchise to the working man. When no one is enthusiastic about a Bill, and its opponents hate it, there is not much difficulty in defeating it, and Derby and Disraeli were not the men to let the opportunity slide. With the aid of the malcontent Whigs they defeated the Reform Bill, and Derby became Prime Minister, with Disraeli as Leader of the House of Commons. It was a conjuncture fraught with consequences vastly more important than anyone foresaw.

In announcing his acceptance of office (which he had obtained by defeating a Reform Bill), Derby amazed his opponents and agitated his friends by saying that he "reserved to himself complete liberty to deal with the question of Parliamentary reform whenever suitable occasion should arise." In February, 1867, Disraeli, on behalf of the Tory Government, brought in the first really democratic Reform Bill which England had ever known. He piloted it through the House of Commons with a daring and a skill of which I was an eye-witness, and, when it went up to the Lords, Derby persuaded his fellow-peers to accept a measure which established household suffrage in the towns.

It was "a revolution by due course of law," nothing less; and to this day people dispute whether Disraeli induced Derby to accept it, or whether the process was reversed. Derby called it "a leap in the dark." Disraeli vaulted that he had "educated his party" up to the point of accepting it. Both alike took comfort in the fact that they had "dished the Whigs"—which, indeed, they had done most effectually. The disgusted Clarendon declared that Derby "had only agreed to the Reform Bill as he would of old have backed a horse at Newmarket. He hates Disraeli, but believes in him as he would have done in an unprincipled trainer: *he wins*—that is all."

On the 15th of August, 1867, the Tory Reform Bill received the Royal Assent, and Derby attained the summit of his career. Inspired by whatever motives, influenced by whatever circumstances, the Tory chief had accomplished that which the most liberal-minded of his predecessors had never even dreamed of doing. He had rebuilt the British Constitution on a democratic foundation.

At this point some account of Lord Derby's personal appearance may be introduced. My impression is that he was only of the middle height, but quite free from the disfigurement of obesity; light in frame, and brisk in movement. Whereas most statesmen were bald, he had an immense crop of curly, and rather untidy, hair and the abundant whiskers of the period. His features were exactly of the type which novelists used to call aristocratic: an aquiline nose, a wide but firmly compressed mouth, and a prominent chin. His dress was, even then, old-fashioned, and his enormous black satin cravat, arranged in I know not how many folds, seemed to be a survival from the days of Count D'Orsay. His air and bearing were such as one expects in a man whose position needs no advertizing; and I have been told that, even in the breeziest moments of unguarded merriment, his chaff was always the chaff of a gentleman.

Lord Beaconsfield, writing to a friend, once said that he had just emerged from an attack of the gout, "of renovating ferocity," and this phrase might have been applied to the long succession of gouty illnesses which were always harassing Lord Derby. Unfortunately, as we advance in life, the "renovating" effects of gout become less conspicuous than its "ferocity;" and Lord Derby, who was born in 1799, was older than his years in 1867. In January and February, 1868, his gout was so severe that it threatened his life. He recovered, but he saw that his health was no longer equal to the strain of office, and on the 24th of February he placed his resignation in the Queen's hands.

But during the year and a half that remained to him he was by no means idle. He had originally broken away from the Whigs on a point which threatened the temporalities of the still-established Church of Ireland; and in the summer of 1868 Gladstone's avowal of the principle of Irish Disestablishment roused all his ire, and seemed to quicken him into fresh life. The General Election was fixed for November, and the Liberal party, almost without exception, prepared to follow Gladstone in his Irish policy. On the 29th of October Bishop Wilberforce noted that Derby was "very keen," and had asked: "What will the Whigs not swallow? Disraeli is very sanguine still about the elections."

The question about the Whigs came comically from the man who had just made the Tories swallow Household Suffrage; and Disraeli's sanguineness was ill-founded. The election resulted in a majority of one hundred for Irish Disestablishment; Disraeli resigned, and Gladstone became for the first time Prime Minister.

The Session of 1869 was devoted to the Irish Bill, and Lord Derby, though on the brink of the grave, opposed the Bill in what some people thought the greatest of his speeches in the House of Lords. He was pale, his voice was feeble, he looked, as he was, a broken man; but he rose to the very height of an eloquence which had already become traditional. His quotation of Meg Merrilies' address to the Laird of Ellangowan, and his application of it to the plight of the Irish Church, were as apt and as moving as anything in English oratory. The speech concluded thus:

"My Lords, I am now an old man, and, like many of your Lordships, I have already passed three score years and ten. My official life is entirely closed; my political life is nearly so; and, in the course of nature, my natural life cannot now be long. That natural life commenced with the bloody suppression of a formidable rebellion in Ireland, which immediately preceded the union between the two countries. And may God grant that its close may not witness a renewal of the one and a dissolution of the other."

This speech was delivered on the 17th of June, 1869, and the speaker died on the 23rd of the following October.

IV

BENJAMIN DISRAEI

I always count it among the happy accidents of my life that I happened to be in London during the summer of 1867. I was going to Harrow in the following September, and for the next five years my chance of hearing Parliamentary debates was small. In the summer of 1866, when the Russell-Gladstone Reform Bill was thrown out, I was in the country, and therefore I had missed the excitement caused by the demolition of the Hyde Park railings, the tears of the terrified Home Secretary, and the litanies chanted by the Reform League under Gladstone's window in Carlton House Terrace. But in 1867 I was in the thick of the fun. My father was the Sergeant-at-Arms attending the House of Commons, and could always admit me to the privileged seats "under the Gallery," then more numerous than now. So it came about that I heard all the most famous debates in Committee on the Tory Reform Bill, and thereby learned for the first time the fascination of Disraeli's genius. The Whigs, among whom I was reared, did not dislike "Dizzy" as they disliked Lord Derby, or as Dizzy himself was disliked by the older school of Tories. But they absolutely miscalculated and misconceived him, treating him as merely an amusing charlatan, whose rococo oratory and fantastic tricks afforded a welcome relief from the dulness of ordinary politics.

To a boy of fourteen thus reared, the Disraeli of 1867 was an astonishment and a revelation—as the modern world would say, an eye-opener. The House of Commons was full of distinguished men—Lord Cranborne, afterwards Lord Salisbury; John Bright and Robert Lowe, Gathorne Hardy, Bernal-Osborne, Goschen, Mill, Kinglake, Renley, Horsman, Coleridge. The list might be greatly prolonged, but of course it culminates in Gladstone, then in the full vigour of his powers. All these people I saw and heard during that memorable summer; but high above them all towers, in my recollection, the strange and sinister figure of the great Disraeli. The Whigs had laughed at him for thirty years; but now, to use a phrase of the nursery, they laughed on the wrong side of their mouths. There was nothing ludicrous about him now, nothing to provoke a smile, except when he wished to provoke it, and gaily unhorsed his opponents of every type—Gladstone, or Lowe, or Beresford-Hope. He seemed, for the moment, to dominate the House of Commons, to pervade it with his presence, and to guide it where he would. At every turn he displayed his reckless audacity, his swiftness in transition, his readiness to throw overboard a stupid colleague, his alacrity to take a hint from an opponent and make it appear his own. The Bill underwent all sorts of changes in Committee; but still it seemed to be Disraeli's Bill, and no one else's. And, indeed, he is entitled to all the credit which he got, for it was his genius that first saw the possibilities hidden in a Tory democracy.

To a boy of fourteen, details of rating, registration, and residential qualification make no strong appeal; but the personality of this strange magician, un-English, inscrutable, irresistible, was profoundly interesting. "Gladstone," wrote Lord Houghton to a friend, "seems quite awed with the diabolical cleverness of Dizzy, who, he says, is gradually driving all ideas of political honour out of the House, and accustoming it to the most revolting cynicism." I had been trained by people who were sensitive about "Political honour," and I knew nothing of "cynicism"; but the "diabolical cleverness" made an impression on me which has lasted to this day.

What was Dizzy in personal appearance? If I had not known the fact, I do not think that I should have recognized him as one of the ancient race of Israel. His profile was not the least what we in England consider Semitic. He might have been a Spaniard or an Italian, but he certainly was not a Briton. He was rather tall than short, but slightly bowed, except when he drew himself up for the more effective delivery of some shrewd blow. His complexion was extremely pale, and the pallor was made more conspicuous by contrast with his hair, steeped in Tyrian dye, worn long, and eked out with artificial additions.

He was very quietly dressed. The green velvet trousers and rings worn outside white kid gloves, which had helped to make his fame in "the days of the dandies," had long since been discarded. He dressed, like other men of his age and class, in a black frock-coat worn open, a waistcoat cut rather deep, light-coloured trousers, and a black cravat tied in a loose bow—and those spring-sided boots of soft material which used to be called "Jemimas." I may remark, in passing, that these details of costume were reproduced with startling fidelity in Mr. Dennis Eadie's wonderful play—the best representation of personal appearance that I have ever seen on the stage.

Disraeli's voice was by nature deep, and he had a knack of deepening it when he wished to be impressive. His articulation was extremely deliberate, so that every word told; and his habitual manner was calm, but not stolid. I say "habitual," because it had variations. When Gladstone, just the other side of the Table, was thundering his protests, Disraeli became absolutely statuesque, eyed his opponent stonily through his monocle, and then congratulated himself, in a kind of stage drawl, that there was a "good broad piece of furniture" between him and the enraged Leader of the Opposition. But when it was his turn to simulate the passion which the other felt, he would shout and wave his arms, recoil from the Table and return to it, and act his part with a vigour which, on one memorable occasion, was attributed to champagne; but this was merely play-acting, and was completely laid aside as he advanced in years.

What I have written so far is, no doubt, an anachronism, for I have been describing what I saw and heard in the Session of 1867, and Disraeli did not become Prime Minister till February, 1868; but six months made no perceptible change in his appearance, speech, or manner. What he had been when he was fighting his Reform Bill through the House, that he was when, as Prime Minister, he governed the country at the head of a Parliamentary minority. His triumph was the triumph of audacity. In 1834 he had said to Lord Melbourne, who enquired his object in life, "I want to be Prime Minister"—and now that object was attained. At Brooks's they said, "The last Government was the Derby; this is the Hoax." Gladstone's discomfiture was thus described by Frederick Greenwood:

"The scorner who shot out the lip and shook the head at him across the Table of the House of Commons last Session has now more than heart could wish; his eyes—speaking in an Oriental manner—stand out with fatness, he speaketh loftily; and pride compasseth him about as with a chain. It is all very well to say that the candle of the wicked is put out in the long run; that they are as stubble before the wind, and as chaff that the storm carries away. So we were told in other times of tribulation. This was the sort of consolation that used to be offered in the jaunty days of Lord Palmerston. People used then to soothe the earnest Liberal by the same kind of argument. 'Only wait,' it was said, 'until he has retired, and all will be well with us.' But no sooner has the storm carried away the wicked Whig chaff than the heavens are forthwith darkened by new clouds of Tory chaff."

Lord Shaftesbury, as became his character, took a sterner view. "Disraeli Prime Minister! He is a Hebrew; this is a good thing. He is a man sprung from an inferior station; another good thing in these days, as showing the liberality of our institutions. But he is a leper, without principle, without feeling, without regard to anything, human or Divine, beyond his own personal ambition."

The situation in which the new Prime Minister found himself was, from the constitutional point of view, highly anomalous. The settlement of the question of Reform, which he had effected in the previous year, had healed the schism in the Liberal party, and the Liberals could now defeat the Government whenever they chose to mass their forces. Disraeli was officially the Leader of a House in which his opponents had a large majority. In March, 1868, Gladstone began his attack on the Irish Church, and pursued it with all his vigour, and with the support of a united party. He moved a series of Resolutions favouring Irish Disestablishment, and the first was carried by a majority of sixty-five against the Government.

This defeat involved explanation. Disraeli, in a speech which Bright called "a mixture of pompousness and servility," described his audiences of the Queen, and so handled the Royal name as to convey the impression that Her Majesty was on his side. Divested of verbiage and mystification, his statement amounted to this—that, in spite of adverse votes, he intended to hold on till the autumn, and then to appeal to the new electorate created by the Reform Act of the previous year. As the one question to be submitted to the electors was that of the Irish Church, the campaign naturally assumed a theological character. On the 20th of August Lord Shaftesbury wrote: "Dizzy is seeking everywhere for support. He is all things to all men, and nothing to anyone. He cannot make up his mind to be Evangelical, Neologian, or Ritualistic; he is waiting for the highest bidder."

Parliament was dissolved in November, and the General Election resulted in a majority of one hundred for Gladstone and Irish Disestablishment. By a commendable innovation on previous practice, Disraeli resigned the Premiership without waiting for a hostile vote of the new Parliament. He declined the Earldom to which, as an ex-Prime Minister, he was by usage entitled; but he asked the Queen to make his devoted wife Viscountess Beaconsfield. As a youth, after hearing the great speakers of the House which he had not yet entered, he had said, "Between ourselves, I could floor them all"—but now Gladstone had "floored" him, and it took him five years to recover his breath.

V

WILLIAM EWART GLADSTONE

Most people remember Gladstone as an old man. He reached the summit of his career when he had just struck seventy. After Easter, 1880, when he dethroned Lord Beaconsfield and formed his second Administration, the eighteen years of life that remained to him added nothing to his fame, and even in some respects detracted from it. Gradually he passed into the stage which was indicated by Labouchere's nickname of "The Grand Old Man"; and he enjoyed the homage which rightly attends the closing period of an exemplary life, wonderfully prolonged, and spent in the service of the nation. He had become historical before he died. But my recollections of him go back to the earlier sixties, when he was Chancellor of the Exchequer in Lord Palmerston's Government, and they become vivid at the point of time when he became Prime Minister—December, 1868.

In old age his appearance was impressive, through the combination of physical wear-and-tear with the unconquerable vitality of the spirit which dwelt within. The pictures of him as a young man represent him as distinctly handsome, with masses of dark hair thrown back from a truly noble forehead, and eyes of singular expressiveness. But in middle life—and in his case middle life was continued till he was sixty—he was neither as good-looking as he once had been, nor, as grand-looking as he eventually became. He looked much older than his age. When he met the new Parliament which had been elected at the end of 1868, he was only as old as Lord Curzon is now; but he looked old enough to be Lord Curzon's father. His life had been, as he was fond of saying, a life of contention; and the contention had left its mark on his face, with its deep furrows and careworn expression. Three years before he had felt, to use his own phrase, "sore with conflicts about the public expenditure" (in which old Palmerston had always beaten him), and to that soreness had been added traces of the fierce strife about Parliamentary Reform and Irish Disestablishment. F. D. Maurice thus described him: "His face is a very expressive one, hard-worked, as you say, and not perhaps specially happy; more indicative of struggle than of victory, though not without promise of that. He has preserved the type which I can remember that he bore at the University thirty-six years ago, though it has undergone curious development."

My own recollection exactly confirms Maurice's estimate. In Gladstone's face, as I used to see it in those days, there was no look of gladness or victory. He had, indeed, won a signal triumph at the General Election of

1868, and had attained the supreme object of a politician's ambition. But he did not look the least as if he enjoyed his honours, but rather as if he felt an insupportable burden of responsibility. He knew that he had an immense amount to do in carrying the reforms which Palmerston had burked, and, coming to the Premiership on the eve of sixty, he realized that the time for doing it was necessarily short. He seemed consumed by a burning and absorbing energy; and, when he found himself seriously hampered or strenuously opposed, he was angry with an anger which was all the more formidable because it never vented itself in an insolent or abusive word. A vulnerable temper kept resolutely under control had always been to me one of the most impressive features in human character.

Gladstone had won the General Election by asking the constituencies to approve the Disestablishment of the Irish Church; and this was the first task to which he addressed himself in the Parliament of 1869. It was often remarked about his speaking that in every Session he made at least one speech of which everyone said, "That was the finest thing Gladstone ever did." This was freely said of it he speech in which he introduced the Disestablishment Bill on the 1st of March, 1869, and again of that in which he wound up the debate on the Second Reading. In pure eloquence he had rivals, and in Parliamentary management superiors; but in the power of embodying principles in legislative form and preserving unity of purpose through a multitude of confusing minutiæ he had neither equal nor second.

The Disestablishment Bill passed easily through the Commons, but was threatened with disaster in the Lords, and it was with profound satisfaction that Mrs. Gladstone, most devoted and most helpful of wives, announced the result of the division on the Second Reading. Gladstone had been unwell, and had gone to bed early. Mrs. Gladstone who had been listening to the debate in the House of Lords, said to a friend, "I could not help it; I gave William a discreet poke. 'A majority of thirty-three, my dear.' 'Thank you, my dear,' he said, and turned round, and went to sleep on the other side." After a stormy passage through Committee, the Bill became law on the 26th of July.

So Gladstone's first great act of legislation ended, and he was athirst for more. Such momentous reforms as the Irish Land Act, the Education Act, the abolition of religious tests in the University, the abolition of purchase in the Army, and the establishment of the Ballot, filled Session after Session with excitement; and Gladstone pursued each in turn with an ardour which left his followers out of breath.

He was not very skilful in managing his party, or even his Cabinet. He kept his friendships and his official relations quite distinct. He never realized the force of the saying that men who have only worked together have only half lived together. It was truly said that he understood MAN, but not men; and meek followers in the House of Commons, who had sacrificed money, time, toil, health, and sometimes conscience, to the support of the Government, turned, like the crushed worm, when they found that Gladstone sternly ignored their presence in the Lobby, or, if forced to speak to them, called them by inappropriate names. His strenuousness of reforming purpose and strength of will were concealed by no lightness of touch, no give-and-take, no playfulness, no fun. He had little of that saving grace of humour which smoothes the practical working of life as much as it adds to its enjoyment. He was fiercely, terribly, incessantly in earnest; and unbroken earnestness, though admirable, exhausts and in the long run alienates.

There was yet another feature of his Parliamentary management which proved disastrous to his cause, and this was his tendency to what the vulgar call hair-splitting and the learned casuistry. At Oxford men are taught to distinguish with scrupulous care between propositions closely similar, but not identical. In the House of Commons they are satisfied with the roughest and broadest divisions between right and wrong; they see no shades of colour between black-and white. Hence arose two unfortunate incidents, which were nicknamed "The Ewelme Scandal" and "The Colliery Explosion"—two cases in which Gladstone, while observing the letter of an Act of Parliament, violated, or seemed to violate, its spirit in order to qualify highly deserving gentlemen for posts to which he wished to appoint them. By law the Rectory of Ewelme (in the gift of the Crown) could only be held by a graduate of the University of Oxford. Gladstone conferred it on a Cambridge man, who had to procure an *ad eundem* degree at Oxford before he could accept the preferment. By law no man could be made a paid member of the Judicial Committee of the Privy Council unless he had served as a judge. Gladstone made his Attorney-General, Sir John Collier, a Judge for three weeks, and then passed him on to the Judicial Committee. Both these appointments were angrily challenged in Parliament. Gladstone defended them with energy and skill, and logically his defence was unassailable. But these were cases where the plain man—and the House of Commons is full of plain men—feels, though he cannot prove, that there has been a departure from ordinary straightforwardness and fair dealing.

Yet again; the United States had a just complaint against us; arising out of the performances of the *Alabama*, which, built in an English dockyard and manned by an English crew, but owned by the Slaveowners' Confederacy, had got out to sea, and, during a two years' cruise of piracy and devastation, had harassed the Government of the United States. The quarrel had lasted for years, with ever-increasing gravity. Gladstone determined to end it; and, with that purpose, arranged for a Board of Arbitration, which sat at

Geneva, and decided against England. We were heavily amerced by the sentence of this International Tribunal. We paid, but we did not like it. Gladstone gloried in the moral triumph of a settlement without bloodshed; but a large section of the nation, including many of his own party, felt that national honour had been lowered, and determined to avenge themselves on the Minister who had lowered it.

Meanwhile Disraeli, whom Gladstone had deposed in 1868, was watching the development of these events with sarcastic interest and effective criticism, till in 1872 he was able to liken the great Liberal, Government to "a range of exhausted volcanoes," and to say of its eminent leader that he "alternated between a menace and a sigh." In 1873 Gladstone introduced a wholly unworkable Bill for the reform of University education in Ireland. It pleased no one, and was defeated on the Second Reading. Gladstone resigned. The Queen sent for Disraeli; but Disraeli declined to repeat the experiment of governing the country without a majority in the House of Commons, and Gladstone was forced to resume office, though, of course, with immensely diminished authority. His Cabinet was all at sixes and sevens. There were resignations and rumours of resignation. He took the Chancellorship of the Exchequer, and, as some authorities contended, vacated his seat by doing so. Election after election went wrong, and the end was visibly at hand.

At the beginning of 1874 Gladstone, confined to his house by a cold, executed a *coup d'état*. He announced the Dissolution of Parliament, and promised, if his lease of power were renewed, to repeal the income-tax. *The Times* observed: "The Prime Minister descends upon Greenwich" (where he had taken refuge after being expelled from South Lancashire) "amid a shower of gold, and must needs prove as irresistible as the Father of the Gods." But this was too sanguine a forecast. Greenwich, which returned two members, placed Gladstone second on the poll, below a local distiller, while his followers were blown out of their seats like chaff before the wind. When the General Election was over, the Tories had a majority of forty-six. Gladstone, after some hesitation, resigned without waiting to meet a hostile Parliament. Disraeli became Prime Minister for the second time; and in addressing the new House of Commons he paid a generous compliment to his great antagonist. "If," he said, "I had been a follower of a Parliamentary chief so eminent, even if I thought he had erred, I should have been disposed rather to exhibit sympathy than to offer criticism. I should remember the great victories which he had fought and won; I should remember his illustrious career; its continuous success and splendour, not its accidental or even disastrous mistakes."

The roost loyal Gladstonian cannot improve upon that tribute, and Gladstone's greatest day was yet to come.

VI

LORD SALISBURY

This set of sketches is not intended for a continuous narrative, but for a series of impressions. I must therefore condense the events of Disraeli's second Administration (during which he became Lord Beaconsfield) and of Gladstone's Administration which succeeded it, hurrying to meet Lord Salisbury, whom so far I have not attempted to describe.

From February, 1874, to May, 1880, Disraeli was not only in office, but, for the first time, in power; for whereas in his first Administration he was confronted by a hostile majority in the House of Commons, he now had a large majority of his own, reinforced, on every critical division, by renegade Whigs and disaffected Radicals. He had, as no Minister since Lord Melbourne had, the favour and friendship, as well as the confidence, of the Queen. The House of Lords and the London mob alike were at his feet, and he was backed by a noisy and unscrupulous Press.

In short, he was as much a dictator as the then existing forms of the Constitution allowed, and he gloried in his power. If only he had risked a Dissolution on his triumphal return from Berlin in July, 1878, he would certainly have retained his dictatorship for life; but his health had failed, and his nerve failed with it. "I am very unwell," he said to Lord George Hamilton, "but I manage to crawl to the Treasury Bench, and when I get there I look as fierce as I can."

Meanwhile Gladstone was not only "looking fierce," but agitating fiercely. After his great disappointment in 1874 he had abruptly retired from the leadership of the Liberal party, and had divided his cast-off mantle between Lord Granville and Lord Hartington. But the Eastern Question of 1876-1879 brought him back into the thick of the fight. Granville and Hartington found themselves practically dispossessed of their respective leaderships, and Gladstonianism dominated the active and fighting section of the Liberal party.

It is impossible to conceive a more passionate or a more skilful opposition than that with which Gladstone, to use his own phrase, "counter-worked the purpose of Lord Beaconsfield" from 1876 to 1880— and he attained his object. Lord Beaconsfield, like other Premiers nearer our own time, imagined that he was indispensable and invulnerable. Gladstone might harangue, but Beaconsfield would still govern. He told the Queen that she might safely go abroad in March, 1880, for, though there was a Dissolution impending, he knew that the country would support him. So the Queen went off in perfect ease of mind, and returned in three weeks' time to find a Liberal majority of one hundred, excluding the Irish members, with Gladstone on the crest of the wave. Lord Beaconsfield resigned without waiting for the verdict of the new Parliament. Gladstone, though the Queen had done all she could to persuade Hartington to form a Government, was found to be inevitable, and his second Administration was formed on the 28th of April, 1880. It lasted till the 25th of June, 1885, and, its achievements, its failures, and its disasters are too well remembered to need recapitulation here.

When, after a defeat on the Budget of 1885, Gladstone determined to resign, it was thought by some that Sir Stafford Northcote, who had led the Opposition in the House of Commons with skill and dignity, would be called to succeed him. But the Queen knew better; and Lord Salisbury now became Prime Minister for the first time. To all frequenters of the House of Commons he had long been a familiar, if not a favourite, figure: first as Lord Robert Cecil and then as Lord Cranborne. In the distant days of Palmerston's Premiership he was a tall, slender, ungainly young man, stooping as short-sighted people always stoop, and curiously untidy. His complexion was unusually dark for an Englishman, and his thick beard and scanty hair were intensely black. Sitting for a pocket-borough, he soon became famous for his anti-democratic zeal and his incisive speech. He joined Lord Derby's Cabinet in 1866, left it on-account of his hostility to the Reform Bill of 1867, and assailed Disraeli both with pen and tongue in a fashion which seemed to make it impossible that the two men could ever again speak to one another—let alone work together. But political grudges are short-lived; or perhaps it would be nearer the mark to say that, however strong those grudges may be, the allurements of office are stronger still. Men conscious of great powers for serving the State will often put up with a good deal which they dislike sooner than decline an opportunity of public usefulness.

Whatever the explanation, the fact remains that Lord Salisbury (who had succeeded to the title in 1868) joined Disraeli's Cabinet in 1874, and soon became a leading figure in it. His oratorical duels with the Duke of Argyll during the Eastern Question of 1876-1879 were remarkably, vigorous performances; and, when he likened a near kinsman to Titus Oates, there were some who regretted that the days of physical duelling were over. In 1878 he accompanied Lord Beaconsfield to the Congress of Berlin, being second Plenipotentiary; and when on their return he drove through the acclaiming streets of London in the back seat of the Triumphal Car, it was generally surmised that he had established his claim to the ultimate reversion of the Premiership. That reversion, as I said just now, he attained in June, 1885, and enjoyed till February, 1886—a short tenure of office, put the earnest of better and longer things to come.

At this period of His career Lord Salisbury was forced to yield to the democratic spirit so far as to "go on the stump" and address popular audiences in great towns. It was an uncongenial employment. His myopia rendered the audience invisible, and no one can talk effectively to hearers whom he does not see. The Tory working men bellowed "For he's a jolly good fellow"; but he looked singularly unlike that festive character. His voice was clear and penetrating, but there was no popular fibre in his speech. He talked of the things which interested him; but whether or not they interested his hearers he seemed not to care a jot. When he rolled off the platform and into the carriage which was to carry him away, there was a general sense of mutual relief.

But in the House of Lords he was perfectly and strikingly at home. The massive bulk, which had replaced the slimness of his youth, and his splendidly developed forehead made him there, as everywhere, a majestic figure. He neither saw, nor apparently regarded, his audience. He spoke straight up to the Reporters' Gallery, and, through it, to the public. To his immediate surroundings he seemed as profoundly indifferent as to his provincial audiences. He spoke without notes and apparently without effort. There was no rhetoric, no declamation, no display. As one listened, one seemed to hear the genuine thoughts of a singularly clever and reflective man, who had strong prejudices of his own in favour of religion, authority, and property, but was quite unswayed by the prejudices of other people. The general tone of his thought was sombre. Lord Lytton described, with curious exactness, the "massive temple," the "large slouching shoulder," and the "prone head," which "habitually stoops"—

> "Above a world his contemplative gaze
> Peruses, finding little there to praise!"

But though he might find little enough to "praise" in a world which had departed so widely from the traditions of his youth, still, this prevailing gloom was lightened, often at very unexpected moments, by flashes of delicious humour, sarcastic but not savage. No one excelled him in the art of making an opponent look ridiculous. Careless critics called him "cynical," but it was an abuse of words. Cynicism is shamelessness, and not a word ever fell from Lord Salisbury which was inconsistent with the highest ideals of patriotic statesmanship.

He was by nature as shy as he was short-sighted. He shrank from new acquaintances, and did not always detect old friends. His failure to recognize a young politician who sat in his Cabinet, and a zealous clergyman whom he had just made a Bishop, supplied his circle with abundant mirth, which was increased when, at the beginning of the South African War, he was seen deep in military conversation with Lord Blyth, under the impression that he was talking to Lord Roberts.

But, in spite of these impediments to social facility, he was an admirable host both at Hatfield and in Arlington Street—courteous, dignified, and only anxious to put everyone at their ease. His opinions were not mine, and it always seemed to me that he was liable to be swayed by stronger wills than his own. But he was exactly what he called Gladstone, "a great Christian statesman."

VII

LORD ROSEBERY

It was in December, 1885, that the present Lord Gladstone; in conjunction with the late Sir Wemyss Reid, sent up "the Hawarden Kite." After a lapse of thirty-two years, that strange creature is still flapping about in a stormy sky; and in the process of time it has become a familiar, if not an attractive, object. But the history of its earlier gyrations must be briefly recalled.

The General Election of 1885 had just ended in a tie, the Liberals being exactly equal to the combined Tories and Parnellites. Suddenly the Liberals found themselves committed, as far as Gladstone could commit them, to the principle of Home Rule, which down to that time they had been taught to denounce. Most of them followed their leader, but many rebelled. The Irish transferred their votes in the House to the statesman whom—as they thought—they had squeezed into compliance with their policy, and helped him to evict Lord Salisbury after six months of office. Gladstone formed a Government, introduced a Home Rule Bill, split his party in twain, was defeated in the House of Commons, dissolved Parliament, and was soundly beaten at the General Election which he had precipitated. Lord Salisbury became Prime Minister for the second time, and ruled, with great authority and success, till the summer of 1892.

Meanwhile, Gladstone, by his indefatigable insistence on Home Rule and by judicious concessions to opponents, had to some extent repaired the damage done in 1886; but not sufficiently. Parliament was dissolved in June, 1892, and, when the Election was over, the Liberals, *plus* the Irish, made a majority of forty for Home Rule. Gladstone realized that this majority, even if he could hold it together, had no chance of coercing the House of Lords into submission; but he considered himself bound in honour to form a Government and bring in a second Home Rule Bill. Lord Rosebery became his Foreign Secretary, and Sir William Harcourt his Chancellor of the Exchequer. The Home Rule Bill struggled through the House of Commons, but was thrown out in the Lords, 41 voting for and 419 against it. Not a single meeting was held to protest against this decisive action of the Lords, and it was evident that the country was sick to death of the Irish Question.

Gladstone knew that his public work was done, and in the spring of 1894 it began to be rumoured that he was going to resign. On the 1st of March he delivered his last speech in the House of Commons, and immediately afterwards it became known that he was really resigning. The next day he went to dine and sleep at Windsor, taking his formal letter of resignation with him. He had already arranged with the Queen that a Council should be held on the 3rd of March. At this moment he thought it possible that the Queen might consult him about the choice of his successor, and, as we now know from Lord Morley's "Life," he had determined to recommend Lord Spencer.

Lord Harcourt's evidence on this point is interesting. According to him— and there could not be a better authority—Sir William Harcourt knew of Gladstone's intention. But he may very well have believed that the Queen would act (as in the event she did) on her own unaided judgment, and that her choice would fall on him as Leader of the House of Commons. The fact that he was summoned to attend the Council on the 3rd of March would naturally confirm the belief. But *Dis aliter visum.* After the Council the Queen sent, through the Lord President (Lord Kimberley), a summons to Lord Rosebery, who kissed hands as Prime Minister at Buckingham Palace on the 9th of March.

Bulwer-Lytton, writing "about political personalities, said with perfect truth:

> "Ne'er of the living can the living judge,
> Too blind the affection, or too fresh the grudge."

In this case, therefore, I must attempt not judgment but narrative. Lord Rosebery was born under what most people would consider lucky stars. He inherited an honourable name, a competent fortune, and abilities far above the average. But his father died when he was a child, and as soon as he struck twenty-one he was "Lord of himself, that heritage of woe."

At Eton he had attracted the notice of his gifted tutor, "Billy Johnson," who described him as "one of those who like the palm without the dust," and predicted that he would "be an orator, and, if not a poet, such a man as poets delight in." It was a remarkably shrewd prophecy. From Eton to Christ Church the transition was natural. Lord Rosebery left Oxford without a degree, travelled, went into society, cultivated the Turf, and bestowed some of his leisure on the House of Lords. He voted for the Disestablishment of the Irish Church, and generally took the line of what was then considered advanced Liberalism.

But it is worthy of note that the first achievement which brought him public fame was not political. "Billy Rogers," the well-known Rector of Bishopsgate, once said to me: "The first thing which made me think that Rosebery had real stuff in him was finding him hard at work in London in August, when everyone else was in a country-house or on the Moors. He was getting up his Presidential Address for the Social Science Congress at Glasgow in 1874." Certainly, it was an odd conjuncture of persons and interests. The Social Science Congress, now happily defunct, had been founded by that omniscient charlatan, Lord Brougham, and its gatherings were happily described by Matthew Arnold: "A great room in one of our dismal provincial towns; dusty air and jaded afternoon light; benches full of men with bald heads, and women in spectacles; and an orator lifting up his face from a manuscript written within and without." One can see the scene. On this occasion the orator was remarkably unlike his audience, being only twenty-seven, very young-looking even for that tender age, smartly dressed and in a style rather horsy than professorial. His address, we are told, "did not cut very deep, but it showed sympathetic study of social conditions, it formulated a distinct yet not extravagant programme, and it abounded in glittering phrases."

Henceforward Lord Rosebery was regarded as a coming man, and his definite adhesion to Gladstone on the Eastern Question of 1876-1879 secured him the goodwill of the Liberal party. The year 1878, important in politics, was not less important in Lord Rosebery's career. Early in the year he made a marriage which turned him into a rich man, and riches, useful everywhere, are specially useful in politics. Towards the close of it he persuaded the Liberal Association of Midlothian to adopt Gladstone as their candidate. There is no need to enlarge on the importance of a decision which secured the Liberal triumph of 1880, and made Gladstone Prime Minister for the second time.

When Gladstone formed his second Government he offered a place in it to Lord Rosebery, who, with sound judgment, declined what might have looked like a reward for services just rendered. In 1881 he consented to take the Under-Secretaryship of the Home Department, with Sir William Harcourt as his chief; but the combination did not promise well, and ended rather abruptly in 1883. When the Liberal Government was in the throes of dissolution, Lord Rosebery returned to it, entering the Cabinet as Lord Privy Seal in 1885. It was just at this moment that Matthew Arnold, encountering him in a country-house, thus described him: "Lord Rosebery is very gay and 'smart,' and I like him very much."

The schism over Home Rule was now approaching, and, when it came, Lord Rosebery threw in his lot with Gladstone, becoming Foreign Secretary in February, 1886, and falling with his chief in the following summer. In 1889 he was chosen Chairman of the first London County Council, and there did the best work of his life, shaping that powerful but amorphous body into order and efficiency. Meanwhile, he was, by judicious speech and still more judicious silence, consolidating his political position; and before he joined Gladstone's last Government in August, 1892, he had been generally recognized as the exponent of a moderate and reasonable Home Rule and an advocate of Social Reform. My own belief is that the Liberal party as a whole, and the Liberal Government in particular, rejoiced in the decision which, on Gladstone's final retirement, made Rosebery Prime Minister.

But it was a difficult and disappointing Premiership. Harcourt, not best pleased by the Queen's choice, was Chancellor of the Exchequer and Leader of the House of Commons. Gladstone, expounding our Parliamentary system to the American nation, once said: "The overweight of the House of Commons is apt, other things being equal, to bring its Leader inconveniently near in power to a Prime Minister who is a Peer. He can play off the House of Commons against his chief, and instances might be cited, though they are happily most rare, when he has served him very ugly tricks."

The Parliamentary achievement of 1894 was Harcourt's masterly Budget, with which, naturally, Lord Rosebery had little to do; the Chancellor of the Exchequer loomed larger and larger, and the Premier vanished more and more completely from the public view. After the triumph of the Budget, everything went wrong with the Government, till, being defeated on a snap division about gunpowder in June, 1895, Lord Rosebery and his colleagues trotted meekly out of office. They might have dissolved, but apparently were afraid to challenge the judgment of the country on the performances of the last three years.

Thus ingloriously ended a Premiership of which much had been expected. It was impossible not to be reminded of Goderich's "transient and embarrassed phantom"; and the best consolation which I could offer to my dethroned chief was to remind him that he had been Prime Minister for fifteen months, whereas Disraeli's first Premiership had only lasted for ten.

VIII

AUTHUR JAMES BALFOUR

When Lord Rosebery brought his brief Administration to an end, Lord Salisbury became Prime Minister for the last time. His physical energy was no longer what it once had been, and the heaviest of all bereavements, which befell him in 1899, made the burden of office increasingly irksome. He retired in 1902, and was succeeded by his nephew, Mr. A. J. Balfour, The Administration formed in 1895 had borne some resemblance to a family party, and had thereby invited ridicule—even, in some quarters, created disaffection. But when Lord Salisbury was nearing the close of his career, the interests of family and of party were found to coincide, and everybody felt that Mr. Balfour must succeed him. Indeed, the transfer of power from uncle to nephew was so quietly effected that the new Prime Minister had kissed hands before the general public quite realized that the old one had disappeared.

Mr. Balfour had long been a conspicuous and impressive figure in public life. With a large estate and a sufficient fortune, with the Tory leader for his uncle, and a pocket-borough bidden by that uncle to return him, he had obvious qualifications for political success. He entered Parliament in his twenty-sixth year, at the General Election of 1874, and his many friends predicted great performances. But for a time the fulfilment of those predictions hung fire. Disraeli was reported to have said, after scrutinizing his young follower's attitude: "I never expect much from a man who sits on his shoulders."

Beyond some rather perplexed dealings with the unpopular subject of Burial Law, the Member for Hertford took no active part in political business. At Cambridge he had distinguished himself in Moral Science. This was an unfortunate distinction. Classical scholarship had been traditionally associated with great office, and a high wrangler was always credited with hardheadedness; but "Moral Science" was a different business, not widely understood, and connected in the popular mind with metaphysics and general vagueness. The rumour went abroad that Lord Salisbury's promising nephew was busy with matters which lay quite remote from politics, and was even following the path of perilous speculation. It is a first-rate instance of our national inclination to talk about books without reading them that, when Mr. Balfour published *A Defence of Philosophic Doubt*, everyone rushed to the conclusion that he was championing agnosticism. His friends went about looking very solemn, and those who disliked him piously hoped that all this "philosophic doubt" might not end in atheism. It was not till he had consolidated his position as a political leader that politicians read the book, and then discovered, to their delight, that, in spite of its alarming name, it was an essay in orthodox apologetic.

The General Election of 1880 seemed to alter the drift of Mr. Balfour's thought and life. It was said that he still was very philosophical behind the scenes, but as we saw him in the House of Commons he was only an eager and a sedulous partisan. Gladstone's overwhelming victory at the polls put the Tories on their mettle, and they were eager to avenge the dethronement of their Dagon. "The Fourth Party" was a birth of this eventful time, and its history has been written by the sons of two of its members. With the performances of Lord Randolph Churchill, Sir John Gorst, and Sir Henry Drummond Wolff I have no concern; but the fourth member of the party was Mr. Balfour, who now, for the first time, began to take a prominent part in public business. I must be forgiven if I say that, though he was an admirable writer, it was evident that Nature had not intended him for a public speaker. Even at this distance of time I can recall his broken sentences, his desperate tugs at the lapel of his coat, his long pauses in search of a word, and his selection of the wrong word after all.

But to the Fourth Party, more than to any other section of the House, was due that defeat over the Budget which, in June, 1885, drove Gladstone from power and enthroned Lord Salisbury. In the new Administration Mr. Balfour was, of course, included, but his sphere of work was the shady seclusion of the Local Government Board, and, for anything that the public knew of his doings, he might have been composing a second treatise on philosophic doubt or unphilosophic cocksureness. The General Election of 1885 marked a stage in his career. The pocket-borough which he had represented since 1874 was merged, and he courageously betook himself to Manchester, where for twenty years he faced the changes and chances of popular election.

The great opportunity of his life came in 1887. The Liberal party, beaten on Home Rule at the Election of 1886, was now following its leader into new and strange courses. Ireland was seething with lawlessness, sedition, and outrage. The Liberals, in their new-found zeal for Home Rule, thought it necessary to condone or extenuate all Irish crime; and the Irish party in the House of Commons was trying to make Parliamentary government impossible.

At this juncture Mr, Balfour became Chief Secretary; and his appointment was the signal for a volume of criticism, which the events of the next four years proved to be ludicrously inapposite. He, was likened to a young lady—"Miss Balfour," "Clara," and "Lucy"; he was called "a palsied, masher" and "a perfumed popinjay"; he was accused of being a recluse, a philosopher, and a pedant; he was pronounced incapable of holding his own in debate, and even more obviously unfit for the rough-and-tumble of Irish administration.

The Irish, party, accustomed to triumph over Chief Secretaries, rejoicingly welcomed a new victim in Mr. Balfour. They found, for the first time, a master. Never was such a tragic disillusionment. He armed himself with anew Crimes Act, which had the special merit of not expiring at a fixed period, but of enduring till it should be repealed, and he soon taught sedition-mongers, Irish and English, that he did not bear this sword in vain. Though murderous threats were rife, he showed an absolute disregard for personal danger, and ruled Ireland with a strong and dexterous hand. His administration was marred by want of human sympathy, and by some failure to discriminate between crime and disorder. The fate of John Mandeville is a black blot on the record of Irish government; and it did not stand alone.

Lord Morley, who had better reasons than most people to dread Mr. Balfour's prowess, thus described it:

"He made no experiments in judicious mixture, hard blows and soft speech, but held steadily to force and tear.... In the dialectic of senate and platform he displayed a strength of wrist, a rapidity, an instant readiness for combat, that took his foes by surprise, and roused in his friends a delight hardly surpassed in the politics of our day."

It is not my business to attack or defend. I only record the fact that Mr. Balfour's work in Ireland established his position as the most important member of the Conservative party. In 1891 he resigned the Chief Secretaryship, and became Leader of the House; was an eminently successful Leader of Opposition between 1892 and 1895; and, as I said before, was the obvious and unquestioned heir to the Premiership which Lord Salisbury laid down in 1902.

As Prime Minister Mr. Balfour had no opportunity for exercising his peculiar gift of practical administration, and only too much opportunity for dialectical ingenuity. His faults as a debater had always been that he loved to "score," even though the score might be obtained by a sacrifice of candour, and that he seemed often to argue merely for arguing's sake. It was said of the great Lord Holland that he always put his opponent's case better than the opponent put it for himself. No one ever said this of Mr. Balfour; and his tendency to sophistication led Mr. Humphrey Paul to predict that his name "would always be had in honour wherever hairs were split." His manner and address (except when he was debating) were always courteous and conciliatory; those who were brought into close contact with him liked him, and those who worked under him loved him. Socially, he was by no means as expansive as the leader of a party should be. He was surrounded by an adoring clique, and reminded one of the dignitaries satirized by Sydney Smith: "They live in high places with high people, or with little people who depend upon them. They walk delicately, like Agag. They hear only one sort of conversation, and avoid bold, reckless men, as a lady veils herself from rough breezes."

But, unfortunately, a Prime Minister, though he may "avoid" reckless men, cannot always escape them, and may sometimes be forced to count them among his colleagues. Lord Rosebery's Administration was sterilized partly by his own unfamiliarity with Liberal sentiment, and partly by the frowardness of his colleagues. Mr. Balfour knew all about Conservative sentiment, so far as it is concerned with order, property, and religion; but he did not realize the economic heresy which always lurks in the secret heart of Toryism; and it was his misfortune to have as his most important colleague a "bold, reckless man" who realized that heresy, and was resolved to work it for his own ends. From the day when Mr. Chamberlain launched his scheme, or dream, of Tariff Reform, Mr. Balfour's authority steadily declined. Endless ingenuity in dialectic, nimble exchanges of posture, candid disquisition for the benefit of the well-informed, impressive phrase-making for the bewilderment of the ignorant—these and a dozen other arts were tried in vain. People began to laugh at the Tory leader, and likened him to Issachar crouching down between two burdens, or to that moralist who said that he always sought "the narrow path which lies between right and wrong." His colleagues fell away from him, and he was unduly ruffled by their secession. "It is time," exclaimed the Liberal leader, "to have done with this fooling"; and though he was blamed by the Balfourites for his abruptness of speech, the country adopted his opinion. Gradually it seemed to dawn on Mr. Balfour that his position was no longer tenable. He slipped out of office as quietly as he had slipped into it; and the Liberal party entered on its ten years' reign.

IX

HENRY CAMPBELL-BANNERMAN

"He put his country first, his party next, and himself last." This, the noblest eulogy which can be pronounced upon a politician, was strikingly applicable to my old and honoured friend whose name stands at the head of this page. And yet, when applied to him, it might require a certain modification, for, in his view, the interests of his country and the interests of his party were almost synonymous terms—so profoundly was he convinced that freedom is the best security for national welfare. When he was entertained at dinner by the Reform Club on his accession to the Premiership, he happened to catch my eye while he was speaking, and he interjected this remark: "I see George Russell there. He is by birth, descent, and training a Whig; but he is a little more than a Whig." Thus describing me he described himself. He was a Whig who had marched with the times from Whiggery to Liberalism; who had never lagged an inch behind his party, but who did not, as a rule, outstep it. His place was, so to speak, in the front line of the main body, and every forward movement found him ready and eager to take his place in it. His chosen form of patriotism was a quiet adhesion to the Liberal party, with a resolute and even contemptuous avoidance of sects and schisms.

He was born in 1836, of a mercantile family which had long flourished in Glasgow, and in 1872 he inherited additional wealth, which transformed his name from Campbell to Campbell-Bannerman—the familiar "C.-B." of more recent times. Having graduated from Trinity College, Cambridge, he entered Parliament as Member for the Stirling Burghs in 1868, and was returned by the same delightful constituency till his death, generally without a contest. He began official life in Gladstone's first Administration as Financial Secretary to the War Office, and returned to the same post after the Liberal victory of 1880. One of the reasons for putting him there was that his tact, good sense, and lightness in hand enabled him to work harmoniously with the Duke of Cambridge—a fiery chief who was not fond of Liberals, and abhorred prigs and pedants. In 1884, when Sir George Trevelyan was promoted to the Cabinet, Campbell-Bannerman was made Chief Secretary for Ireland, and in that most difficult office acquitted himself with notable success. Those were not the days of "the Union of Hearts," and it was not thought necessary for a Liberal Chief Secretary to slobber over murderers and outrage-mongers. On the other hand, the iron system of coercion, which Mr. Balfour administered so unflinchingly, had not been invented; and the Chief Secretary had to rely chiefly on his own resources of firmness, shrewdness, and good-humour. With these Campbell-Bannerman was abundantly endowed, and his demeanour in the House of Commons was singularly well adapted to the situation. When the Irish members insulted him, he turned a deaf ear. When they pelted him with controversial questions, he replied with brevity. When they lashed themselves into rhetorical fury, he smiled and "sat tight" till the storm was over. He was not a good speaker, and he had no special skill in debate; but he invariably mastered the facts of his case. He neither overstated nor understated, and he was blessed with a shrewd and sarcastic humour which befitted his comfortable aspect, and spoke in his twinkling eyes even when he restrained his tongue.

The Liberal Government came to an end in June, 1885. The "Home Rule split" was now nigh at hand, and not even Campbell-Bannerman's closest friends could have predicted the side which he would take. On the one hand, there was his congenital dislike of rant and gush, of mock-heroics and mock-pathetics; there was his strong sense for firm government, and there was his recent experience of Irish disaffection. These things might have tended to make him a Unionist, and he had none of those personal idolatries which carried men over because Mr. Gladstone, or Lord Spencer, or Mr. Morley had made the transition. On the other hand, there was his profound conviction—which is indeed the very root of Whiggery—that each nation has the right to choose its own rulers, and that no government is legitimate unless it rests on the consent of the governed.

This conviction prevailed over all doubts and difficulties, and before long it became known that Campbell-Bannerman had, in his own phrase, "found salvation." There were those who were scandalized when they heard the language of Revivalism thus applied, but it exactly hit the truth as regards a great many of the converts to Home Rule. In a very few cases—*e.g.*, in Gladstone's own—there had peen a gradual approximation to the idea of Irish autonomy, and the crisis of December, 1885, gave the opportunity of avowing convictions which had long been forming. But in the great majority of cases the conversion was instantaneous. Men, perplexed by the chronic darkness of the Irish situation, suddenly saw, or thought they saw, a light from heaven, and were converted as suddenly as St. Paul himself. I remember asking the late Lord Ripon the reason which had governed his decision. He answered: "I always have been for the most advanced thing in the Liberal programme, and Home Rule is the most advanced thing just now, so I'm for it." I should not wonder if a similar sentiment had some influence in the decision, arrived at by Campbell-Bannerman, who, when Gladstone formed his Home Rule Cabinet in 1886, entered it as Secretary of State for War. He went out with his chief in the following August, and in the incessant clamour for and against Home Rule which occupied the next six years he took a very moderate part.

When Gladstone formed his last Administration, Campbell-Bannerman returned to the War Office, and it was on a hostile vote concerning his Department that the Government was defeated in June, 1895. He resented this defeat more keenly than I should have expected from the habitual composure of his character; but it was no doubt the more provoking because in the previous spring he had wished to succeed Lord Peel as Speaker. He told me that the Speakership was the one post in public life which he should have most enjoyed, and which would best have suited his capacities. But his colleagues declared that he could not be spared from the Cabinet, and, true to his fine habit of self-effacement, he ceased to press his claim.

In October, 1896, Lord Rosebery, who had been Premier from 1894 to 1895, astonished his party by resigning the Liberal leadership. Who was to succeed him? Some cried one thing and some another. Some were for Harcourt, some for Morley, some for a leader in the House of Lords. Presently these disputations died down; what logicians call "the process of exhaustion" settled the question, and Campbell-Bannerman—the least self-seeking man in public life—found himself the accepted leader of the Liberal party. The leadership was an uncomfortable inheritance. There was a certain section of the Liberal party which was anxious that Lord Rosebery should return on his own terms. There were others who wished for Lord Spencer, and even in those early days there were some who already saw the makings of a leader in Mr. Asquith. And, apart from these sectional preferences, there was a crisis at hand, "sharper than any two-edged sword, piercing even to the dividing asunder of soul and spirit, and of the joints and marrow."

The Eastern Question of 1876 had rent the Liberal party once; the Irish Question of 1886 had rent it again; and now for the third time it was rent by the South African Question. Holding that the South African War was a wanton crime against freedom and humanity, I wished that my leader could declare himself unequivocally against it, but he felt bound to consider the interests of the Liberal party as a whole rather than those of any particular section which he might personally favour. As the campaign advanced, and the motives with which it had been engineered became more evident, his lead became clearer and more decisive. What we read about Concentration Camps and burnt villages and Chinese labour provoked his emphatic protest against "methods of barbarism," and those Liberals who enjoyed the war and called themselves "Imperialists" openly revolted against his leadership. He bore all attacks and slights and impertinences with a tranquillity which nothing could disturb, but, though he said very little, he saw very clearly. He knew exactly the source and centre of the intrigues against his leadership, and he knew also that those intrigues were directed to the end of making Lord Rosebery again Prime Minister. The controversy about Tariff Reform distracted general attention from these domestic cabals, but they were in full operation when Mr. Balfour suddenly resigned, and King Edward sent for Campbell-Bannerman. Then came a critical moment.

If Mr. Balfour had dissolved, the Liberal leader would have come back at the head of a great majority, and could have formed his Administration as he chose; but, by resigning, Mr. Balfour compelled his successor to form his Administration out of existing materials. So the cabals took a new form. The Liberal Imperialists were eager to have their share in the triumph, and had not the slightest scruple about serving under a leader whom, when he was unpopular, they had forsaken and traduced. Lord Rosebery put himself out of court by a speech which even Campbell-Bannerman could not regard as friendly; but Mr. Asquith, Mr. Haldane, and Sir Edward Grey were eager for employment. The new Premier Was the most generous-hearted of men, only too ready to forgive and forget. His motto was *Alors comme alors*, and he dismissed from consideration all memories of past intrigues. But, when some of the intriguers calmly told him that they would not join his Government unless he consented to go to the House of Lords and leave them to work their will in the House of Commons, he acted with a prompt decision which completely turned the tables.

The General Election of January, 1906, gave him an overwhelming majority; but in one sense it came too late. His health was a good deal impaired, and he was suffering from domestic anxieties which doubled the burden of office. Lady Campbell-Bannerman died, after a long illness, in August, 1906, but he struggled on bravely till his own health rather suddenly collapsed in November, 1907. He resigned office on the 6th of April, 1908, and died on the 22nd.

His brief Premiership had not been signalized by any legislative triumphs. He was unfortunate in some of his colleagues, and the first freshness of 1906 had been wasted on a quite worthless Education Bill. But during his term of office he had two signal opportunities of showing the faith that was in him. One was the occasion when, in defiance of all reactionary forces, he exclaimed, "La Duma est morte! Vive la Duma!" The other was the day when he gave self-government to South Africa, and won the tribute thus nobly rendered by General Smuts: "The Boer War was supplemented, and compensated for, by one of the wisest political settlements ever made in the history of the British Empire, and in reckoning up the list of Empire-builders I hope the name of Sir Henry Campbell-Bannerman, who brought into being a united South Africa, will never be forgotten."

II
IN HONOUR OF FRIENDSHIP

I

GLADSTONE—AFTER TWENTY YEARS

The 19th of May, 1898, was Ascension Day; and, just as the earliest Eucharists were going up to God, William Ewart Gladstone passed out of mortal suffering into the peace which passeth understanding. For people who, like myself, were reared in the Gladstonian tradition, it is a shock to be told by those who are in immediate contact with young men that for the rising generation he is only, or scarcely, a name. For my own part, I say advisedly that he was the finest specimen of God's handiwork that I have ever seen; and by this I mean that he combined strength of body, strength of intellect, and spiritual attainments, in a harmony which I have never known equalled. To him it was said when he lay dying, "You have so lived and wrought that you have kept the soul alive in England." Of him it was said a few weeks later, "On the day that Gladstone died the world lost its greatest citizen." Mr. Balfour called him "the greatest member of the greatest deliberative assembly that the world has ever seen"; and Lord Salisbury said, "He will be long remembered as a great example, to which history hardly furnishes a parallel of a great Christian statesman."

I have written so often and so copiously of Mr. Gladstone, who was both my religious and my political leader, that I might have found it difficult to discover any fresh aspects of his character and work; but the Editor[*] has kindly relieved me of that difficulty. He has pointed out certain topics which strikingly connect Gladstone's personality with the events and emotions of the present hour. I will take them as indicated, point by point.

[Footnote *: Of the *Red Triangle*.]

1. THE LOVE OF LIBERTY.

I have never doubted that the master-passion of Gladstone's nature was his religiousness—his intensely-realized relation with God, with the Saviour, and with "the powers of the world to come." This was inborn. His love of liberty was acquired. There was nothing in his birth or education or early circumstances to incline him in this direction. He was trained to "regard liberty with jealousy and fear, as something which could not wholly be dispensed with, but which was continually to be watched for fear of excesses." Gradually—very gradually—he came to regard it as the greatest of temporal blessings, and this new view affected every department of his public life. In financial matters it led him to adopt the doctrine of Free Exchanges. In politics, it induced him to extend the suffrage, first to the artisan and then to the labourer. In foreign affairs, it made him an unrelenting foe of the Turkish tyranny. In Ireland, it converted him to Home Rule. In religion, it brought him nearer and nearer to the ideal of the Free Church in the Free State.

2. BELGIUM AND THE FRANCO-PRUSSIAN WAR.

Gladstone hated war. He held, as most people hold, that there are causes, such as Life and Home and Freedom, for which the gentlest and most humane of men must be prepared to draw the sword. But he was profoundly anxious that it should never be drawn except under the absolute compulsion of national duty, and during the Crimean War he made this memorable declaration:

"If, when you have attained the objects of the war, you continue it for the sake of mere military glory, I say you tempt the justice of Him in whose hands the fates of armies are as absolutely lodged as the fate of the infant slumbering in its cradle."

This being his general view of war, it was inevitable that he should regard with horror the prospect of intervention in the Franco-German War, which broke out with startling suddenness, when he was Prime Minister, in the summer of 1870. He strained every nerve to keep England out of the struggle, and was profoundly thankful that Providence enabled him to do so. Yet all through that terrible crisis he saw quite clearly that either of the belligerent Powers might take a step which would oblige England to intervene, and he made a simultaneous agreement with Prussia and France that, if either violated the neutrality of Belgium, England would co-operate with the other to defend the little State. Should Belgium, he said, "go plump down the maw of another country to satisfy dynastic greed," such a tragedy would "come near to an extinction of public right in Europe, and I do not think we could look on while the sacrifice of freedom and independence was in course of consummation."

3. WAR-FINANCE AND ECONOMY.

A colleague once said about Gladstone, "The only two things which really interest him are Religion and Finance." The saying is much too unguarded, but it conveys a certain truth. My own opinion is that Finance was the field of intellectual effort in which his powers were most conspicuously displayed; and it was always remarked that, when he came to deal with the most prosaic details of national income and expenditure, his eloquence rose to an unusual height and power. At the same time, he was a most vigilant guardian of the public purse, and he was incessantly on the alert to prevent the national wealth, which his finance had done so much to increase, from being squandered on unnecessary and unprofitable objects. This jealousy of foolish expenditure combined with his love of peace to make him very chary of spending money on national defences. When he was Chancellor of the Exchequer under Lord Palmerston, his eagerness in this regard caused his chief to write to the Queen that "it would be better to lose Mr. Gladstone than to run the risk of losing Portsmouth or Plymouth." At the end of his career, his final retirement was precipitated by his reluctance to sanction a greatly increased expenditure on the Navy, which the Admiralty considered necessary. From first to last he sheltered himself under a dogma of his financial master—Sir Robert Peel—to the effect that it is possible for a nation, as for an individual, so to over-insure its property as to sacrifice its income. "My name," he said at the end, "stands in Europe as a symbol of the policy of peace, moderation, and non-aggression. What would be said of my active participation in a policy that will be taken as plunging England into the whirlpool of Militarism?"

4. ARBITRATION AND THE "ALABAMA."

Gladstone's hatred of war, and his resolve to avoid it at all hazards unless national duty required it, determined his much criticized action in regard to the *Alabama*. That famous and ill-omened vessel was a privateer, built in an English dockyard and manned by an English crew, which during the American Civil War got out to sea, captured seventy Northern vessels, and did a vast deal of damage to the Navy and commerce of the Union. The Government of the United States had a just quarrel with England in this matter, and the controversy—not very skilfully handled on either side— dragged on till the two nations seemed to be on the edge of war. Then Gladstone agreed to submit the case to arbitration, and the arbitration resulted in a judgment hostile to England. From that time—1872— Gladstone's popularity rapidly declined, till it revived, after an interval of Lord Beaconsfield's rule, at the General Election of 1880. In the first Session of that Parliament, he vindicated the pacific policy which had been so severely criticized in the following words:

"The dispositions which led us to become parties to the arbitration of the *Alabama* case are still with us the same as ever; we are not discouraged, we are not damped in the exercise of these feelings by the fact that we were amerced, and severely amerced, by the sentence of the international tribunal; and, although we may think the sentence was harsh in its extent and unjust in its basis, we regard the fine imposed on this country as dust in the balance compared with the moral value of the example set when these two great nations of England and America, who are among the most fiery and the most jealous in the world with regard to anything that touches national honour, went in peace and concord before a judicial tribunal to dispose of these painful differences, rather than resort to the arbitrament of the sword."

5. NATIONALITY—THE BALKANS AND IRELAND.

Gladstone was an intense believer in the principle of nationality, and he had a special sympathy with the struggles of small and materially feeble States. "Let us recognize," he said, "and recognize with frankness, the equality of the weak with the strong, the principles of brotherhood among nations, and of their sacred independence. When we are asking for the maintenance of the rights which belong to our fellow-subjects, resident abroad, let us do as we would be done by, and let us pay that respect to a feeble State, and to the infancy of free institutions, which we would desire and should exact from others, towards their maturity and their strength."

He was passionately Phil-Hellene. Greece, he said in 1897, is not a State "equipped with powerful fleets, large armies, and boundless treasure supplied by uncounted millions. It is a petty Power, hardly counting in the list of European States. But it is a Power representing the race that fought the battles of Thermopylæ and Salamis, and hurled back the hordes of Asia from European shores."

Of the Christian populations in Eastern Europe which had the misfortune to live under "the black hoof of the Turkish invader," he was the chivalrous and indefatigable champion, from the days of the Bulgarian atrocities in 1875 to the Armenian massacres of twenty years later. "If only," he exclaimed, "the spirit of little Montenegro had animated the body of big Bulgaria," very different would have been the fate of Freedom and Humanity in those distracted regions. The fact that Ireland is so distinctly a nation—not a mere province of Great Britain—and the fact that she is economically poor, reinforced that effort to give her self-government which had originated in his late-acquired love of political freedom.

6. THE IDEA OF PUBLIC RIGHT.

Of the "Concert of Europe" as it actually lived and worked (however plausible it might sound in theory) Gladstone had the poorest opinion, and, indeed, he declared that it was only another and a finer name for "the mutual distrust and hatred of the Powers." It had conspicuously failed to avert, or stop, or punish the Armenian massacres, and it had left Greece unaided in her struggle against Turkey. Lord Morley has finely said of him that "he was for an iron fidelity to public engagements and a stern regard for public law, which is the legitimate defence for small communities against the great and powerful"; and yet again: "He had a vision, high in the heavens, of the flash of an uplifted sword and the gleaming arm of the Avenging Angel."

I have now reached the limits of the task assigned me by the Editor, and my concluding word must be more personal.

I do not attempt to anticipate history. We cannot tell how much of those seventy years of strenuous labour will live, or how far Gladstone will prove to have read aright the signs of the times, the tendencies of human thought, and the political forces of the world. But we, who were his followers and disciples, know perfectly well what we owe to him. If ever we should be tempted to despond about the possibilities of human nature and human life, we shall think of him and take courage. If ever our religious faith should be perplexed by the

> "Blank misgivings of a creature,
> Moving about in worlds not realized,"

the memory of his strong confidence will reassure us. And if ever we are told by the flippancy of scepticism that "Religion is a disease," then we can point to him who, down to the very verge of ninety years, displayed a fulness of vigorous and manly life beyond all that we had ever known.

II

HENRY SCOTT HOLLAND[*]

[Footnote *: Written in 1907.]

The Hollands spring from Mobberley, in Cheshire, and more recently from the town of Knutsford, familiar to all lovers of English fiction as "Cranford." They have made their mark in several fields of intellectual effort. Lord Knutsford, Secretary of State for the Colonies from 1887 to 1892, was a son of Sir Henry Holland, M.D. (1788-1873), who doctored half the celebrities of Europe; and one of Sir Henry's first cousins was the incomparable Mrs. Gaskell. Another first-cousin was George Henry Holland (1818-1891), of Dumbleton Hall, Evesham, who married in 1844 the Hon. Charlotte Dorothy Gifford, daughter of the first Lord Gifford.

George Holland was an enthusiastic fox-hunter, and frequently changed his abode for the better enjoyment of his favourite sport. In 1847 he was living at a place called Underdown, near Ledbury; and there, on the 27th of January in that year, his eldest son was born.

The first Lord Gifford (1779-1826), who was successively Lord Chief Justice and Master of the Rolls, had owed much in early life to the goodwill of Lord Eldon, and, in honour of his patron, he named one of his sons' Scott. This Scott Gifford was Mrs. George Holland's brother, and his name was bestowed on her eldest son, who was christened "Henry Scott," but has always been known by his second name. This link with George III.'s Tory Chancellor is pleasingly appropriate.

Let it be remarked in passing that the hyphen so often introduced into the name is solely a creation of the newspapers, which, always rejoicing in double-barrelled surnames, gratify a natural impulse by writing about "Canon Scott-Holland."

I regret that the most exhaustive research has failed to discover any recorded traits of "Scotty" Holland in the nursery, but his career in the schoolroom is less obscure. His governess was a Swiss lady, who pronounced her young pupil "the most delightful of boys; not clever or studious, but full of fun and charm." This governess must have been a remarkable woman, for she is, I believe, the only human being who ever pronounced Scott Holland "not clever." It is something to be the sole upholder of an opinion, even a wrong one, against a unanimous world. By this time George Holland had established himself at Wellesbourne Hall, near Warwick, and there his son Scott was brought up in the usual habits of a country home where hunting and shooting are predominant interests. From the Swiss lady's control he passed to a private school at Allesley, near Coventry, and in January, 1860, he went to Eton. There he boarded at the house of Mrs. Gulliver,[*] and was a pupil of William Johnson (afterwards Cory), a brilliant and eccentric scholar, whose power of eliciting and stimulating a boy's intellect has never been surpassed.

[Footnote *: Of Mrs. Gulliver and her sister, H. S. H. writes: "They allowed football in top passage twice a week, which still seems to be the zenith of all joy."]

From this point onwards, Scott Holland's history—the formation of his character, the development of his intellect, the place which he attained in the regard of his friends—can be easily and exactly traced; for the impression which he made upon his contemporaries has not been effaced, or even dimmed, by the lapse of seven-and-forty years.

"My recollection of him at Eton," writes one of his friends, "is that of a boy most popular and high-spirited, strong, and full of life; but not eminent at games." Another writes: "He was very popular with a certain set, but not exactly eminent." He was not a member of "Pop," the famous Debating Society of Eton, but his genius found its outlet in other spheres. "He once astonished us all by an excellent performance in some private theatricals in his house." For the rest, he rowed, steered the *Victory* twice, played cricket for his House, and fives and football, and was a first-rate swimmer.

With regard to more important matters, it must suffice to say that then, as always, his moral standard was the highest, and that no evil thing dared manifest itself in his presence. He had been trained, by an admirable mother, in the best traditions of the Tractarian school, and he was worthy of his training. Among his intimate friends were Dalmeny, afterwards Lord Rosebery; Henry Northcote, now Lord Northcote; Freddy Wood, afterwards Meynell; Alberic Bertie; and Francis Pelham, afterwards Lord Chichester. He left Eton in July, 1864, and his tutor, in a letter to a friend, thus commented on his departure: "There was nothing to comfort me in parting with Holland; and he was the picture of tenderness. He and others stayed a good while, talking in the ordinary easy way. M. L. came, and his shyness did not prevent my saying what I wished to say to him. But to Holland I could say nothing; and now that I am writing about it I cannot bear to think that he is lost."

On leaving Eton, Holland went abroad to learn French, with an ultimate view to making his career in diplomacy. Truly the Canon of St. Paul's is an "inheritor of unfulfilled renown." What an Ambassador he would have made! There is something that warms the heart in the thought of His Excellency Sir Henry Scott Holland, G.C.B., writing despatches to Sir

Edward Grey in the style of *The Commonwealth*, and negotiating with the Czar or the Sultan on the lines of the Christian Social Union.

Returning from his French pilgrimage, he wept to a private tutor in Northamptonshire, who reported that "Holland was quite unique in charm and goodness, but would never be a scholar." In January, 1866, this charming but unscholarly youth went up to Balliol, and a new and momentous chapter in his life began.

What was he like at this period of his life? A graphic letter just received enables me to answer this question. "When I first met him, I looked on him with the deepest interest, and realized the charm that everyone felt. He had just gone up to Oxford, and was intensely keen on Ruskin and Browning, and devoted to music. He would listen with rapt attention when we played Chopin and Schumann to him. I used to meet him at dinner-parties when I first came out, by which time he was very enthusiastic on the Catholic side, and very fond of St. Barnabas, Pimlico, and was also deeply moved by social questions, East End poor, etc.; always unconventional, and always passionately interested in whatever he talked of. Burne-Jones once told me: 'It was perfectly delicious to see Holland come into a room, laughing before he had even said a word, and always bubbling over with life and joy.' Canon Mason said to me many years ago that he had hoped I kept every scrap Scotty ever wrote to me, as he was quite sure he was the most remarkable man of his generation. But there was a grave background to all this merriment. I remember that, as we were coming out of a London party, and looked on the hungry faces in the crowd outside the door, I rather foolishly said: 'One couldn't bear to look at them unless one felt that there was another world for them.' He replied: 'Are we to have both, then?' I know how his tone and the look in his face haunted me more than I can say."

A contemporary at Oxford writes, with reference to the same period: "When we went up, Liddon was preaching his Bamptons, and we went to them together, and were much moved by them. There were three of us who always met for Friday teas in one another's rooms, and during Lent we used to go to the Special Sermons at St. Mary's. We always went to Liddon's sermons, and sometimes to his Sunday evening lectures in the Hall of Queen's College. We used to go to the Choral Eucharist in Merton Chapel, and, later, to the iron church at Cowley, and to St. Barnabas, and enjoyed shouting the Gregorians."

On the intellectual side, we are told that Holland's love of literature was already marked. "I can remember reading Wordsworth with him, and Carlyle, and Clough; and, after Sunday breakfasts, Boswell's *Life of Johnson*." Then, as always, he found a great part of his pleasure in music.

No record, however brief, of an undergraduate life can afford to disregard athletics; so let it be here recorded that Holland played racquets and fives, and skated, and "jumped high," and steered the *Torpid*, and three times rowed in his College Eight. He had innumerable friends, among whom three should be specially recalled: Stephen Fremantle and R. L. Nettleship, both of Balliol, and W. H. Ady, of Exeter. In short, he lived the life of the model undergraduate, tasting all the joys of Oxford, and finding time to spare for his prescribed studies. His first encounter with the examiners, in "Classical Moderations," was only partially successful. "He did not appreciate the niceties of scholarship, and could not write verses or do Greek or Latin prose at all well;" and he was accordingly placed in the Third Class. But as soon as the tyranny of Virgil and Homer and Sophocles was overpast, he betook himself to more congenial studies. Of the two tutors who then made Balliol famous, he owed nothing to Jowett and everything to T. H. Green. That truly great man "simply fell in love" with his brilliant pupil, and gave him of his best.

"Philosophy's the chap for me," said an eminent man on a momentous occasion. "If a parent asks a question in the classical, commercial, or mathematical-line, says I gravely, 'Why, sir, in the first place, are you a philosopher?' 'No, Mr. Squeers,' he says, 'I ain't.' 'Then, sir,' says I, 'I am sorry for you, for I shan't be able to explain it.' Naturally, the parent goes away and wishes he was a philosopher, and, equally naturally, thinks I'm one."

That is the Balliol manner all over; and the ardent Holland, instructed by Green, soon discovered, to his delight, that he was a philosopher, and was henceforward qualified to apply Mr. Squeer's searching test to all questions in Heaven and earth. "It was the custom at Balliol for everyone to write an essay once a week, and I remember that Holland made a name for his essay-writing and originality. It was known that he had a good chance of a 'First in Greats,' if only his translations from Greek and Latin books did not pull him down. He admired the ancient authors, especially Plato, and his quick grasp of the meaning of what he read, good memory, and very remarkable powers of expression, all helped him much. He was good at History and he had a great turn for Philosophy" (*cf.* Mr. Squeers, *supra*), "Plato, Hegel; etc., and he understood, as few could, Green's expositions, and counter-attack on John Stuart Mill and the Positivist School, which was the dominant party at that time."

In the summer Term of 1870 Holland went in for his final examination at Oxford. A friend writes: "I remember his coming out from his paper on, Moral Philosophy in great exaltation; and his *viva voce* was spoken of as a most brilliant performance. One of the examiners, T. Fowler (afterwards President of Corpus), said he had never heard anything like it." In fine, a new and vivid light had appeared in the intellectual sky—a new planet had swum into the ken of Oxford Common Rooms; and it followed naturally that Holland, having obtained his brilliant First, was immediately elected to a Studentship at Christ Church, which, of course, is the same as a Fellowship anywhere else. He went into residence at his new home in January, 1871, and remained there for thirteen years, a "don," indeed, by office, but so undonnish in character, ways, and words, that he became the subject of a eulogistic riddle: "When is a don not a don? When he is Scott Holland."

Meanwhile, all dreams of a diplomatic career had fled before the onrush of Aristotle and Plato, Hegel and Green. The considerations which determined Holland's choice of a profession I have not sought to enquire. Probably he was moved by the thought that in Holy Orders he would have the best chance of using the powers, of which by this time he must have become conscious, for the glory of God and the service of man. I have been told that the choice was in some measure affected by a sermon of Liddon's on the unpromising subject of Noah;[*] and beyond doubt the habitual enjoyment of Liddon's society, to which, as a brother-Student, Holland was now admitted, must have tended in the same direction.

[Footnote *: Preached at St. Mary the Virgin, Oxford, on the 11th of March, 1870.]

Perhaps an even stronger influence was that of Edward King, afterwards Bishop of Lincoln, and then Principal of Cuddesdon, in whom the most persuasive aspects of the priestly character were beautifully displayed, and who made Cuddesdon a sort of shrine to which all that was spiritual and ardent in young Oxford was irresistibly attracted. Preaching, years afterwards, at a Cuddesdon Festival, Holland uttered this moving panegyric of the place to which he owed so much: "Ah! which of us does not know by what sweet entanglement Cuddesdon threw its net about our willing feet? Some summer Sunday, perhaps, we wandered here, in undergraduate days, to see a friend; and from that hour the charm was at work. How joyous, how

enticing, the welcome, the glad brotherhood! So warm and loving it all seemed, as we thought of the sharp skirmishing of our talk in College; so buoyant and rich, as we recalled the thinness of our Oxford interests. The little rooms, like college rooms just shrinking into cells; the long talk on the summer lawn; the old church with its quiet country look of patient peace; the glow of the evening chapel; the run down the hill under the stars, with the sound of Compline Psalms still ringing in our hearts—ah! happy, happy day! It was enough. The resolve that lay half slumbering in our souls took shape; it leapt out. We would come to Cuddesdon when the time of preparation should draw on!" Readers of this glowing passage have naturally imagined that the writer of it must himself have been a Cuddesdon man, but this is a delusion; and, so far as I know, Holland's special preparation for Ordination consisted of a visit to Peterborough, where he essayed the desperate task of studying theology under Dr. Westcott.

In September, 1872, he was ordained deacon by Bishop Mackarness, in Cuddesdon Church, being chosen to read the Gospel at the Ordination; and he was ordained priest there just two years later. It was during his diaconate that I, then a freshman, made his acquaintance. We often came across one another, in friends' rooms and at religious meetings, and I used to listen with delight to the sermons which he preached in the parish churches of Oxford. They were absolutely original; they always exhilarated and uplifted one; and the style was entirely his own, full of lightness and brightness, movement and colour. Scattered phrases from a sermon at SS. Philip and James, on the 3rd of May, 1874, and from another at St. Barnabas, on the 28th of June in the same year, still haunt my memory.[*]

[Footnote *: An Oxford Professor, who had some difficulty with his aspirates, censured a theological essay as "Too 'ollandy by 'alf."]

Holland lived at this time a wonderfully busy and varied life. He lectured on Philosophy in Christ Church; he took his full share in the business of University and College; he worked and pleaded for all righteous causes both among the undergraduates and among the citizens. An Oxford tutor said not long ago: "A new and strong effort for moral purity in Oxford can be dated from Holland's Proctorship."

This seems to be a suitable moment for mentioning his attitude towards social and political questions. He was "suckled in a creed outworn" of Eldonian Toryism, but soon exchanged it for Gladstonian Liberalism, and this, again, he suffused with an energetic spirit of State Socialism on which Mr. Gladstone would have poured his sternest wrath. A friend writes: "I don't remember that H. S. H., when he was an undergraduate, took much interest in politics more than chaffing others for being so Tory." (He never spoke at the Union, and had probably not realized his powers as a speaker.) "But when, in 1872, I went to be curate to Oakley (afterwards Dean of Manchester) at St. Saviour's, Hoxton, Holland used to come and see me there, and I found him greatly attracted to social life in the East End of London. In 1875 he came, with Edward Talbot and Robert Moberly, and lodged in Hoxton, and went about among the people, and preached in the church. I have sometimes thought that this may have been the beginning of the Oxford House."

All through these Oxford years Holland's fame as an original and independent thinker, a fascinating preacher, an enthusiast for Liberalism as the natural friend and ally of Christianity, was widening to a general recognition. And when, in April, 1884, Mr. Gladstone nominated him to a Residentiary Canonry at St. Paul's, everyone felt that the Prime Minister had matched a great man with a great opportunity.

From that day to this, Henry Scott Holland has lived in the public eye, so there is no need for a detailed narrative of his more recent career. All London has known him as a great and inspiring preacher; a literary critic of singular skill and grace; an accomplished teacher in regions quite outside theology; a sympathetic counsellor in difficulty and comforter in distress; and one of the most vivid and joyous figures in our social life. It is possible to trace some change in his ways of thinking, though none in his ways of feeling and acting. His politics have swayed from side to side under the pressure of conflicting currents. Some of his friends rejoice—and others lament—that he is much less of a partisan than he was; that he is apt to see two and even three sides of a question; and that he is sometimes kind to frauds and humbugs, if only they will utter the shibboleths in which he himself so passionately believes. But, through all changes and chances, he has stood as firm as a rock for the social doctrine of the Cross, and has made the cause of the poor, the outcast, and the overworked his own. He has shown the glory of the Faith in its human bearings, and has steeped Dogma and, Creed and Sacrament and Ritual in his own passionate love of God and man.

Stupid people misunderstand him. Wicked people instinctively hate him. Worldly people, sordid people, self-seekers, and promotion-hunters, contemn him as an amiable lunatic. But his friends forget all measure and restraint when they try to say what they feel about him. One whom I have already quoted writes again: "I feel Holland is little changed from what he was as a schoolboy and an undergraduate—the same joyous spirit, unbroken good temper, quick perception and insight, warm sympathy, love of friends, kind interest in lives of all sorts, delight in young people—these never fail. He never seems to let the burden of life and the sadness of things depress his cheery, hopeful spirit. I hope that what I send may be of some use. I cannot express what I feel. I love him too well."

This is the tribute of one friend; let me add my own. I do not presume to say what I think about him as a spiritual guide and example; I confine myself to humbler topics. Whatever else he is, Henry Scott Holland is, beyond doubt, one of the most delightful people in the world. In fun and geniality and warm-hearted, hospitality, he is a worthy successor of Sydney Smith, whose official house he inhabits; and to those elements of agreeableness he adds certain others which his famous predecessor could scarcely have claimed. He has all the sensitiveness of genius, with its sympathy, its versatility, its unexpected turns, its rapid transitions from grave to gay, its vivid appreciation of all that is beautiful in art and nature, literature and life. No man in London, I should think, has so many and such devoted friends in every class and station; and those friends acknowledge in him not only the most vivacious and exhilarating of social companions, but one of the moral forces which have done most to quicken their consciences and lift their lives.

By the death of Henry Scott Holland a great light is quenched,[*] or, to use more Christian language, is merged in "the true Light which lighteth every man that cometh into the world."

[Footnote *: Written in 1918.]

Light is the idea with which my beloved friend is inseparably associated in my mind. His nature had all the attributes of light—its revealing power, its cheerfulness, its salubrity, its beauty, its inconceivable rapidity. He had the quickest intellect that I have ever known. He saw with a flash into the heart of an argument or a situation. He diffused joy by his own joy in living; he vanquished morbidity by his essential wholesomeness; whatever he touched became beautiful under his handling. "He was not the Light, but he came to bear witness of that Light," and bore it for seventy years by the mere force of being what he was. My friendship with Dr. Holland began in my second term at Oxford, and has lasted without a cloud or a break from that day to this. He was then twenty-five years old, and was already a conspicuous figure in the life of the University. In 1866 he had come up from Eton to Balliol with a high reputation for goodness and charm, but with no report of special cleverness. He soon became extremely popular in his own College and outside it. He rowed and played games and sang, and was recognized as a delightful companion wherever he went. But all the time a process of mental development was going on, of which none but his intimate friends were aware. "I owed nothing to Jowett," he was accustomed to say; "everything to Green." From that great teacher he caught his Hegelian habit of thought, his strong sense of ethical and spiritual values, and that practical habit of mind which seeks to apply moral principles to the problems of actual life. In 1870 came the great surprise, and Holland, who had no pretensions to scholarship, and whose mental development had only been noticed by a few, got a First Class of unusual brilliancy in the searching school of *Literæ Humaniores.* Green had triumphed; he had made a philosopher without spoiling a Christian. Christ Church welcomed a born Platonist, and made him Senior Student, Tutor, and Lecturer.

Holland had what Tertullian calls the *anima naturaliter Christiana*, and it had been trained on the lines of the Tractarian Movement. When he went up to Oxford he destined himself for a diplomatic career, but he now realized his vocation to the priesthood, and was ordained deacon in 1872 and priest two years later. He instantly made his mark as a preacher. Some of the sermons preached in the parish churches of Oxford in the earliest years of his ministry stand out in my memory among his very best. He had all the preacher's gifts—a tall, active, and slender frame, graceful in movement, vigorous in action, abundant in gesture, a strong and melodious voice, and a breathless fluency of speech. Above all, he spoke with an energy of passionate conviction which drove every word straight home. He seemed a young apostle on fire with zeal for God and humanity. His fame as an exponent of metaphysic attracted many hearers who did not usually go much to church, and they were accustomed—then as later—to say that here was a Christian who knew enough about the problems of thought to make his testimony worth hearing. Others, who cared not a rap for Personality or Causation, Realism or Nominalism, were attracted by his grace, his eloquence, his literary charm. His style was entirely his own. He played strange tricks with the English language, heaped words upon words, strung adjective to adjective; mingled passages of Ruskinesque description with jerky fragments of modern slang. These mannerisms grew with his growth, but in the seventies they were not sufficiently marked to detract from the pure pleasure which we enjoyed when we listened to his preaching as to "a very lovely song."

Judged by the canons of strict art, Holland was perhaps greater as a speaker than as a preacher. He differed from most people in this—that whereas most of us can restrain ourselves better on paper than when we are speaking, his pen ran away with him when he, was writing a sermon, but on a platform he could keep his natural fluency in bounds. Even then he was fluent enough in all conscience; but he did not so overdo the ornaments, and the absence of a manuscript and a pulpit-desk gave ampler scope for oratorical movement.

I have mentioned Holland's intellectual and moral debt to T. H. Green. I fancy that, theologically and politically, he owed as much to Mr. Gladstone. The older and the younger man had a great deal in common. They both were "patriot citizens of the kingdom of God"; proud and thankful to be members of the Holy Church Universal, and absolutely satisfied with that portion of the Church in which their lot was cast; passionate adherents of the Sacramental theology; and yet, in their innermost devotion to the doctrine of the Cross, essentially Evangelical. In politics they both worshipped freedom; they both were content to appeal to the popular judgment; and they both were heart and soul for the Christian cause in the

East of Europe. Holland had been brought up by Tories, but in all the great controversies of 1886 to 1894 he followed the Gladstonian flag with the loyalty of a good soldier and the faith of a loving son.

When in 1884 Gladstone appointed Holland to a Canonry at St. Paul's, the announcement was received with an amount of interest which is not often bestowed upon ecclesiastical promotions. Everyone felt that it was a daring experiment to place this exuberant prophet of the good time coming at what Bishop Lightfoot called "the centre of the world's concourse." Would his preaching attract or repel? Would the "philosophy of religion," which is the perennial interest of Oxford, appeal to the fashionable or business-like crowd which sits under the Dome? Would his personal influence reach beyond the precincts of the Cathedral into the civil and social and domestic life of London? Would the Mauritian gospel of human brotherhood and social service—in short, the programme of the Christian Social Union—win the workers to the side of orthodoxy? These questions were answered according to the idiosyncrasy or bias of those to whom they were addressed, and they were not settled when, twenty-seven years later, Holland returned from St. Paul's to Oxford. Indeed, several answers were possible. On one point only there was an absolute agreement among those who knew, and this was that the Church in London had been incalculably enriched by the presence of a genius and a saint.

In one respect, perhaps, Holland's saintliness interfered with the free action of his genius. His insight, unerring in a moral or intellectual problem, seemed to fail him when he came to estimate a human character. His own life had always been lived on the highest plane, and he was in an extraordinary degree "unspotted from the world." His tendency was to think—or at any rate to speak and act—as if everyone were as simply good as himself, as transparent, as conscientious, as free from all taint of self-seeking. This habit, it has been truly said, "disqualifies a man in some degree for the business of life, which requires for its conduct a certain degree of prejudice"; but it is pre-eminently characteristic of those elect and lovely souls

> "Who, through the world's long day of strife,
> Still chant their morning song."

III

LORD HALIFAX

There can scarcely be two more typically English names than Wood and Grey. In Yorkshire and Northumberland respectively, they have for centuries been held in honour, and it was a happy conjunction which united them in 1829. In that year, Charles Wood, elder son of Sir Francis Lindley Wood, married Lady Mary Grey, youngest daughter of Charles, second Earl Grey, the hero of the first Reform Bill. Mr. Wood succeeded his father in the baronetcy, in 1846, sat in Parliament as a Liberal for forty years, filled some of the highest offices of State in the Administrations of Lord Palmerston and Mr. Gladstone, and was raised to the peerage as Viscount Halifax in 1866.

Lord and Lady Halifax had seven children, of whom the eldest was Charles Lindley Wood—the subject of the present sketch—born in 1839; and the second, Emily Charlotte, wife of Hugo Meynell-Ingram, of Hoar Cross and Temple Newsam. I mention these two names together because Mrs. Meynell-Ingram (whose qualities of intellect and character made a deep impression on all those who were brought in contact with her) was one of the formative influences of her brother's life. The present Lord Halifax (who succeeded to his father's peerage in 1885) writes thus about his early days:

"My sister was everything to me. I never can remember the time when it was not so between us. I hardly ever missed writing to her every day when we were away from one another; and for many years after her marriage, and as long as her eyes were good, I don't think she and I ever omitted writing to one another, as, indeed, we had done all through my school and college life. She is never out of my mind and thoughts. Her birthday, on the 19th of July, and mine, on the 7th of June, were days which stood out amongst all the days of the year."

This extract illustrates the beautiful atmosphere of mutual love and trust in which the family of Sir Charles and Lady Mary Wood were reared. In other respects their upbringing was what one would naturally expect in a Yorkshire country-house, where politics were judiciously blended with fox-hunting. From the enjoyments of a bright home, and the benign sway of the governess, and the companionship of a favourite sister, the transition to a private school is always depressing. In April, 1849, Charles Wood was sent to the Rev. Charles Arnold's, at Tinwell, near Stamford. "What I chiefly remember about the place is being punished all one day, with several canings, because I either could not or would not learn the Fifth Declension of the Greek Nouns."

So much for the curriculum of Tinwell; but it only lasted for one year, and then, after two years with a private tutor at home, Charles Wood went to Eton in January, 1853. He boarded at the house of the Rev. Francis Vidal, and his tutor was the famous William Johnson, afterwards Cory. "Billy Johnson" was not only a consummate scholar and a most stimulating teacher, but the sympathetic and discerning friend of the boys who were fortunate enough to be his private pupils. In his book of verses—*Ionica*—he made graceful play with a casual word which Charles Wood had let fall in the ecstasy of swimming—"Oh, how I wish I could fly!"

"Fresh from the summer wave, under the beech,
    Looking through leaves with a far-darting eye,
Tossing those river-pearled locks about,
    Throwing those delicate limbs straight out,
Chiding the clouds as they sailed out of reach,
    Murmured the swimmer, 'I wish I could fly!'

"Laugh, if you like, at the bold reply,
    Answer disdainfully, flouting my words:
How should the listener at simple sixteen
Guess what a foolish old rhymer could mean,
Calmly predicting, 'You will surely fly'—
    Fish one might vie with, but how be like birds?

"Genius and love will uplift thee; not yet;
    Walk through some passionless years by my side,
Chasing the silly sheep, snapping the lily-stalk,
Drawing my secrets forth, witching my soul with talk.
When the sap stays, and the blossom is set,
    Others will take the fruit; I shall have died."

Surely no teacher ever uttered a more beautiful eulogy on a favourite pupil; and happily the poet lived long enough to see his prophecy fulfilled.

The principal charm of a Public School lies in its friendships; so here let me record the names of those who are recalled by contemporaries as having been Charles Wood's closest friends, at Eton—Edward Denison, Sackville Stopford, George Palmer, George Lane-Fox, Walter Campion, Lyulph Stanley,[1] and Augustus Legge.[2] With Palmer, now Sir George, he "messed," and with Stopford, now Stopford-Sackville, he shared a private boat. As regards his pursuits I may quote his own words:

[Footnote 1: Now (1918) Lord Sheffield.]
[Footnote 2: Afterwards Bishop of Lichfield.]

"I steered the *Britannia* and the *Victory*. I used to take long walks with friends in Windsor Park, and used sometimes to go up to the Castle, to ride with the present King.[3] I remember, in two little plays which William Johnson wrote for his pupils, taking the part of an Abbess in a Spanish Convent at the time of the Peninsular War; and the part of the Confidante of the Queen of Cyprus, in an historical in which Sir Archdale Palmer was the hero, and a boy named Chafyn Grove, who went into the Guards, the heroine. In Upper School, at Speeches on the 4th of June, I acted with Lyulph Stanley in a French piece called *Femme à Vendre*. In 1857, I and George Cadogan,[4] and Willy Gladstone, and Freddy Stanley[5] went with the present King for a tour in the English Lakes; and in the following August we went with the King to Koenigs-winter. I was in 'Pop' (the Eton Debating Society) at the end of my time at Eton, and I won the 'Albert,' the Prince Consort's Prize for French."

[Footnote 3: Edward VII.]
[Footnote 4: Afterwards Lord Cadogan.]
[Footnote 5: The late Lord Derby.]

A younger contemporary adds this pretty testimony:

"As you can imagine, he was very popular both among the boys and the masters. One little instance remains with me. There was a custom of a boy, when leaving, receiving what one called 'Leaving Books,' from boys remaining in the school; these books were provided by the parents, and were bound in calf, etc. The present Lord Eldon went to Eton with me, and when Charles Wood left, in July, 1858, he wanted to give him a book; but knowing nothing of the custom of parents providing books, he went out and bought a half-crown copy of *The Pilgrim's Progress*, and sent it to C. Wood's room. Two shillings and sixpence was a good deal to a Lower Boy at the end of the half; and it was, I should think, an almost unique testimony from a small boy to one at the top of the house."

In October, 1858, Charles Wood went up to Christ Church. There many of his earlier friendships were renewed and some fresh ones added: Mr. Henry Chaplin coming up from Harrow; Mr. H. L. Thompson, afterwards Vicar of St. Mary-the-Virgin, Oxford, from Westminster; and Mr. Henry Villiers, afterwards Vicar of St. Paul's, Knightsbridge, from a private tutor's. Charles Wood took his full share in the social life of the place, belonging both to "Loder's" and to "Bullingdon"—institutions of high repute in the Oxford world; and being then, as now, an admirable horseman, he found his chief joy in hunting. In his vacations he visited France and Italy, and made some tours nearer home with undergraduate friends. In 1861 he took his degree, and subsequently travelled Eastward as far as Suez, and spent a winter in Rome. In 1862 he was appointed Groom of the Bedchamber to the Prince of Wales, and in this capacity attended his royal master's wedding at St. George's, Windsor, on the 10th of March, 1863, and spent two summers with him at Abergeldie. At the same time he became Private Secretary to his mother's cousin, Sir George Grey, the Secretary of State for the Home Department, and retained that post until the fall of Lord Russell's Administration in 1866.

"There was," writes Lord Halifax, "a question of my standing for some Yorkshire constituency; but with my convictions it was not easy to come out on the Liberal side, and the project dropped. I never can remember the time when I did not feel the greatest devotion to King Charles I. and Archbishop Laud. I can recall now the services for the Restoration at Eton, when everyone used to wear an oak-leaf in his button-hole, and throw it down on the floor as the clock struck twelve."

This may be a suitable moment for a word about Lord Halifax's "convictions" in the sphere of religion. His parents were, like all the Whigs, sound and sturdy Protestants. They used to take their children to Church at Whitehall Chapel, probably the least ecclesiastical-looking place of worship in London; and the observances of the Parish Church at Hickleton—their country home near Doncaster—were not calculated to inspire a delight in the beauty of holiness. However, when quite a boy, Charles Wood, who had been confirmed at Eton by Bishop Wilberforce, found his way to St. Barnabas, Pimlico, then newly opened, and fell much under the influence of Mr. Bennett at St. Paul's, Knightsbridge, and Mr. Richards, at All Saints', Margaret Street. At Oxford he became acquainted with Dr. Pusey and the young and inspiring Liddon, and frequented the services at Merton College Chapel, where Liddon used often to officiate. By 1863 his religious opinions must have been definitely shaped; for in that year his old tutor, William Johnson, when paying a visit to Hickleton, writes as follows:

"He told me of Mr. Liddon, the saintly and learned preacher; of the devout worshippers at All Saints', whose black nails show they are artisans; of the society formed to pray daily for the restoration of Christian unity."

And again:

"His father and mother seem to gather virtue and sweetness from looking at him and talking to him, though they fight hard against his unpractical and exploded Church views, and think his zeal misdirected.... And all the while his mother's face gets brighter and kinder because she is looking at him. Happy are the parents who, when they have reached that time of life in which the world is getting too strong and virtue is a thing of routine, are quickened by the bold, restless zeal of their sons and daughters, and so renew their youth."

In 1866 he was induced by his friend Mr. Lane-Fox, afterwards Chancellor of the Primrose League, to join the English Church Union.

"At that time," he writes, "I was much concerned with the affairs of the House of Charity in Soho and the Newport Market Refuge. 1866 was the cholera year, and I recollect coming straight back from Lorne's[*] coming of age to London, where I saw Dr. Pusey, with the result that I set to work to help Miss Sellon with her temporary hospital in Commercial Street, Whitechapel."

[Footnote *: Afterwards Duke of Argyll.]

In this connexion it is proper to recall the devoted services which he rendered to the House of Mercy at Horbury, near Wakefield; and those who know what religious prejudice was in rural districts forty years ago will realize the value of the support accorded to an institution struggling against calumny and misrepresentation by the most popular and promising young man in the West Riding. There lies before me as I write a letter written by an Evangelical mother—Lady Charles Russell—to her son, then just ordained to a curacy at Doncaster.

"I want to hear more about Lord and Lady Halifax. I knew them pretty well as Sir Charles and Lady Mary Wood, but I have lived in retirement since before he was raised to the peerage. His eldest son was not only very good-looking, but inclined to be very good, as I dare say Dr. Vaughan may have heard. Do you know anything about him?"

That "very good" and "very good-looking" young man was now approaching what may be called the decisive event of his life. In April, 1867, Mr. Colin Lindsay resigned the Presidency of the English Church Union, and Mr. Charles Lindley Wood was unanimously chosen to fill his place. Eleven years later Dr. Pusey wrote: "As to his being President of the E.C.U., he is the sense and moderation of it." He has administered its affairs and guided its policy through fifty anxious years. Indeed, the President and the Union have been so completely identified that the history of the one has been the history of the other. His action has been governed by a grand and simple consistency. Alike in storms and in fair weather, at times of crisis and at times of reaction, he has been the unswerving and unsleeping champion of the spiritual claims of the English Church, and the alert, resourceful, and unsparing enemy of all attempts, from whatever quarter, to subject her doctrine and discipline to the control of the State and its secular tribunals. The eager and fiery enthusiasm which pre-eminently marks his nature awakes a kindred flame in those who are reached by his influence; and, even when the reason is unconvinced, it is difficult to resist the leadership of so pure and passionate a temper.

It would be ridiculous for an outsider, like myself, to discuss the interior working of the E.C.U., so I avail myself of the testimony which has reached me from within.

"Like most men of his temperament, Lord Halifax seems now and again to be a little before his time. On the other hand, it is remarkable that Time generally justifies him. There is no question that he has always enjoyed the enthusiastic and affectionate support of the Union as a whole."

It is true that once with reference to the book called *Lux Mundi*, and once with reference to the "Lambeth Opinions" of 1899, there was some resistance in the Union to Lord Halifax's guidance; and that, in his negotiations about the recognition of Anglican Orders, he would not, if he had been acting officially, have carried the Union with him. But these exceptions only go to confirm the general truth that his policy has been as successful as it has been bold and conscientious.

It is time to return, for a moment, to the story of Lord Halifax's private life. In 1869 he married Lady Agnes Courtenay, daughter of the twelfth Earl of Devon, and in so doing allied himself with one of the few English families which even the most exacting genealogists recognize as noble.[1] His old tutor wrote on the 22nd of April:

[Footnote 1: "The purple of three Emperors who have reigned at Constantinople will authorize or excuse a digression on the origin and singular fortunes of the House of Courtenay" (Gibbon, chapter xii.).]

"This has been a remarkable day—the wedding of Charles Wood and Lady Agnes Courtenay. It was in St. Paul's Church, Knightsbridge, which was full, galleries and all, the central passage left empty, and carpeted with red. It was a solemn, rapt congregation; there was a flood of music and solemn tender voices. The married man and woman took the Lord's Supper, with hundreds of witnesses who did not Communicate.... Perhaps a good many were Church Union folk, honouring their Chairman."

Of this marriage I can only say that it has been, in the highest aspects, ideally happy, and that the sorrows which have chequered it have added a new significance to the saying of Ecclesiastes that "A threefold cord is not quickly broken."[2]

[Footnote 2: Charles Reginald Lindley Wood died 1890; Francis Hugh Lindley Wood died 1889; Henry Paul Lindley Wood died 1886.]

In 1877 Mr. Wood resigned his office in the household of the Prince of Wales. It was the time when the affairs of St. James's, Hatcham, and the persecution of Mr. Tooth, were first bringing the Church into sharp collision with the courts of law. The President of the Church Union was the last man to hold his peace when even the stones were crying out against this profane intrusion of the State into the kingdom of God; and up and down the country he preached, in season and out of season, the spiritual independence of the Church, and the criminal folly of trying to coerce Christian consciences by deprivation and imprisonment. The story went that an Illustrious Personage said to his insurgent Groom of the Bedchamber: "What's this I hear? I'm told you go about the country saying that the Queen is not the Head of the Church. Of course, she's the Head of the Church, just the same as the Pope is the Head of his Church, and the Sultan the Head of *his* Church.'" But this may only be a creation of that irresponsible romancist, Ben Trovato; and it is better to take Lord Halifax's account of the transaction:

"I remember certain remonstrances being made to me in regard to disobedience to the law and suchlike, and my saying at once that I thought it quite unreasonable that the Prince should be compromised by anyone in his household taking a line of which he himself did not approve; and that I honestly thought I had much better resign my place. Nothing could have been nicer or kinder than the Prince was about it; and, if I resigned, I thought it much better for him on the one side, while, as regards myself, as you may suppose, I was not going to sacrifice my own liberty of saying and doing what I thought right."

In those emphatic words speaks the true spirit of the man. To "say and do what he thinks right," without hesitation or compromise or regard to consequences, has been alike the principle and the practice of his life. And here the reader has a right to ask, What manner of man is he whose career you have been trying to record?

First and foremost, it must be said—truth demands it, and no conventional reticence must withhold it—that the predominant feature of his character is his religiousness. He belongs to a higher world than this. His "citizenship is in Heaven." Never can I forget an address which, twenty years ago, he delivered, by request, in Stepney Meeting-House. His subject was "Other-worldliness." The audience consisted almost exclusively of Nonconformists. Many, I imagine, had come with itching ears, or moved by a natural curiosity to see the man whose bold discrimination between the things of Cæsar and the things of God was just then attracting, general attention, and, in some quarters, wrathful dismay. But gradually, as the high theme unfolded itself, and the lecturer showed the utter futility of all that this world has to offer when compared with the realities of the Supernatural Kingdom, curiosity was awed into reverence, and the address closed amid a silence more eloquent than any applause."

"That strain I heard was of a higher mood."

As I listened, I recalled some words written by Dr. Pusey in 1879, about

"One whom I have known intimately for many years, who is one of singular moderation as well as wisdom, who can discriminate with singular sagacity what is essential from is not essential—C. Wood."

The Doctor went on:

"I do not think that I was ever more impressed than by a public address which I heard him deliver now many years ago, in which, without controversy or saying anything which could have offended anyone, he expressed his own faith on deep subjects with a precision which reminded me of Hooker's wonderful enunciation of the doctrine of the Holy Trinity and of the Person of our Lord Jesus Christ."

After so solemn a tribute from so great a saint, it seems almost a profanity—certainly a bathos—to add any more secular touches. Yet, if the portrait is even to approach completeness, it must be remembered that we are not describing an ascetic or a recluse, but the most polished gentleman, the most fascinating companion, the most graceful and attractive figure, in the Vanity Fair of social life. He is full of ardour, zeal, and emotion, endowed with a physical activity which corresponds to his mental alertness, and young with that perpetual youth which is the reward of "a conscience void of offence toward God and toward man."

Clarendon, in one of his most famous portraits, depicts a high-souled Cavalier, "of inimitable sweetness and delight in conversation, of a glowing and obliging humanity and goodness to mankind, and of a primitive simplicity and integrity of life." He was writing of Lord Falkland: he described Lord Halifax.

IV

LORD AND LADY RIPON[*]

[Footnote *: George Frederick Samuel Robinson, first Marquess of Ripon, K.G. (1827-1909); married in 1851 his cousin Henrietta Ann Theodosia Vyner.]

The *Character of the Happy Warrior* is, by common consent, one of the noblest poems in the English language. A good many writers and speakers seem to have discovered it only since the present war began, and have quoted it with all the exuberant zeal of a new acquaintance. But, were a profound Wordsworthian in general, and a devotee of this poem in particular, to venture on a criticism, it would be that, barring the couplet about Pain and Bloodshed, the character would serve as well for the "Happy Statesman" as for the "Happy Warrior." There is nothing specially warlike in the portraiture of the man

> "Who, with a toward or untoward lot,
> Prosperous or adverse, to his mind or not,
> Plays in the many games of life, that one
> Where what he most doth value must be won;
> Whom neither shape of danger can dismay,
> Not thought of tender happiness betray;
> Who, not content that former worth stand fast,
> Looks forward, persevering to the last,
> From well to better, daily self-surpast."

These lines always recurred to my memory when circumstances brought me into contact with the second Lord Ripon, whose friendship I enjoyed from my first entrance into public life.

I know few careers in the political life of modern England more interesting or more admirable than his, and none more exactly consonant with Wordsworth's eulogy:

> "Who, not content that former worth stand fast,
> Looks forward, persevering to the last,
> From well to better, daily self-surpast."

The first Lord Ripon, who was born in 1782 and died in 1859, entered public life as soon as he had done with Cambridge, filled pretty nearly every office of honour and profit under the Crown (including, for four troubled months, the Premiership), and served impartially under moderate Whigs and crusted Tories, finding, perhaps, no very material difference between their respective creeds. The experiences of the hen that hatches the duckling are proverbially pathetic; and great must have been the perplexity of this indeterminate statesman when he discovered that his only son was a young man of the most robust convictions, and that those convictions were frankly democratic. To men possessed by birth of rank and wealth, one has sometimes heard the question addressed, in the sheer simplicity of snobbery, "Why are you a Liberal?" and to such a question Lord Goderich (for so the second Lord Ripon was called till he succeeded to his father's title) would probably have replied, "Because I can't help it." He was an only child, educated at home, and therefore free to form his own opinions at an age when most boys are subject to the stereotyping forces of a Public School and a University. Almost before his arrival at man's estate, he had clearly marked out his line of political action, and to that line he adhered with undeviating consistency.

He was supremely fortunate in an early and ideally happy marriage. Tennyson might well have drawn the heroine of *The Talking Oak* from Henrietta, Lady Ripon:

> "Yet, since I first could cast a shade,
> Did never creature pass,
> So slightly, musically made,
> So light upon the grass."

Her mental constitution corresponded to her physical frame; she was the brightest of companions and the most sympathetic of friends. She shared to the full her husband's zeal for the popular cause, and stimulated his efforts for social as well as political reform.

From the earliest days of their married life, Lord and Lady Goderich made their home a centre and a rallying-point for all the scattered forces which, within the Liberal party or beyond its pale, were labouring to promote the betterment of human life. There the "Christian Socialists," recovering from the shocks and disasters of '48, re-gathered their shattered hosts, and reminded a mocking world that the People's Cause was not yet lost. There was Maurice with his mystical eloquence, and Kingsley with his fiery zeal, and Hughes and Vansittart and Ludlow with their economic knowledge and powerful pens. They were reinforced by William Edward Forster, a young Radical M.P., whose zeal for social service had already marked him out from the ruck of mechanical politicians; and from time to time Carlyle himself would vouchsafe a growl of leonine approval to enterprises which, whether wise or foolish, were at least not shams. In 1852 the Amalgamated Society of Engineers conducted in London and Lancashire a strike which had begun in some engineering works at Oldham.

The Christian Socialists gave it their support, and Lord Goderich subscribed £500 to the maintenance of the strikers. But, although he lived in this highly idealistic society, surrounded by young men who saw visions and old men who dreamed dreams, Lord Goderich was neither visionary nor dreamer. He passed, under Lord Russell, Lord Palmerston, and Mr. Gladstone, through a long series of practical and laborious offices. He became Secretary of State for India, and for War; and, when Lord President of the Council, attained perhaps the highest honour of his life in being appointed Chairman of the Joint Commission on American Affairs, which in 1871 saved us from the unimaginable calamity of war with the United States. Ten years later, as Viceroy of India, he made his permanent mark on the history of the British Empire; and from that day forward no Liberal Government would have been considered complete unless it could show the sanction of his honoured name. When, in February, 1886, Gladstone formed the Administration which was to establish Home Rule, Lord Ripon, who became First Lord of the Admiralty, explained his position to me with happy candour: "I have always been in favour of the most advanced thing in the Liberal Programme. Just now the most advanced thing is Home Rule; so I'm a Home Ruler."

In the last year of Lord Ripon's life, when he had just retired from the Cabinet and the leadership of the House of Lords, he was entertained at luncheon by the Eighty Club, and the occasion was marked by some more than usually interesting speeches. It always is satisfactory to see public honours rendered, not to a monument or a tomb, but to the living man; and, in Lord Ripon's case, the honours, though ripe, were not belated. George Eliot has reminded us that "to all ripeness under the sun there comes a further stage of development which is less esteemed in the market." The Eighty Club avoided that latent peril, and paid its honours, while they were still fresh and worth having, to the living representative of a Liberalism "more high and heroical than the present age affecteth." One could not help feeling that the audience which Lord Ripon faced when he was addressing the Club was Radical to the backbone. Radicals themselves, and eager to set the world right, they paid reverence to a Radical who, sixty years ago, was inspired by the same passion, and in all that long stretch of time has never failed the cause. The applause, hearty, genuine, emotional, was even more expressive than the oratory, for it was evoked by the presence of a man who, in his earliest youth, had burst the trammels of station and environment, and had sworn himself to the service of the poor, the ill-fed, and the unrepresented, in days when such devotion was far more difficult than now. It is probable that not a few of Lord Ripon's hearers, while they acclaimed his words and waved their salutations, may have added in the depths of their hearts some aspiration such as this: "When I come to my eightieth year, may I be able to look back upon a career as consistent, as unselfish, and as beneficent."

Thrice happy is the man, be he Warrior or Statesman, who, in spite of lessened activity and increasing burdens and the loss of much that once made life enjoyable, still

"Finds comfort in himself and in his cause,
And, while the mortal mist is gathering, draws
His breath in confidence of Heaven's applause."

V

"FREDDY LEVESON"

When a man has died in his eighty-ninth year, it seems irreverent to call him by his nickname. And yet the irreverence is rather in seeming than in reality, for a nickname, a pet-name, an abbreviation, is often the truest token of popular esteem. It was so with the subject of this section, whose perennial youthfulness of heart and mind would have made formal appellation seem stiff and out of place.

Edward Frederick Leveson-Gower was the third son of Granville Leveson-Gower, first Earl Granville, by his marriage with Henrietta Elizabeth Cavendish, daughter of the third Duke of Devonshire. The very names breathe Whiggery, and in their combination they suggest a considerable and an important portion of our social and political history.

I have always maintained that Whiggery, rightly understood, is not a political creed, but a social caste. The Whig, like the poet, is born, not made. It is as difficult to become a Whig as to become a Jew. Macaulay was probably the only man who, being born outside the privileged enclosure, ever penetrated to its heart and assimilated its spirit. It is true that the Whigs, as a body, have held certain opinions and pursued certain tactics, which were analysed in chapters xix. and xxi. of the unexpurgated *Book of Snobs*. But those opinions and those tactics have been accidents of Whiggery. Its substance has been relationship. When Lord John Russell formed his first Administration, his opponents alleged that it was mainly composed of his cousins, and the lively oracles of Sir Bernard Burke confirmed the allegation. A. J. Beresford-Hope, in one of his novels, made excellent fun of what he called the "Sacred Circle of the Great-Grandmotherhood." He showed—what, indeed, the Whigs themselves knew uncommonly well—that from John, Earl Gower, who died in 1754, descend all the Gowers, Levesons, Howards, Cavendishes, Grosvenors, Harcourts, and Russells, who walk on the face of the earth. Truly a noble and a highly favoured progeny. "They *are* our superiors," said Thackeray; "and that's the fact. I am not a Whig myself (perhaps it is as unnecessary to say so as to say that I'm not King Pippin in a golden coach, or King Hudson, or Miss Burdett-Coutts)—I'm not a Whig; but oh, how I should like to be one!"

It argues no political bias to maintain that, in the earlier part of the nineteenth century, Toryism offered to its neophytes no educational opportunities equal to those which a young Whig enjoyed at Chatsworth and Bowood and Woburn and Holland House. Here the best traditions of the previous century were constantly reinforced by accessions of fresh intellect. The circle was, indeed, an aristocratic Family Party, but it paid a genuine homage to ability and culture. Genius held the key, and there was a *carrière ouverte aux talents*.

Into this privileged society Frederick Leveson-Gower was born on the 3rd of May, 1819, and within its precincts he "kept the noiseless tenour of his way" for nearly ninety years. Recalling in 1905 the experiences of his boyhood, and among them a sharp illness at Eton, he was able to add, "Never during my long life have I again been seriously ill." To that extraordinary immunity from physical suffering was probably due the imperturbable serenity which all men recognized as his most characteristic trait, and which remained unruffled to the end.

It is recorded of the fastidious Lady Montfort in *Endymion* that, visiting Paris in 1841, she could only with difficulty be induced to call on the British Ambassador and Ambassadress. "I dined," she said, "with those people once; but I confess that, when I thought of those dear Granvilles, their *entrées* stuck in my throat." The "dear Granvilles" in question were the parents of the second Lord Granville, whom we all remember as the most urbane of Foreign Secretaries, and of Frederick Leveson-Gower. The first Lord Granville was a younger son of the first Marquess of Stafford and brother of the second Marquess, who was made Duke of Sutherland. He was born in 1773, entered Parliament at twenty-two, and "found himself a diplomatist as well as a politician before he was thirty years of age." In 1804 he was appointed Ambassador to St. Petersburg, where he remained till 1807. In 1813 he was created Viscount Granville, and in 1824 became Ambassador to the Court of France. "To the indignation of the Legitimist party in France, he made a special journey from Paris to London in order to vote for the Reform Bill of 1832, and, to their astonishment, returned alive to glory in having done so." For this and similar acts of virtue he was raised to an earldom in 1833; he retired from diplomacy in 1841, and died in 1846.

Before he became an Ambassador, this Lord Granville had rented a place called Wherstead, in Suffolk. It was there that Freddy Leveson passed the first years of his life, but from 1824 onwards the British Embassy at Paris was his home. Both those places had made permanent dints in his memory. At Wherstead he remembered the Duke of Wellington shooting Lord Granville in the face and imperilling his eyesight; at Paris he was presented to Sir Walter Scott, who had come to dine with the Ambassador. When living at the Embassy, Freddy Leveson was a playmate of the Duc de Bordeaux, afterwards Comte de Chambord; and at the age of eight he was sent from Paris to a Dr. Everard's school at Brighton, "which was called the House of Lords, owing to most of the boys being related to the peerage, many of them future peers, and among them several dukes." Here, again, the youthful Whig found himself a playmate of Princes. Prince George of Hanover and Prince George of Cambridge were staying with King William IV. at the Pavilion; their companions were chosen from Dr. Everard's seminary; and the King amused his nephews and their friends with sailor's stories, "sometimes rather coarse ones." In his holidays little Freddy enjoyed more refined society at Holland House. In 1828 his mother wrote with just elation: "He always sits next to Lord Holland, and they talk without ceasing all dinner-time."

From Brighton, Frederick Leveson was promoted in due course to Eton, where he played no games and made no friends, had poor health, and was generally unhappy. One trait of Eton life, and only one, he was accustomed in old age to recall with approbation, and that was the complete indifference to social distinctions.

"There is," he wrote, "a well-known story about my friend, the late Lord Bath, who, on his first arrival at Eton was asked his name, and answered, 'I am Viscount Weymouth, and I shall be Marquis of Bath.' Upon which he received two kicks, one for the Viscount and the other for the Marquis. This story may not be true, but at any rate it illustrates the fact that if at Eton a boy boasted of his social advantages, he would have cause to repent it!"

Leaving Eton at sixteen, Frederick Leveson went to a private tutor in Nottinghamshire, and there he first developed his interest in politics. "Reform," he wrote, "is my principal aim." Albany Fonblanque, whose vivacious articles, reprinted from the *Examiner*, may still be read in *England under Seven Administrations*, was his political instructor, and indoctrinated him with certain views, especially in the domain of Political Economy, which would have been deemed heretical in the Whiggish atmosphere of Trentham or Chatsworth. In 1832 he made his appearance in society at Paris, and his mother wrote: "As to Freddy, he turns all heads, and his own would be if it was to last more than a week longer. His dancing *fait fureur*."

In October, 1837, he went up to Christ Church, then rather languishing under Dean Gaisford's mismanagement. Here for three years he enjoyed himself thoroughly. He rode with the drag, was President of the Archery Club, played whist, gave and received a great deal of hospitality, and made some lifelong friendships. Among his contemporaries was Ruskin, of whom his recollection was certainly depressing. "He seemed to keep himself aloof from everybody, to seek no friends, and to have none. I never met him in anyone else's rooms, or at any social gathering. I see him now, looking rather crazy, taking his solitary walks."

That Freddy Leveson was "thoroughly idle" was his own confession; and perhaps, when we consider all the circumstances, it is not surprising. What is surprising, and what he himself recorded with surprise, is that neither he nor his contemporaries paid the least attention to the Oxford Movement, then just at its height, although—and this makes it stranger still—they used to attend Newman's Sermons at St. Mary's. They duly admired his unequalled style, but the substance of his teaching seems to have passed by them like the idle wind.

After taking a "Nobleman's Degree," Frederick Leveson spent an instructive year in France, admitted, by virtue of his father's position, to the society of such men as Talleyrand and Thiers, Guizot and Mole, Berryer and Eugene Sue; and then he returned to England with the laudable, though uninspiring, intention of reading for the Bar. His profession was chosen for him by his father, and the choice was determined by a civil speech of George Canning, who, staying at the British Embassy at Paris, noticed little Freddy, and pleasantly said to Lord Granville, "Bring that boy up as a lawyer, and he will one day become Lord Chancellor." As a first step towards that elevation, Frederick Leveson entered the chambers of an eminent conveyancer called Plunkett, where he had for his fellow-pupils the men who became Lord Iddesleigh and Lord Farrer. Thence he went to a Special Pleader, and lastly to a leading member of the Oxford Circuit. As Marshal to Lord Denman and to Baron Parke, he acquired some knowledge of the art of carving; but with regard to the total result of his legal training, he remarked, with characteristic simplicity, "I cannot say I learnt much law." When living in lodgings in Charles Street, and eating his dinners at Lincoln's Inn, Frederick Leveson experienced to the full the advantage of having been born a Whig. His uncle, the sixth Duke of Devonshire, a benevolent magnifico, if ever there was one, treated him like a son, giving him the run of Devonshire House and Chiswick; while Lady Holland, the most imperious of social dames, let him make a second home of Holland House.

"I dined with her whenever I liked. I had only to send word in the morning that I would do so. Of course, I never uttered a word at dinner, but listened with delight to the brilliant talk—to Macaulay's eloquence and varied information, to Sydney Smith's exquisite joke which made me die of laughing, to Roger's sarcasms and Luttrell's repartees."

Frederick Leveson was called to the Bar in 1843, and went the Oxford Circuit in the strangely-assorted company of G. S. Venables, J. G. Phillimore, and E. V. Kenealy. This proved to be his last stage in the anticipated progress towards the Woolsack. Lord Granville died at the beginning of 1846, and the change which this event produced in Frederick Leveson's position can best be described in his own quaint words:

"My father was greatly beloved by us all, and was the most indulgent parent—possibly too indulgent. Himself a younger son, although I cannot say that his own case was a hard one, he sympathized with me for being one of that unfortunate class. It may have been this feeling, combined with much affection, that made him leave me well provided for. I much question whether, if I had been left to earn my own bread by my own exertions as a lawyer, I should have succeeded."

His friends had no difficulty in answering the question, and answering it affirmatively; but the practical test was never applied, for on succeeding to his inheritance he glided—"plunged" would be an unsuitable word—into a way of living which was, more like the [Greek: scholae] of the Athenian citizen than the sordid strife of professional activity. He was singularly happy in private life, for the "Sacred Circle of the Great-Grandmotherhood" contained some delightful women as well as some distinguished men. Such was his sister-in-law Marie, Lady Granville; such was his cousin Harriet, Duchess of Sutherland; such was his mother, the Dowager Lady Granville; and such, pre-eminently, was his sister, Lady Georgiana Fullerton, of whom a competent critic said that, in the female characters of her novel *Ellen Middleton*, she had drawn "the line which is so apt to be overstepped, and which Walter Scott never clearly saw, between *naïveté* and vulgarity." Myself a devoted adherent of Sir Walter, I can yet recall some would-be pleasantries of Julia Mannering, of Isabella Wardour, and even of Die Vernon, which would have caused a shudder in the "Sacred Circle." Happiest of all was Freddy Leveson in his marriage with Lady Margaret Compton; but their married life lasted only five years, and left behind it a memory too tender to bear translation to the printed page.

Devonshire House was the centre of Freddy Leveson's social life—at least until the death of his uncle, the sixth Duke, in 1858. That unsightly but comfortable mansion was then in its days of glory, and those who frequented it had no reason to regret the past. "Poodle Byng," who carried down to 1871 the social conditions of the eighteenth century, declared that nothing could be duller than Devonshire House in his youth. "It was a great honour to go there, but I was bored to death. The Duchess was usually stitching in one corner of the room, and Charles Fox snoring in another." Under the splendid but arbitrary rule of the sixth Duke no one stitched or snored. Everyone who entered his saloons was well-born or beautiful or clever or famous, and many of the guests combined all four characteristics. When Prince Louis Napoleon, afterwards Napoleon III., first came to live in London, his uncle Jerome asked the Duke of Devonshire to invite his *mauvais sujet* of a nephew to Devonshire House, "so that he might for once be seen in decent society"; and the Prince, repaid the Duke by trying to borrow five thousand pounds to finance his descent on Boulogne. But the Duke, though magnificent, was business-like, and the Prince was sent empty away.

The society in which Freddy Leveson moved during his long career was curiously varied. There was his own family in all its ramifications of cousinship; and beyond its radius there was a circle of acquaintances and associates which contained Charles Greville the diarist and his more amiable brother Henry, Carlyle and Macaulay, Brougham and Lyndhurst, J. A. Roebuck and Samuel Wilberforce, George Grote and Henry Reeve, "that good-for-nothing fellow Count D'Orsay," and Disraeli, "always courteous, but his courtesy sometimes overdone."

For womankind there were Lady Morley the wit and Lady Cowper the humorist, and Lady Ashburton, who tamed Carlyle; Lady Jersey, the queen of fashion, and the two sister-queens of beauty, Lady Canning and Lady Waterford; Lady Tankerville, who as a girl had taken refuge in England from the matrimonial advances of the Comte d'Artois; the three fascinating Foresters, Mrs. Robert Smith, Mrs. Anson, and Lady Chesterfield; and Lady Molesworth and Lady Waldegrave, who had climbed by their cleverness from the lowest rung of the social ladder to a place not very far from the top.

Beyond this circle, again, there was a miscellaneous zone, where dwelt politicians ranging from John Bright to Arthur Balfour; poets and men of letters, such as Tennyson and Browning, Thackeray and Motley and Laurance Oliphant; Paxton the gardener-architect and Hudson the railway-king; stars of the musical world, such as Mario and Grisi and Rachel; blue-stockings like Lady Eastlake and Madame Mohl; Mademoiselle de Montijo, who captivated an Emperor, and Lola Montez, who ruled a kingdom. No advantages of social education will convert a fool or a bore or a prig or a churl into an agreeable member of society; but, where Nature has bestowed a bright intelligence and a genial disposition, her gifts are cultivated to perfection by such surroundings as Frederick Leveson enjoyed in early life. And so it came about that alike as a young man, in middle life (which was in his case unusually prolonged), and in old age, he enjoyed a universal and unbroken popularity.

It is impossible to connect the memory of Freddy Leveson with the idea of ambition, and it must therefore have been the praiseworthy desire to render unpaid service to the public which induced him to embark on the unquiet sea of politics. At a bye-election in the summer of 1847 he was returned, through the interest of his uncle the Duke of Devonshire, for Derby. A General Election immediately ensued; he was returned again, but was unseated, with his colleague, for a technical irregularity. In 1852 he was returned for Stoke-upon-Trent, this time by the aid of his cousin the Duke of Sutherland (for the "Sacred Circle" retained a good deal of what was termed "legitimate influence"). In 1854, having been chosen to second the Address at the opening of Parliament, he was directed to call on Lord John Russell, who would instruct him in his duties. Lord John was the shyest of human beings, and the interview was brief: "I am glad you are going to second the Address. You will know what to say. Good-morning."

At the General Election of 1857 he lost his seat for Stoke. "Poor Freddy," writes his brother, Lord Granville, "is dreadfully disappointed by his failure in the Potteries. He was out-jockeyed by Ricardo." All who knew "poor Freddy" will easily realize that in a jockeying contest he stood no chance. In 1859 he was returned for Bodmin, this time by the good offices, not of relations, but of friends—Lord Robartes and Lady Molesworth— and he retained the seat by his own merits till Bodmin ceased to be a borough. Twice during his Parliamentary career Mr. Gladstone offered him important office, and he declined it for a most characteristic reason—"I feared it would be thought a job." The gaps in his Parliamentary life were occupied by travelling. As a young man he had been a great deal on the Continent, and he had made what was then the adventurous tour of Spain. The winter of 1850-1851 he spent in India; and in 1856 he accompanied his brother Lord Granville (to whom he had been "précis-writer" at the Foreign Office) on his Special Mission to St. Petersburg for the Coronation of Alexander II. No chapter in his life was fuller of vivid and entertaining reminiscences, and his mind was stored with familiar memories of Radziwill, Nesselrode, and Todleben. "Freddy," wrote his brother, "is supposed to have distinguished himself greatly by his presence of mind when the Grande Duchesse Hélène got deep into politics with him."

A travelling experience, which Freddy Leveson used to relate with infinite gusto, belongs to a later journey, and had its origin in the strong resemblance between himself and his brother. Except that Lord Granville shaved, and that in later years Freddy Leveson grew a beard, there was little facially to distinguish them. In 1865 Lord Granville was Lord President of the Council, and therefore, according to the arrangement then prevailing, head of the Education Office. In that year Matthew Arnold, then an Inspector of Schools, was despatched on a mission to enquire into the schools and Universities of the Continent. Finding his travelling allowances insufficient for his needs, he wrote home to the Privy Council Office requesting an increase. Soon after he had despatched this letter, and before he could receive the official reply, he was dining at a famous restaurant in Paris, and he chose the most highly priced dinner of the day. Looking up from his well-earned meal, he saw his official chief, Lord Granville, who chanced to be eating a cheaper dinner. Feeling that this gastronomical indulgence might, from the official point of view, seem inconsistent with his request for increased allowances, he stepped across to the Lord President, explained that it was only once in a way that he thus compensated himself for his habitual abstinence, and was delighted by the facile and kindly courtesy with which his official chief received the *apologia.* His delight was abated when he subsequently found that he had been making his confession, not to Lord Granville, but to Mr. Leveson-Gower.

Looking back from the close of life upon its beginning, Freddy Leveson noted that as an infant he used to eat his egg "very slowly, and with prolonged pleasure." "Did this," he used to ask, "portend that I should grow up a philosopher or a *gourmand?* I certainly did not become the former, and I hope not the latter." I am inclined to think that he was both; for whoso understands the needs of the body has mastered at least one great department of philosophy, and he who feeds his fellow-men supremely well is in the most creditable sense of the word a *gourmand.* Freddy Leveson's dinners were justly famous, and, though he modestly observed that "hospitality is praised more than it deserves," no one who enjoyed the labours of Monsieur Beguinot ever thought that they could be overpraised. The scene of these delights was a house in South Audley Street, which, though actually small, was so designed as to seem like a large house in miniature; and in 1870 the genial host acquired a delicious home on the Surrey hills, which commands a view right across Sussex to the South Downs. "Holm-bury" is its name, and "There's no place like Home-bury" became the grateful watchword of a numerous and admiring society.

People distinguished in every line of life, and conspicuous by every social charm, found at Holm-bury a constant and delightful hospitality. None appreciated it more thoroughly than Mr. and Mrs. Gladstone, whose friendship was one of the chief happinesses of Freddy Leveson's maturer life. His link with them was Harriet, Duchess of Sutherland, who, in spite of all Whiggish prejudices against the half-converted Tory, was one of Gladstone's most enthusiastic disciples. In "Cliveden's proud alcove," and in that sumptuous villa at Chiswick where Fox and Canning died, Mr. and Mrs. Gladstone were her constant guests; and there they formed their affectionate intimacy with Freddy Leveson. Every year, and more than once a year, they stayed with him at Holmbury; and one at least of those visits was memorable. On the 19th of July, 1873, Mr. Gladstone wrote in his diary:

"Off at 4.25 to Holmbury, We were enjoying that beautiful spot and expecting Granville with the Bishop of Winchester,[*] when the groom arrived with the message that the Bishop had had a bad fall. An hour and a half later Granville entered, pale and sad: 'It's all over.' In an instant the thread of that precious life was snapped, We were all in deep and silent grief."

[Footnote *: Samuel Wilberforce.]

And now, for the sake of those who never knew Freddy Leveson, a word of personal description must be added. He was of middle height, with a slight stoop, which began, I fancy from the fact that he was short-sighted and was obliged to peer rather closely at objects which he wished to see. His growing deafness, which in later years was a marked infirmity—he had no others—tended to intensify the stooping habit, as bringing him nearer to his companions voice. His features were characteristically those of the House of Cavendish, as may be seen by comparing his portrait with that of his mother. His expression was placid, benign, but very far from inert; for his half-closed eyes twinkled with quiet mirth. His voice was soft and harmonious, with just a trace of a lisp, or rather of that peculiar intonation which is commonly described as "short-tongued." His bearing was the very perfection of courteous ease, equally remote from stiffness and from familiarity. His manners it would be impertinent to eulogize, and the only dislikes which I ever heard him express were directed against rudeness, violence, indifference to other people's feelings, and breaches of social decorum. If by such offences as these it was easy to displease him, it was no less easy to obtain his forgiveness, for he was as amiable as he was refined. In old age he wrote, with reference to the wish which some people express for sudden death: "It is a feeling I cannot understand, as I myself shall feel anxious before I die to take an affectionate leave of those I love." His desire was granted, and there my story ends. I have never known a kinder heart; I could not imagine a more perfect gentleman.

VI

SAMUEL WHITBREAD

The family of Whitbread enjoyed for several generations substantial possessions in North Bedfordshire. They were of the upper middle class, and were connected by marriage with John Howard the Prison-Reformer, whose property near Bedford they inherited. As years went on, their wealth and station increased. Samuel Whitbread, who died in 1796, founded the brewery in Chiswell Street, E.C., which still bears his name, was Member for the Borough of Bedford, and purchased from the fourth Lord Torrington a fine place near Biggleswade, called Southill, of which the wooded uplands supplied John Bunyan, dwelling on the flats of Elstow, with his idea of the Delectable Mountains.

This Samuel Whitbread was succeeded as M.P. for Bedford by a more famous Samuel, his eldest son, who was born in 1758, and married Lady Elizabeth Grey; sister of

"That Earl who taught his compeers to be just,
And wrought in brave old age what youth had planned."

Samuel Whitbread became one of the most active and influential members of the Whig party, a staunch ally of Fox and a coadjutor of Wilberforce in his attack on the Slave Trade. He was closely and unfortunately involved in the affairs of Drury Lane Theatre, and, for that reason, figures frequently in *Rejected Addresses*. He died before his time in 1815, and his eldest son, William Henry Whitbread, became M.P. for Bedford. This William Henry died without issue, and his nephew and heir was the admirable man and distinguished Parliamentarian who is here commemorated.

Samuel Whitbread was born in 1830, and educated at Rugby, where he was a contemporary of Lord Goschen, and at Trinity College, Cambridge, where one of his closest friends was James Payn, the novelist. He married Lady Isabella Pelham, daughter of the third Earl of Chichester. In those days Bedford returned two members, and at the General Election of 1852, which scotched Lord Derby's attempt to revive Protection, "Young Sam Whitbread" was returned as junior Member for the Borough, and at the elections of 1857, 1859, 1865, 1868, 1874, 1880, 1885, 1886, and 1892 he was again elected, each time after a contest and each time at the top of the poll. Had he stood again in 1895, and been again successful, he would have been "Father of the House."

It may be said, without doubt or exaggeration, that Samuel Whitbread was the ideal Member of Parliament. To begin with physical attributes, he was unusually tall, carried himself nobly, and had a beautiful and benignant countenance. His speaking was calm, deliberate, dignified; his reasoning close and strong; and his style, though unadorned, was perfectly correct. His truly noble nature shone through his utterance, and his gentle humour conciliated the goodwill even of political opponents. His ample fortune and large leisure enabled him to devote himself to Parliamentary work, though the interests of his brewery and of his landed estate were never neglected. He was active in all local business, and had a singularly exact knowledge of all that concerned his constituents, their personalities and desires. A man thus endowed was clearly predestined for high office, and, in 1859 Lord Palmerston, who believed in political apprenticeship, made Samuel Whitbread a Lord of the Admiralty. But this appointment disclosed the one weak joint in the young politician's armour. His circulation was not strong enough for his vast height, and sedulous attention to the work of an office, superadded to the normally unwholesome atmosphere of the House of Commons, was more than he could stand. "I cannot," he said, "get a living out of the London air;" and so in 1863, just on the threshold of high preferment, he bade farewell to official ambition and devoted himself thence-forward to the work of a private Member. But the leaders of the Liberal party did not resign such a recruit without repeated efforts to retain him. Three times he refused the Cabinet and twice the Speakership; while every suggestion of personal distinctions or hereditary honours he waved aside with a smile.

The knowledge that these things were so gave Whit bread a peculiar authority in the House of Commons. His independence was absolute and assured. He was, if any politician ever was, unbuyable; and though he was a sound Party man, on whom at a pinch his leaders could rely, he yet seemed to rise superior to the lower air of partisanship, and to lift debate into the atmosphere of conviction. The *St. James's Gazette* once confessed that his peculiar position in the House of Commons was one of those Parliamentary mysteries which no outsider could understand. He seemed, even amid the hottest controversies, to be rather an arbiter than an advocate. Once Mr. T. W. Russell, in a moment of inspiration, described him as "an umpire, perfectly impartial—except that he never gives his own side out." Whereupon Whitbread, with a quaint half-smile, whispered to the man sitting next to him: "That hit of 'T. W.'s' was *not very bad.*" A singular tribute to Whitbread's influence, and the weight attaching to his counsel, is found in the fact that, in the autumn of 1885, before Mr. Gladstone had announced his conversion to Home Rule, Whitbread was one of the very few people (Goschen was another) to whom he confided his change of view. Of the estimation in which Whitbread was held by his neighbours, even after he had ceased to represent them in Parliament, the present writer once heard a ludicrous, but illuminating, instance. Among the men sentenced to death after the Jameson Raid was one connected by ties of family with Bedford. For a while his kinsfolk could not believe that he was really in danger; but, when ominous rumours began to thicken, one of his uncles said, with an air of grave resolve: "This is becoming serious about my nephew. If it goes on much longer, I shall have to write to Mr. Whitbread."

In the general course of politics Whitbread was a Whig, holding to the great principles of Civil and Religious Liberty, Peace, Retrenchment, and Reform; but he was a Whig with a difference. He stuck to the party after it had been permeated by Gladstonianism, advanced in Liberalism as he advanced in years, and became a convinced Home Ruler. His political prescience, founded on long experience and close observation, was remarkable. Soon after Lord Salisbury's accession to power in the summer of 1895, he said to the present writer: "I fancy that for two or three years the Government will go on quietly enough; and then, when they find their popularity waning, they will pick a quarrel with somebody, and go to war. It is always difficult for an Opposition to attack a Government which is conducting a war, and I think Chamberlain is just the man to take advantage of that difficulty."

In religion Whitbread was an Evangelical of the more liberal type, mistrusting extremes, and always on the friendliest terms with Nonconformists. As regards the affairs of common life, he was a most hospitable and courteous host; a thorough agriculturist, and a keen sportsman. His size and weight debarred him from hunting, but he was a first-rate shot, whether on the moor or in the stubble, and a keen yachtsman. At home and abroad, everywhere and in all things, he was a gentleman of the highest type, genial, dignified, and unassuming. Probity, benevolence, and public spirit were embodied in Samuel Whitbread.

VII

HENRY MONTAGU BUTLER

The loved and honoured friend whose name stands at the head of this section was the fourth son and, youngest child of Dr. George Butler, Dean of Peterborough, and sometime Head Master of Harrow. Montagu Butler was himself-educated at Harrow under Dr. Vaughan, afterwards the well-known Master of the Temple, and proved to be in many respects the ideal schoolboy. He won all the prizes for composition, prose and verse, Greek, Latin, and English. He gained the principal scholarship, and was Head of the School. Beside all this, he was a member of the Cricket Eleven and made the highest score for Harrow in the match against Eton at Lord's.

In July, 1851, Montagu Butler left Harrow, and in the following October entered Trinity College, Cambridge, as a Scholar. He won the Bell University Scholarship, the Battie University Scholarship, the Browne Medal for a Greek Ode twice, the Camden Medal, Porson Prize, and First Member's Prize for a Latin Essay, and graduated as Senior Classic in 1855. Of such an undergraduate career a Fellowship at Trinity was the natural sequel, but Butler did not long reside at Cambridge. All through his boyhood and early manhood he had set his heart on a political career. He had a minute acquaintance with the political history of modern England, and his memory was stored with the masterpieces of political eloquence.

In 1856 he accepted the post of Private Secretary to the Right Hon. W. F. Cowper, afterwards Lord Mount Temple, and then President of the Board of Health in Lord Palmerston's Administration. In this office he served for two years, and then, retiring, he spent eleven months in foreign travel, visiting in turn the Tyrol, Venice, the Danube, Greece, Rome, Florence, and the Holy Land. During this period, he changed his plan of life, and in September, 1859, he was ordained Deacon by Bishop Lonsdale of Lichfield, on Letters Dimissory from Bishop Turton of Ely. His title was his Fellowship; but it was settled that the College should present him to the Vicarage of Great St. Mary's, Cambridge; and till it was vacant he was to have worked as a classical tutor in Trinity. Then came another change. "Dr. Vaughan's retirement," he wrote, "from the Head Mastership of Harrow startled us. We all took quietly for granted that he would stay on for years." However, this "startling" retirement took place, and there was a general agreement among friends of the School that Vaughan's favourite pupil, Montagu Butler, was the right man to succeed him. Accordingly, Butler was elected in November, 1859, though only twenty-six years old; and, with a view to the pastoral oversight of Harrow School, he was ordained priest, again by Bishop Lonsdale, at Advent, 1859.

In January, 1860, Montagu Butler entered on his new duties at Harrow, and there he spent five-and-twenty years of happy, strenuous, and serviceable life. He found 469 boys in the School; under his rule the numbers increased till they reached 600.

Butler's own culture was essentially classical, for he had been fashioned by Vaughan, who "thought in Greek," and he himself might almost have been said to think and feel in Latin elegiacs. But his scholarship was redeemed from pedantry by his wide reading, and by his genuine enthusiasm for all that is graceful in literature, modern as well as ancient. Under his rule the "grand, old, fortifying, classical curriculum," which Matthew Arnold satirized, fought hard and long for its monopoly; but gradually it had to yield. Butler's first concession was to relax the absurd rule which had made Latin versification obligatory on every boy in the School, whatever his gifts or tastes. At the same time he introduced the regular teaching of Natural Science, and in 1869 he created a "Modern Side." An even more important feature of his rule was the official encouragement given to the study of music, which, from an illicit indulgence practised in holes and corners, became, under the energetic management of Mr. John Farmer, a prime element in the life of the School.

In January, 1868, Butler admitted me to Harrow School. My father had introduced me to him in the previous September, and I had fallen at once under his charm. He was curiously unlike what one had imagined a Head Master to be—not old and pompous and austere, but young and gracious, friendly in manner, and very light in hand. His leading characteristic was gracefulness. He was graceful in appearance, tall and as yet slender; graceful in movement and gesture; graceful in writing, and pre-eminently graceful in speech. He was young—thirty-four—and looked younger, although (availing himself of the opportunity afforded by an illness in the summer of 1867) he had just grown a beard. He had a keen sense of humour, and was not afraid to display it before boys, although he was a little pampered by a sense of the solemn reverence due not only to what was sacred, but to everything that was established and official. To breakfast with a Head Master is usually rather an awful experience, but there was no awe about the pleasant meals in Butler's dining-room (now the head Master's study), for he was unaffectedly kind, overflowing with happiness, and tactful in adapting his conversation to the capacities of his guests.

It was rather more alarming to face him at the periodical inspection of one's Form. ("Saying to the Head Master" was the old phrase, then lapsing out of date.) We used to think that he found a peculiar interest in testing the acquirements of such boys as he knew personally, and of those whose parents were his friends; so that on these occasions it was a doubtful privilege to "know him," as the phrase is, "at home." Till one reached the Sixth Form these social and official encounters with Butler were one's only opportunities of meeting him at close quarters; but every Sunday evening we heard him preach in the Chapel, and the cumulative effect of his sermons was, at least in many cases, great. They were always written in beautifully clear and fluent English, and were often decorated with a fine quotation in prose or verse. In substance they were extraordinarily simple, though not childish. For example, he often preached on such practical topics as Gambling, National Education; and the Housing of the Poor, as well as on themes more obviously and directly religious. He was at his best in commemorating a boy who had died in the School, when his genuine sympathy with sorrow made itself unmistakably felt. But whatever was the subject, whether public or domestic, he always treated it in the same simply Christian spirit. I know from his own lips that he had never passed through those depths of spiritual experience which go to make a great preacher; but his sermons revealed in every sentence a pure, chivalrous, and duty-loving heart. One of his intimate friends once spoke of his "Arthur-like" character, and the epithet was exactly right.

His most conspicuous gift was unquestionably his eloquence. His fluency, beauty of phrase, and happy power of turning "from grave to gay, from lively to severe," made him extraordinarily effective on a platform or at a social gathering. Once (in the autumn of 1870) he injured his right arm, and so was prevented from writing his sermons. For three or four Sundays he preached extempore, and even boys who did not usually care for sermons were fascinated by his oratory.

In the region of thought I doubt if he exercised any great influence. To me he never seemed to have arrived at his conclusions by any process of serious reasoning. He held strongly and conscientiously a certain number of conventions—a kind of Palmerstonian Whiggery, a love of "spirited foreign policy;" an admiration for the military character, an immense regard for the Crown, for Parliament, and for all established institutions (he was much shocked when the present Bishop of Oxford spoke in the Debating Society in favour of Republicanism); and in every department of life he paid an almost superstitious reverence to authority. I once ventured to tell him that even a beadle was a sacred being in his eyes, and he did not deny the soft impeachment.

His intellectual influence was not in the region of thought, but in that of expression. His scholarship was essentially literary. He had an instinctive and unaffected love of all that was beautiful, whether in prose or verse, in Greek, Latin, or English. His reading was wide and thorough. Nobody knew Burke so well, and he had a contagious enthusiasm for Parliamentary oratory. In composition he had a *curiosa felicitas* in the strictest meaning of the phrase; for his felicity was the product of care. To go through a prize-exercise with him was a real joy, so generous was his appreciation, so fastidious his taste, so dexterous his substitution of the telling for the ineffective word, and so palpably genuine his enjoyment of the business.

As a ruler his most noticeable quality was his power of discipline. He was feared—and a Head Master who is not feared is not fit for his post; and by bad boys he was hated, and by most good boys he was loved. By most, but not by all. There were some, even among the best, who resented his system of minute regulation, his "Chinese exactness" in trivial detail, his tendency to treat the tiniest breach of a School rule as if it were an offence against the moral law.

I think it may be said, in general terms, that those who knew him best loved him most. He had by nature a passionate temper, but it was grandly controlled, and seldom, if ever, led him into an injustice. His munificence in giving was unequalled in my experience. He was the warmest and staunchest of friends; through honour and dishonour, storm and sunshine, weal or woe, always and exactly the same. His memory for anything associated with his pupils careers was extraordinarily retentive, and he was even passionately loyal to *Auld Lang Syne*. And there is yet another characteristic which claims emphatic mention in any attempt to estimate his influence. He was conspicuously and essentially a gentleman. In appearance, manner, speech, thought, and act, this gentlemanlike quality of his nature made itself felt; and it roused in such as were susceptible of the spell an admiration which the most meritorious teachers have often, by sheer boorishness forfeited.

Time out of mind, a Head Mastership has been regarded as a stepping-stone to a Bishopric—with disastrous results to the Church—and in Butler's case it seemed only too likely that the precedent would be followed. Gladstone, when Prime Minister, once said to a Harrovian colleague, "What sort of Bishop would your old master, Dr. Butler, make?" "The very worst," was the reply. "He is quite ignorant of the Church, and would try to discipline his clergy like school-boys. But there is one place for which he is peculiarly qualified—the Mastership of Trinity." And the Prime Minister concurred. In June, 1885, Gladstone was driven from office, and was succeeded by Lord Salisbury. In October, 1886, the Master of Trinity (Dr. W. H. Thompson) died, and Salisbury promptly offered the Mastership to Dr. Butler, who had for a year been Dean of Gloucester. It is not often that a man is designated for the same great post by two Prime Ministers of different politics.

At Trinity, though at first he had to live down certain amount of jealousy and ill-feeling, Butler's power and influence increased steadily from year to year, and towards the end he was universally respected and admired. A resident contemporary writes: "He was certainly a Reformer, but not a violent one. His most conspicuous services to the College were, in my opinion, these: (1) Sage guidance of the turbulent and uncouth democracy of which a College Governing body consists. (2) A steady aim at the highest in education, being careful to secure the position of literary education from the encroachments of science and mathematics. (3) Affectionate stimulus to all undergraduates who need it, especially Old Harrovians. (4) The maintenance of the dignity and commanding position of Trinity and consequently of the University in the world at large."

To Cambridge generally Butler endeared himself by his eager interest in all good enterprises, by his stirring oratory and persuasive preaching, and by his lavish hospitality. As Vice-Chancellor, in 1889 and 1890, he worthily maintained the most dignified traditions of academical office. Those who knew him both on the religious and on the social side will appreciate the judgment said to have been pronounced by Canon Mason, then Master of Pembroke: "Butler will be saved, like Rahab, by hospitality and faith."

VIII

BASIL WILBERFORCE[*]

[Footnote *: A Memorial Address delivered in St. John's Church, Westminster.]

In the House of God the praise of man should always be restrained. I, therefore, do not propose to obey the natural instinct which would prompt me to deliver a copious eulogy of the friend whom we commemorate—an analysis of his character or a description of his gifts.

But, even in church, there is nothing out of place in an attempt to recall the particular aspects of truth which presented themselves with special force to a particular mind. Rather, it is a dutiful endeavour to acknowledge the gifts, whether in the way of spiritual illumination or of practical guidance, which God gave us through His servant; and, it is on some of those aspects as they presented themselves to the mind of Basil Wilberforce that I propose to speak—not, indeed, professing to treat them exhaustively, but bearing in mind that true saying of Jeremy Taylor: "In this world we believe in part and prophesy in part; and this imperfection shall never be done away, till we be transplanted to a more glorious state."

1. I cannot doubt about the point which should be put most prominently.

Wilberforce's most conspicuous characteristic was his vivid apprehension of the Spiritual World. His eyes, like Elisha's, were always open to see "the mountain full of horses and chariots of fire." Incorporeal presences were to him at least as real as those which are embodied in flesh and blood. Material phenomena were the veils of spiritual realities; and "the powers of the world to come" were more actual and more momentous than those which operate in time and space. Perhaps the most important gift which God gave to the Church through his ministry was his lifelong testimony against the darkness of Materialism.

2. Second only to his keen sense of the Unseen World was his conviction of God's love.

Other aspects of the Divine Nature as it is revealed to us—Almightiness, Justice, Awfulness (though, of course, he recognized them all)—did not colour his heart and life as they were coloured by the sense of the Divine Love. That Love seemed to him to explain all the mysteries of existence, to lift

"the heavy and the weary weight
Of all this unintelligible world";

to make its dark places light, its rough places plain, its hard things easy, even its saddest things endurable. His Gospel was this: God, Who made us in His own Image, loves us like a Father; and therefore, in life and in death, in time and in eternity, all is, and must be, well.

3. "He prayeth best, who lovest best
All things both great and small.
For the dear God Who loveth us,
He made and loveth all."

Those familiar words of Coleridge perfectly express Wilberforce's attitude towards his fellow-creatures, and when I say "fellow-creatures," I am not thinking only of his brothers and sisters in the human family.

He was filled with a God-like love of all that God has made. Hatred and wrath and severity were not "dreamt of" in his "philosophy." Towards the most degraded and abandoned of the race he felt as tenderly as St. Francis felt towards the leper on the roadside at Assisi, when he kissed the scarred hand, and then found that, all unwittingly, he had ministered to the Lord, disguised in that loathsome form. This was the motive which impelled Wilberforce to devote himself, uncalculatingly and unhesitatingly, to the reclamation of lives that had been devastated by drunkenness, and which stimulated his zeal for all social and moral reforms.

But his love extended far beyond the bounds of the human family; and (in this again resembling St. Francis) he loved the birds and beasts which God has provided as our companions in this life, and perhaps—for aught we know—in the next. In a word, he loved all God's creatures for God's sake.

4. No one had a keener sense of the workings of the Holy Spirit in regions beyond the precincts of all organized religion; and yet, in his own personal heart and life, Wilberforce belonged essentially to the Church of England. It is difficult to imagine him happy and content in any communion except our own. Nowhere else could he have found that unbroken chain which links us to Catholic antiquity and guarantees the validity of our sacraments, combined with that freedom of religious speculation and that elasticity of devotional forms which were to him as necessary as vital air. Various elements of his teaching, various aspects of his practice will occur to different minds; but (just because it is sometimes overlooked) I feel bound to remind you of his testimony to the blessings which he had received through Confession, and to the glory of the Holy Eucharist, as the Sun and Centre of Catholic worship. His conviction of the

reality and nearness of the spiritual world gave him a singular ease and "access" in intercessory prayer, and his love of humanity responded to that ideal of public worship which is set forth in *John Inglesant*: "The English Church, as established by the law of England, offers the Supernatural to all who choose to come. It is like the Divine Being Himself, Whose sun shines alike on the evil and on the good."

5. In what theology did Wilberforce, whose adult life had been one long search for truth, finally repose? Assuredly he never lost his hold on the central facts of the Christian revelation as they are stated in the creed of Nicæa and Constantinople. Yet, as years went on, he came to regard them less and less in their objective aspect; more and more as they correspond to the work of the Spirit in the heart and conscience. Towards the end, all theology seemed to be for him comprehended in the one doctrine of the Divine Immanence, and to find its natural expression in that significant phrase of St. Paul: "Christ in you, the hope of glory."

Spiritually-minded men do not, as a rule, talk much of their spiritual experiences; but, if one had asked Wilberforce to say what he regarded as the most decisive moment of his religious life, I can well believe that he would have replied, "The moment when 'it pleased God to reveal His Son *in* me.'"

The subject expands before us, as is always the case when we meditate on the character and spirit of those whom we have lost; and I must hasten to a close.

I have already quoted from a writer with whom I think Wilberforce would have felt a close affinity, though, as a matter of fact, I never heard him mention that writer's name; I mean J. H. Shorthouse; and I return to the same book—the stimulating story of *John Inglesant*—for my concluding words, which seem to express, with accidental fidelity, the principle of Wilberforce's spiritual being: "We are like children, or men in a tennis-court, and before our conquest is half-won, the dim twilight comes and stops the game; nevertheless, let us keep our places, and above all hold fast by the law of life we feel within. This was the method which Christ followed, and He won the world by placing Himself in harmony with that law of gradual development which the Divine wisdom has planned. Let us follow in His steps, and we shall attain to the ideal life; and, without waiting for our mortal passage, tread the free and spacious streets of that Jerusalem which is above."

IX

EDITH SICHEL

This notice is more suitably headed with a name than with a title. Edith Sichel was greater than anything she wrote, and the main interest of the book before us[*] is the character which it reveals. Among Miss Sichel's many activities was that of reviewing, and Mr. Bradley tells that "her first object was to let the reader know what kind of matter he might expect to find in the book, and, if necessary, from what point of view it is treated there." Following this excellent example, let us say that in *New and Old* the reader will find an appreciative but not quite adequate "Introduction"; some extracts from letters; some "thoughts" or aphorisms; some poems; and thirty-two miscellaneous pieces of varying interest-and merit. This is what we "find in the book," and the "point of view" is developed as we read.

[Footnote *: *New and Old*. By Edith Sichel. With an Introduction by A. C. Bradley. London: Constable and Co.]

To say that the Introduction is not quite adequate is no aspersion on Mr. Bradley. He tells us that he only knew Miss Sichel "towards the close of her life" (she was born in 1862 and died in 1914), and in her case pre-eminently the child was mother of the woman. Her blood was purely Jewish, and the Jewish characteristic of precocity was conspicuous in her from the first. At ten she had the intellectual alertness of sixteen, and at sixteen she could have held her own with ordinary people of thirty. To converse with her even casually always reminded me of Matthew Arnold's exclamation: "What women these Jewesses are! with a *force* which seems to triple that of the women of our Western and Northern races."

From the days of early womanhood to the end, Edith Sichel led a double life, though in a sense very different from that in which this ambiguous phrase is generally employed. "She was known to the reading public as a writer of books and of papers in magazines.... Her principal books were warmly praised by judges competent to estimate their value as contributions to French biography and history;" and her various writings, belonging to very different orders and ranging over a wide variety of topics, were always marked by vigour and originality. Her versatility was marvellous; and, "though she had not in youth the severe training that makes for perfect accuracy," she had by nature the instinct which avoids the commonplace, and which touches even hackneyed themes with light and fire. Her humour was exuberant, unforced, untrammelled; it played freely round every object which met her mental gaze—sometimes too freely when she was dealing with things traditionally held sacred. But her flippancy was of speech rather than of thought, for her fundamental view of life was serious. "Life, in her view, brings much that is pure and unsought joy, more, perhaps, that needs transforming effort, little or nothing that cannot be made to contribute to an inward and abiding happiness."

Some more detailed account of her literary work may be given later on; at this point I must turn to the other side of her double life. She was only twenty-two when she began her career of practical benevolence among the poor girls of Bethnal Green, Shoreditch, and Shadwell. She established in the country Homes for the girl-children of an East End work-house, and maintained them till she died. For twenty-two years she was treasurer of a Boys' Home. She was a manager of Elementary Schools in London. She held a class for female prisoners at Holloway. She was deeply impressed by the importance of starting young people in suitable employment, and threw all her energies into the work, "in case of need, supplying the money required for apprenticeship." In this and in all her other enterprises she was generous to a fault, always being ready to give away half her income—and yet not "to a fault," for her strong administrative and financial instinct restrained her from foolish or mischievous expenditure. All this work, of body and mind, was done in spite of fragile health and frequent suffering; yet she never seemed overburdened, or fussed, or flurried, and those who enjoyed her graceful hospitality in Onslow Gardens would never have suspected either that her day had been spent in what she called "the picturesque mire of Wapping," or that she had been sitting up late at night, immersed in *Human Documents from the Four Centuries preceding the Reformation.*

We have spoken of her humour. Those who would see a sample of it are referred to her description of the Eisteddfod on p. 22; and this piece of pungent fun may be profitably read in contrast with her grim story of *Gladys Leonora Pratt.* In that story some of the writer's saddest experiences in the East End are told with an unshrinking fidelity, which yet has nothing mawkish or prurient in it. Edith Sichel was too good an artist to be needlessly disgusting. "It might," she said, "be well for the modern realist to remember that literalness is not the same as truth, nor curiosity as courage."

She was best known as a writer of books about the French Renaissance, on which she became an acknowledged authority. She was less well known, but not less effective, as a reviewer—no one ever dissected Charlotte Yonge so justly—and she excelled in personal description. Her accounts of her friends Miss Emily Lawless, Miss Mary Coleridge, and Joseph Joachim, are masterpieces of characterization. All her literary work was based on a wide and strong foundation of generous culture. German was to her a second mother-tongue, and she lectured delightfully on *Faust.* Though she spoke of herself as talking "fluent and incomprehensible bad French," she was steeped in French scholarship. She had read Plato and Sophocles under the stimulating guidance of William Cory, and her love of Italy had taught her a great deal of Italian. The authors whom she enjoyed and quoted were a motley crowd—Dante and Rabelais, Pascal and Montaigne, George Sand and Sainte-Beuve, Tolstoi and George Borrow, "Mark Rutherford" and Samuel Butler, Fénelon and Renan and Anatole France. Her vein of poetic feeling was strong and genuine. In addressing some young girls she said: "We all think a great deal of the importance of opening our windows and airing our rooms. I wish we thought as much of airing our imaginations. To me poetry is quite like that. It is like opening the window daily, and looking out and letting in the air and the sunlight into an otherwise stuffy little room; and if I cannot read some poetry in the day I feel more uncomfortable than I can tell you." She might have put the case more strongly; for poetry, and music, and painting, and indeed all art at its highest level, made a great part of her religion. Her family had long ago conformed to the Church of England, in which she was brought up; but she never shook off her essential Judaism. She had no sympathy with rites or ordinances, creeds or dogmas, and therefore outward conformity to the faith of her forefathers would have been impossible to her; but she looked with reverent pride on the tombs in the Jewish cemetery at Prague. "It gave me a strange feeling to stand at the tombstone of our tribe—900 A.D. The oldest scholar's grave is 600 A.D., and Heaven knows how many great old Rabbis lie there, memorable and forgotten. The wind and the rain were sobbing all round the place, and all the melancholy of my race seemed to rise up and answer them." Though she was a Churchwoman by practice, her own religion was a kind of undefined Unitarianism. "The Immanence of God and the life of Christ are my treasures." "I am a heretic, you know, and it seems to me that all who call Christ Master with adoration of that life are of the same band." Her favourite theologians were James Martineau, Alfred Ainger (whose Life she wrote admirably), and Samuel Barnett, whom she elevated into a mystic and a prophet. The ways of the Church of England did not please her. She had nothing but scorn for "a joyless curate prating of Easter joy with limpest lips," or for "the Athanasian Creed sung in the highest of spirits in a prosperous church" filled with "sealskin-jacketed mammas and blowsy old gentlemen." But the conclusion of the whole matter was more comfortable—"All the clergymen in the world cannot make one disbelieve in God."

X

"WILL" GLADSTONE

"He bequeathed to his children the perilous inheritance of a name which the Christian world venerates." The words were originally used by Bishop Samuel Wilberforce with reference to his father, the emancipator of the negro. I venture to apply them to the great man who, in days gone by, was my political leader, and I do so the more confidently because I hold that Gladstone will be remembered quite apart from politics, and, as Bishop Westcott said, "rather for what he was than for what he did." He was, in Lord Salisbury's words, "an example, to which history hardly furnishes a parallel, of a great Christian, Statesman." It was no light matter for a boy of thirteen to inherit a name which had been so nobly borne for close on ninety years, and to acquire, as soon as he came of age, the possession of a large and difficult property, and all the local influence which such ownership implies. Yet this was the burden which was imposed on "Will" Gladstone by his father's untimely death. After an honourable career at Eton and Oxford, and some instructive journeyings in the East and in America (where he was an attaché at the British Embassy), he entered Parliament as Member for the Kilmarnock Boroughs. His Parliamentary career was not destined to be long, but it was in many respects remarkable.

In some ways he was an ideal candidate. He was very tall, with a fair complexion and a singular nobility of feature and bearing. To the most casual observer it was palpable that he walked the world

"With conscious step of purity and pride."

People interested in heredity tried to trace in him some resemblance to his famous grandfather; but, alike in appearance and in character, the two were utterly dissimilar. In only one respect they resembled each other, and that was the highest. Both were earnest and practical Christians, walking by a faith which no doubts ever disturbed, and serving God in the spirit and by the methods of the English Church. And here we see alike Will Gladstone's qualifications and his drawbacks as a candidate for a Scottish constituency. His name and his political convictions commended him to the electors; his ecclesiastial opinions they could not share. His uprightness of character and nobility of aspect commanded respect; his innate dislike of popularity-hunting and men-pleasing made him seem for so young a man— he was only twenty-seven—austere and aloof. Everyone could feel the intensity of his convictions on the points on which he had made up his mind; some were unreasonably distressed when he gave expression to that intensity by speech and vote. He was chosen to second the Address at the opening of the Session of 1912, and acquitted himself, as always, creditably; but it was in the debates on the Welsh Disestablishment Bill that he first definitely made his mark. "He strongly supported the principle, holding that it had been fully justified by the results of the Irish Disestablishment Act on the Irish Church. But, as in that case, generosity should characterize legislation; disendowment should be clearly limited to tithes. Accordingly, in Committee, he took an independent course. His chief speech on this subject captivated the House. For a very young Member to oppose his own party without causing irritation, and to receive the cheers of the Opposition without being led to seek in them solace for the silence of his own side, and to win general admiration by transparent sincerity and clear, balanced statement of reason, was a rare and notable performance."

When Will Gladstone struck twenty-nine, there were few young men in England who occupied a more enviable position. He had a beautiful home; sufficient, but not overwhelming, wealth; a property which gave full scope for all the gifts of management and administration which he might possess; the devoted love of his family, and the goodwill even of those who did not politically agree with him. His health, delicate in childhood, had improved with years. "While he never neglected his public duties, his natural, keen, healthy love of nature, sport, fun, humour, company, broke out abundantly. In these matters he was still a boy"—but a boy who, as it seemed, had already crossed the threshold of a memorable manhood. Such was Will Gladstone on his last birthday—the 12th of July, 1914. A month later the "Great Tribulation" had burst upon the unthinking world, and all dreams of happiness were shattered. Dreams of happiness, yes; but not dreams of duty. Duty might assume a new, a terrible, and an unlooked-for form; but its essential and spiritual part—the conviction of what a man owes to God, to his fellow-men, and to himself—became only more imperious when the call to arms was heard: *Christus ad arma vocat.*

Will Gladstone loved peace, and hated war with his whole heart. He was by conviction opposed to intervention in the quarrels of other nations. "His health was still delicate; he possessed neither the training nor instincts of a soldier; war and fighting were repugnant to his whole moral and physical fibre." No one, in short, could have been by nature less disposed for the duty which now became urgent. "The invasion of Belgium shattered his hopes and his ideals." He now realized the stern truth that England must fight, and, if England must fight, he must bear his part in the fighting. He had been made, when only twenty-six, Lord-Lieutenant of Flintshire, and as such President of the Territorial Force Association. It was his official duty to "make personal appeals for the enlistment of young men. But how could he urge others to join the Army while he, a young man not disqualified for military service, remained at home in safety? It was his duty to lead, and his best discharge of it lay in personal example." His decision was quickly and quietly made. "He was the only son of his mother, and what it meant to her he knew full well;" but there was no hesitation, no repining, no looking back. He took a commission in the 3rd Battalion of the Royal Welsh Fusiliers, and on the 15th of March, 1915, he started with a draft for France. On the 12th of April he was killed. "It is not"—he had just written to his mother—"the length of existence, that counts, but what is achieved during that existence, however short." These words of his form his worthiest epitaph.

XI

LORD CHARLES RUSSELL

A man can have no better friend than a good father; and this consideration warrants, I hope, the inclusion of yet one more sketch drawn "in honour of friendship."

Charles James Fox Russell (1807-1894) was the sixth son of the sixth Duke of Bedford. His mother was Lady Georgiana Gordon, daughter of the fourth Duke of Gordon and of the adventurous "Duchess Jane," who, besides other achievements even more remarkable, raised the "Gordon Highlanders" by a method peculiarly her own. Thus he was great-great-great-grandson of the Whig martyr, William, Lord Russell, and great-nephew of Lord George Gordon, whose Protestant zeal excited the riots of 1780. He was one of a numerous family, of whom the best remembered are John, first Earl Russell, principal author of the Reform Act of 1832, and Louisa, Duchess of Abercorn, grandmother of the present Duke.

Charles James Fox was a close friend, both politically and privately, of the Duke and Duchess of Bedford, and he promised them that he would be godfather to their next child; but he died before the child was born, whereupon his nephew, Lord Holland, took over the sponsorship, and named his godson "Charles James Fox." The child was born in 1807, and his birthplace was Dublin Castle.[*] The Duke of Bedford was then Viceroy of Ireland, and became involved in some controversy because he refused to suspend the Habeas Corpus Act. When Lord Charles Russell reached man's estate, he used, half in joke but quite half in-earnest, to attribute his lifelong sympathy with the political demands of the Irish people to the fact that he was a Dublin man by birth.

[Footnote *: He was christened from a gold bowl by the Archbishop of Dublin, Lord Normanton.]

The Duke of Bedford was one of the first Englishmen who took a shooting in Scotland (being urged thereto by his Highland Duchess); and near his shooting-lodge a man who had been "out" with Prince Charlie in 1745 was still living when Charles Russell first visited Speyside. Westminster was the Russells' hereditary school, and Charles Russell was duly subjected to the austere discipline which there prevailed. From the trials of gerund-grinding and fagging and flogging a temporary relief was afforded by the Coronation of George IV., at which he officiated as Page to the acting Lord Great Chamberlain. It was the last Coronation at which the procession was formed in Westminster Hall and moved across to the Abbey. Young Russell, by mischievousness or carelessness, contrived to tear his master's train from the ermine cape which surmounted it; and the procession was delayed till a seamstress could be found to repair the damage. "I contrived to keep that old rascal George IV. off the throne for half an hour," was Lord Charles-Russell's boast in maturer age.[*]

[Footnote *: J, W. Croker, recording the events of the day, says: "The King had to wait full half an hour for the Great Chamberlain, Lord Gwydyr, who, it seems, had torn his robes, and was obliged to wait to have them mended. I daresay the public lays the blame of the delay on to the King, who was ready long before anyone else,"—*The Croker Papers*, vol. i., p. 195.]

From Westminster Lord Charles passed to the University of Edinburgh, where his brother John had preceded him. He boarded with Professor Pillans, whom Byron gibbeted as "paltry"[*] in "English Bards and Scotch Reviewers," and enjoyed the society of the literary circle which in those days made Edinburgh famous. The authorship of the Waverley Novels was not yet revealed, and young Russell had the pleasure of discussing with Sir Walter Scott the dramatic qualities of *The Bride of Lammermoor.* He was, perhaps, less unfitted for such high converse than most lads would be, because, as Lord Holland's godson, he had been from his schooldays a frequenter of Holland House in its days of glory.[**]

[Footnote *: Why?]
[Footnote **: On his first visit Lord Holland told him that he might order his own dinner. He declared for a roast duck with green peas, and an apricot tart; whereupon the old Amphitryon said: "Decide as wisely on every question in life, and you will never go far wrong."]

On leaving Edinburgh, Lord Charles Russell joined the Blues, then commanded by Ernest, Duke of Cumberland, afterwards King of Hanover; and he was able to confirm, by personal knowledge, the strange tales of designs which the Duke entertained for placing himself or his son upon the throne of England.[*] He subsequently exchanged into the 52nd Light Infantry, from which he retired, with the rank of Lieutenant-Colonel, in order to enter Parliament. In December, 1832, he was returned at the head of the poll for Bedfordshire, and on Christmas Eve a young lady (who in 1834 became his wife) wrote thus to her sister:

"Lord Charles Russell is returned for this County. The Chairing, Dinner, etc., take place to-day. Everybody is interested about him, as he is very young and it is his first appearance in the character. His speeches have delighted the whole County, and he is, of course, very much pleased." This faculty of public speaking was perhaps his most remarkable endowment. He had an excellent command of cultivated English, a clear and harmonious voice, a keen sense of humour, and a happy knack of apt quotation.

[Footnote *: *Cf. Tales of my Father*, by A. F. Longmans, 1902.]

On the 23rd of February, 1841, Disraeli wrote, with reference to an impending division on the Irish Registration Bill: "The Whigs had last week two hunting accidents; but Lord Charles Russell, though he put his collar-bone out, and we refused to pair him, showed last night." He sate for Bedfordshire till the dissolution of that year, when he retired, feeling that Free Trade was indeed bound to come, but that it would be disastrous for the agricultural community which he represented. "Lord Charles Russell," wrote Cobden, "is the man who opposed even his brother John's fixed duty, declaring at the time that it was to throw two millions of acres out of cultivation." He returned to Parliament for a brief space in 1847, and was then appointed Serjeant-at-Arms—not, as he always insisted, "Serjeant-at-Arms to the House of Commons," but "one of the Queen's Serjeants-at-Arms, directed by her to attend on the Speaker during the sitting of Parliament." In 1873 the office and its holder were thus described by "Jehu Junior" in *Vanity Fair*.

"For the filling of so portentous an office, it is highly important that one should be chosen who will, by personal mien and bearing not less than by character, detract nothing from its dignity. Such a one is Lord Charles Russell, who is a worthy representative of the great house of Bedford from which he springs.

"For a quarter of a century he has borne the mace before successive Speakers. From his chair he has listened to Peel, to Russell, to Palmerston, to Disraeli, and to Gladstone, and he still survives as a depository of their eloquence. He is himself popular beyond the fair expectations of one who has so important a part to play in the disciplinary arrangements of a popular assembly; for he is exceptionally amiable and genial by nature, is an excellent sportsman, and has cultivated a special taste for letters.[*] It is rarely that in these times a man can be found so thoroughly fitted to fill an office which could be easily invested with ridicule, or so invariably to invest it, as he has, with dignity."

[Footnote *: He was the best Shakespearean I ever knew, and founded the "Shakespeare Medal" at Harrow. Lord Chief Justice Coleridge wrote thus: "A munificent and accomplished nobleman, Lord Charles Russell, has, by the wise liberality which dictated the foundation of his Shakespeare Medal at Harrow, secured that at least at one great Public School the boys may be stimulated in youth to an exact and scholarlike acquaintance with the poet whom age will show them to be the greatest in the world."]

Sir George Trevelyan writes: "You can hardly imagine how formidable and impressive Lord Charles seemed to the mass of Members, and especially to the young; and how exquisite and attractive was the moment when he admitted you to his friendly notice, and the absolute assurance that, once a friend, he would be a friend for ever."

Lord Charles Russell held the Serjeancy till 1875; and at this point I had better transcribe the record in *Hansard*:

Monday, April 5, 1875:

Mr. Speaker acquainted the House that he had received from Lord Charles James Fox Russell the following letter:

> HOUSE OF COMMONS,
> *April* 5*th*, 1875.

SIR,

I have the honour to make application to you that you will be pleased to sanction my retirement from my office, by Patent, of Her Majesty's Serjeant-at-Arms attending the Speaker of the House of Commons. I have held this honourable office for twenty-seven years, and I feel that the time is come when it is desirable that I should no longer retain it.

> I have the honour to be, Sir,
> Your very obedient servant,
> CHARLES J. F. RUSSELL,
> *Serjeant-at-Arms.*

THE RIGHT HONBLE. THE SPEAKER.

Thursday, April 8, 1875:

Mr. DISRAELI: I beg to move, Sir, that the letter addressed to you by Lord Charles Russell, the late Serjeant-at-Arms, be read by the Clerk at the Table.

Letter [5th April] read.

Mr. DISRAELI: Mr. Speaker, we have listened to the resignation of his office by one who has long and ably served this House. The office of Serjeant-at-Arms is one which requires no ordinary qualities; for it requires at the same time patience, firmness, and suavity, and that is a combination of qualities more rare than one could wish in this world. The noble Lord who filled the office recently, and whose resignation has just been read at the Table, has obtained our confidence by the manner in which he has discharged his duties through an unusually long period of years; and we should remember, I think, that occasions like the present are almost the only opportunity we have of expressing our sense of those qualities, entitled so much to our respect, which are possessed and exercised by those who fill offices attached to this House, and upon whose able fulfilment of their duties much of our convenience depends. Therefore, following the wise example of those who have preceded me in this office, I have prepared a Resolution which expresses the feeling of the House on this occasion, and I now place it, Sir, in your hands.

Mr. Speaker, read the Resolution, as follows: "That Mr. Speaker be requested to acquaint Lord Charles James Fox Russell that this House entertains a just sense of the exemplary manner in which he has uniformly discharged the duties of the Office of Serjeant-at-Arms during his long attendance on this House."

The MARQUESS OF HARTINGTON: Sir, on behalf of the Members who sit on this side of the House, I rise to second the Motion of the Right Hon. Gentleman. He has on more than one occasion gracefully, but at the same time justly, recognized the services rendered to the State by the house of Russell. That house will always occupy a foremost place in the history of the Party to which I am proud to belong, and I hope it will occupy no insignificant place in the history of the country. Of that house the noble Lord who has just resigned his office is no unworthy member. There are, Sir, at the present moment but few Members who can recollect the time when he assumed the duties of his office; but I am glad that his resignation has been deferred long enough to enable a number of new Members of this House to add their testimony to that of us who are better acquainted with him, as to the invariable dignity and courtesy with which he has discharged his duties.

The Resolution was adopted by the House, *nemine contradicente.*

Lord Charles now retired to his home at Woburn, Bedfordshire, where he spent the nineteen years of his remaining life. He had always been devoted to the duties and amusements of the county, and his two main joys were cricket and hunting. He was elected to M.C.C. in 1827, and for twenty years before his death I had been its senior member. Lilywhite once said to him: "For true cricket, give *me* bowling, *Pilch* in, *Box* at the wicket, and your Lordship looking on."[*] He was a good though uncertain shot, but in the saddle he was supreme—a consummate horseman, and an unsurpassed judge of a hound. He hunted regularly till he was eighty-one, irregularly still later, and rode till his last illness began. Lord Ribblesdale writes: "The last time I had the good fortune to meet your father we went hunting together with the Oakley Hounds, four or five years before his death. We met at a place called Cranfield Court, and Lord Charles was riding a young mare, five years old—or was she only four?—which kicked a hound, greatly to his disgust! She was not easy to ride, nor did she look so, but he rode her with the ease of long proficiency—not long years—and his interest in all that goes to make up a day's hunting was as full of zest and youth as I recollect his interest used to be in all that made up a cricket-match in my Harrow days."

[Footnote *: See *Lords and the M.C.C.*, p. 86.]

In religion Lord Charles Russell was an Evangelical, and he was a frequent speaker on religious platforms. In politics he was an ardent Liberal; always (except in that soon-repented heresy about Free Trade) rather in advance of his party; a staunch adherent of Mr. Gladstone, and a convinced advocate of Home Rule, though he saw from the outset that the first Home Rule Bill, without Chamberlain's support, was, as he said, "No go." He took an active part in electioneering, from the distant days when, as a Westminster boy, he cheered for Sir Francis Burdett, down to September, 1892, when he addressed his last meeting in support of Mr. Howard Whitbread, then Liberal candidate for South Bedfordshire. A speech which he delivered at the General Election of 1886, denouncing the "impiety" of holding that the Irish were incapable of self-government, won the enthusiastic applause of Mr. Gladstone. When slow-going Liberals complained of too-rapid reforms, he used to say: "When I was a boy, our cry was 'Universal Suffrage, Triennial Parliaments, and the Ballot.' That was seventy years ago, and we have only got one of the three yet."

In local matters, he was always on the side of the poor and the oppressed, and a sturdy opponent of all aggressions on their rights. "Footpaths," he wrote, "are a precious right of the poor, and consequently much encroached on."

It is scarcely decent for a son to praise his father, but even a son may be allowed to quote the tributes which his father's death evoked. Let some of these tributes end my tale.

June 29th, 1894.

My DEAR G. RUSSELL,

I am truly grieved to learn this sad news. It is the disappearance of an illustrious figure to us, but of much more, I fear, to you.

> Yours most sincerely,
> ROSEBERY.

June 30th, 1894.

DEAR G. RUSSELL,

I saw with sorrow the announcement of your father's death. He was a good and kind friend to me in the days long ago, and I mourn his loss. In these backsliding days he set a great example of steadfastness and loyalty to the faith of his youth and his race.

Yours very truly,

W. V. HARCOURT.

July 31*rd* 1894.

DEAR RUSSELL,

I was very grieved to hear of your revered father's death.

He was a fine specimen of our real aristocracy, and such specimens are becoming rarer and rarer in these degenerate days.

There was a true ring of the "Grand Seigneur" about him which always impressed me.

Yours sincerely,
REAY.

July 1*st*, 1894.

My DEAR RUSSELL,

I thank you very much for your kindness in writing to me.

You may, indeed, presume that it is with painful interest and deep regret that I hear of the death of your father, and that I value the terms in which you speak of his feelings towards myself.

Though he died at such an advanced age, it is, I think, remarkable that his friends spoke of him to the last as if he were still in the full intercourse of daily life, without the disqualification or forgetfulness that old age sometimes brings with it.

For my part I can never forget my association with him in the House of Commons and elsewhere, nor the uniform kindness which he always showed me.

Believe me, most truly yours,
ARTHUR W. PEEL.

June 29*th*, 1894.

My DEAR RUSSELL,

I have seen, with the eyes of others, in newspapers of this afternoon the account of the death—shall I say?—or of the ingathering of your father. And of what he was to you as a father I can reasonably, if remotely, conceive from knowing what he was in the outer circle, as a firm, true, loyal friend.

He has done, and will do, no dishonour to the name of Russell. It is a higher matter to know, at a supreme moment like this, that he had placed his treasure where moth and dust do not corrupt, and his dependence where dependence never fails. May he enjoy the rest, light, and peace of the just until you are permitted to rejoin him. With growing years you will feel more and more that here everything is but a rent, and that it is death alone which integrates.

On Monday I hope to go to Pitlochrie, N. B., and in a little time to return southward, and resume, if it please God, the great gift of working vision.

      Always and sincerely yours,
      W. E. GLADSTONE.

III
RELIGION AND THE CHURCH

I

A STRANGE EPIPHANY

Whenever the State meddles with the Church's business, it contrives to make a muddle. This familiar truth has been exemplified afresh by the decree which dedicated last Sunday[*] to devotions connected with the War. The Feast of the Epiphany has had, at least since the fourth century, its definite place in the Christian year, its special function, and its peculiar lesson. The function is to commemorate the revelation of Christianity to the Gentile world; and the lesson is the fulfilment of all that the better part of Heathendom had believed in and sought after, in the religion which emanates from Bethlehem. To confuse the traditional observance of this day with the horrors and agonies of war, its mixed motives and its dubious issues, was indeed a triumph of ineptitude.

[Footnote *: January 6th, 1918.]

Tennyson wrote of

> "this northern island,
> Sundered once from all the human race";

and when Christians first began to observe the Epiphany, or Theophany (as the feast was indifferently called), our own forefathers were among the heathen on whom the light of the Holy Manger was before long to shine. It has shone on us now for a good many centuries; England has ranked as one of the chiefest of Christian nations, and has always professed, and often felt, a charitable concern for the races which are still lying in darkness. Epiphany is very specially the feast of a missionary Church, and the strongest appeal which it could address to Heathendom would be to cry, "See what Christianity has done for the world! Christendom possesses the one religion. Come in and share its blessings."

There have been times and places at which that appeal could be successfully made. Indeed, as Gibbon owned, it was one of the causes to which the gradual triumph of Christianity was due. But for Europe at the present moment to address that appeal to Africa or India or China would be to invite a deadly repartee. In the long ages, Heathendom might reply, which have elapsed since the world "rose out of chaos," you have improved very little on the manners of those primeval monsters which "tare each other in the slime." Two thousand years of Christianity have not taught you to beat your swords into plough-shares. You still make your sons to pass through the fire to Moloch, and the most remarkable developments of physical science are those which make possible the destruction of human life on the largest scale. Certainly, in Zeppelins and submarines and poisonous gas there is very little to remind the world of Epiphany and what it stands for.

Thirty years ago the great Lord Shaftesbury wrote: "The present is terrible, the future far more so; every day adds to the power and facility of the means of destruction. Science is hard at work (science, the great—nay, to some the only—God of these days) to discover and concentrate the shortest and easiest methods to annihilate the human race." We see the results of that work in German methods of warfare.

Germany has for four centuries asserted for herself a conspicuous place in European religion. She has been a bully there as in other fields, and the lazy and the timid have submitted to her theological pretensions. Now, by the mouth of her official pastors she has renounced the religion of sacrifice for the lust of conquest, and has substituted the creed of Odin for the faith of Christ. A country which, in spite of learning and opportunity, has wilfully elapsed from civilization into barbarism can scarcely evangelize Confucians or Buddhists.

If we turn from the Protestant strongholds of the North to the citadel of Authority at Rome, the signs of an Epiphany are equally lacking. The Infallibility which did not save the largest section of Christendom from such crimes as the Inquisition and the massacre of St. Bartholomew has proved itself equally impotent in these latter days. No one could have expected the Pope, who has spiritual children in all lands, to take sides in an international dispute; but one would have thought that a divinely-given infallibility would have denounced, with the trumpet-tone of Sinai, the orgies of sexual and sacrilegious crime which have devastated Belgium.

Is the outlook in allied Russia any more hopeful than in hostile Germany and in neutral Rome? I must confess that I cannot answer. We were always told that the force which welded together in one the different races and tongues of the Russian Empire was a spiritual force; that the Russian held his faith dearer than his life; and that even his devotion to the Czar had its origin in religion. At this moment of perplexity and peril, will the Holy Orthodox Church manifest her power and instil into her children the primary conceptions of Christian citizenship?

And if we look nearer home, we must acknowledge that the condition of England has not always been such as to inspire Heathendom with a lively desire to be like us. A century and a half ago Charles Wesley complained that his fellow-citizens, who professed Christianity, "the sinners unbaptized out-sin." And everyone who remembers the social and moral state of England during the ten years immediately preceding the present War will be inclined to think that the twentieth century had not markedly improved on the eighteenth. Betting and gambling, and the crimes to which they lead, had increased frightfully, and were doing as much harm as drunkenness used to do. There was an open and insolent disregard of religious observance, especially with respect to the use of Sunday, the weekly Day of Rest being perverted into a day of extra amusement and resulting labour. There was a general relaxation of moral tone in those classes of society which are supposed to set a good example. There was an ever-increasing invasion of the laws which guard sexual morality, illustrated in the agitation to make divorce even easier than it is now. Other and darker touches might be added; but I have said enough to make my meaning clear. Some say that the war is teaching us to repent of and to forsake those national offences. If so, but not otherwise, we can reasonably connect it with the lessons of Epiphany.

II

THE ROMANCE OF RENUNCIATION

"What is Romance? The world well lost for an ides." I know no better definition; and Romance in this sense is perpetually illustrated in the history of the Church. The highest instance-save One—is, of course, the instance of the Martyrs. When in human history has Romance been more splendidly displayed than when the young men and maidens of Pagan Rome suffered themselves to be flung to the wild beasts of the arena sooner than abjure the religion of the Cross? And close on the steps of the Martyrs follow the Confessors, the "Martyrs-Elect," as Tertullian calls them, who, equally willing to lay down their lives, yet denied that highest privilege, carried with them into exile and imprisonment the horrible mutilations inflicted by Severus and Licinius. In days nearer our own time, "many a tender maid, at the threshold of her young life, has gladly met her doom, when the words that accepted Islam would have made her in a moment a free and honoured member of a dominant community." Then there is the Romance of the Hermitage and the Romance of the Cloister, illustrated by Antony in the Egyptian desert, and Benedict in his cave among the Latin hills, and Francis tending the leper by the wayside of Assisi. In each of these cases, as in thousands more, the world was well lost for an idea.

The world is well lost—and supremely well lost—by the Missionary, whatever be his time or country or creed. Francis Xavier lost it well when he made his response to the insistent question: "What shall it profit a man, if he shall gain the whole world, and lose his own soul?" Henry Martyn lost it well when, with perverse foolishness as men accounted it, he sacrificed the most brilliant prospects which a University offers to preach and fail among the heathen, and to die at thirty, forsaken and alone. John Coleridge Patterson lost it well when, putting behind him all the treasures of Eton and Oxford, and powerful connexions and an opulent home, he went out to spread the light of the Gospel amid the isles of the Pacific, and to meet his death at the hands of the heathen whom he loved and served.

These, indeed, are the supreme Romances of Renunciation, but others there are, which, though less "high and heroical," are not less Teal and not less instructive. The world was well lost (though for a cause which is not mine) by the two thousand ministers who on "Black Bartholomew," in the year 1662, renounced their benefices in the Established Church sooner than accept a form of worship which their conscience disallowed. And yet again the world was gloriously lost by the four hundred ministers and licentiates of the Church of Scotland who, in the great year of the Disruption, sacrificed home and sanctuary land subsistence rather than compromise the "Headship of Christ over His own house."

One more instance I must give of these heroic losses, and in giving it I recall a name, famous and revered in my young days, but now, I suppose, entirely forgotten—the name of the Honble. and Revd. Baptist Noel (1798-1873). "His more than three-score years and ten were dedicated, by the day and by the hour, to a ministry not of mind but of spirit; his refined yet vigorous eloquence none who listened to it but for once could forget; and, having in earliest youth counted birth and fortune, and fashion but loss 'for Christ,' in later age, at the bidding of the same conscience, he relinquished even the church which was his living and the pulpit which was his throne, because he saw danger to Evangelical truth in State alliance, and would go forth at the call of duty, he knew not and he cared not whither."

After these high examples of the Romance of Renunciation, it may seem rather bathetic to cite the instance which has given rise to this chapter. Yet I cannot help feeling that Mr. William Temple, by resigning the Rectory of St. James's, Piccadilly, in order to devote himself to the movement for "Life and Liberty," has established a strong claim on the respect of those who differ from him. I state on p. 198 my reason for dissenting from Mr. Temple's scheme. To my thinking, it is just one more attempt to stave off Disestablishment. The subjection of the Church to the State is felt by many to be an intolerable burden. Mr. Temple and his friends imagine that, while retaining the secular advantages of Establishment and endowment, they can obtain from Parliament the self-governing powers of a spiritual society. I doubt it, and I do not desire it. My own ideal is Cavour's—the Free Church in the Free State; and all such schemes as Mr. Temple's seem to me desperate attempts to make the best of two incompatible worlds. By judicious manipulation our fetters might be made to gall less painfully, but they would be more securely riveted than ever. So in this new controversy Mr. Temple stands on one side and I on the other; but this does not impair my respect for a man who is ready to "lose the world for an idea"—even though that idea be erroneous and Impracticable.

To "lose the world" may seem too strong a phrase for the occasion, but it is not in substance inappropriate. Mr. Temple has all the qualifications which in our Established Church lead on to fortune. He has inherited the penetrating intelligence and the moral fervour which in all vicissitudes of office and opinion made his father one of the conspicuous figures of English life. Among dons he was esteemed a philosopher, but his philosophy did not prevent him from being an eminently practical Head Master. He is a vigorous worker, a powerful preacher, and the diligent rector of an important parish. Of such stuff are Bishops made. There is no shame in the wish to be a Bishop, or even an Archbishop, as we may see by the biographies of such prelates as Wilberforce and Tait and Magee, and in the actual history of some good men now sitting on Episcopal thrones. But Mr. Temple has proved himself a man capable of ideals, and has given that irrefragable proof of sincerity which is afforded by the voluntary surrender of an exceptionally favoured position.

That the attempt to which he is now devoting himself may come to naught is my earnest desire; and then, when the Church, at length recognizing the futility of compromise, acquires her complete, severance from the secular power, she may turn to him for guidance in the use of her new-born freedom.

III

PAN-ANGLICANISM

It is an awful word. Our forefathers, from Shakespeare downwards, ate pan-cakes, and trod the pantiles at Tunbridge Wells; but their "pan" was purely English, and they linked it with other English words. The freedom of the "Ecclesia Anglicana" was guaranteed by the Great Charter, and "Anglicanism" became a theological term. Then Johnson, making the most of his little Greek, began to talk about a "pancratical" man, where we talk of an all-round athlete; and, a little later, "Pantheist" became a favourite missile with theologians who wished to abuse rival practitioners, but did not know exactly how to formulate their charge. It was reserved for the journalists of 1867 to form the terrible compound of two languages, and, by writing of the "Pan-Anglican Synod," to prepare the way for "Pan-Protestant" and "Pan-denominational." Just now the "Lively Libertines" (as their detractors style the promoters of "Life and Liberty") seem to be testing from their labours, and they might profitably employ their leisure by reading the history of their forerunners half a century ago.

The hideously named "Pan-Anglican Synod," which assembled at Lambeth in September, 1867, and terminated its proceedings in the following December, was a real movement in the direction of Life and Liberty for the Church of England. The impulse came from the Colonies, which, themselves enjoying the privilege of spiritual independence, were generously anxious to coalesce at a time of trial with the fettered Church at home. The immediate occasion of the movement was the eccentricity of Bishop Colenso—"the arithmetical Bishop who could not forgive Moses for having written a Book of Numbers." The faith of some was seriously perturbed when they heard of a Bishop who, as Matthew Arnold said, "had learnt among the Zulus that only a certain number of people can stand in a doorway at once, and that no man can eat eighty-eight pigeons a day; and who tells us, as a consequence, that the Pentateuch is all fiction, which, however, the author may very likely have composed without meaning to do wrong, and as a work of poetry, like Homer's."

Certainly the tremors of a faith so lightly overset were justly obnoxious to Arnold's ridicule; but Colenso's negations went deeper than the doorway and the pigeons; and the faithful of his diocese, being untrammelled by the State, politely dismissed him from his charge. In England steady-going Christians had been not less perturbed by that queer collection of rather musty discourses which was called *Essays and Reviews*; and the Church of

England had made an attempt to rid itself, by synodical action, of all complicity in the dubious doctrine. But the Judicial Committee of the Privy Council had justified the essayists, and had done its best to uphold Colenso. By so doing, it had, of course, delighted all Erastians; but Churchmen, whether at home or abroad, who believed in the English Church as a spiritual society, with a life of its own apart from all legal establishment, felt that the time had come when this belief should be publicly proclaimed. In February, 1866, the Anglican Bishops of Canada addressed a Memorial to Dr. Longley, then Archbishop of Canterbury, requesting him to summon a conference of all the Bishops of the Anglican Communion; and, after some characteristic hesitation, this was done. A Letter of Invitation was issued in February, 1867. The more dogged Erastians held aloof; but those who conceived of the Church as a spiritual society obeyed the summons; the "Conference of Bishops" assembled, and the priceless word "Pan-Anglicanism" was added to the resources of the language.

What did these good men do when they were come together? Not, it must be admitted, very much. They prayed and they preached, and debated and divided, and, in the matter of Colenso, quarrelled. They issued a Pastoral Letter which, as Bishop Tait said, was "the expression of essential agreement and a repudiation of Infidelity and Romanism." If this had been the sole result of the Conference, it would have been meagre enough; but under this official ineffectiveness there had been a real movement towards "Life and Liberty." The Conference taught the Established Bishops of England and Ireland that the Bishops of Free Churches—Scottish, American, Colonial—were at least as keen about religious work and as jealous for the spiritual independence of the Christian society as the highly placed and handsomely paid occupants of Lambeth and Bishopthorpe. Bishop Hamilton of Salisbury (whom the Catholic-minded section of the English Church regarded as their special champion) "thought that we had much to learn from contact with the faith and vigour of the American Episcopate"; and Bishop Wilberforce thus recorded his judgment: "The Lambeth gathering was a very great success. Its strongly anti-Erastian tone, rebuking the Bishop of London (Tait), was quite remarkable. We are now sitting in Committee trying to complete our work—agree to a voluntary Court of English Doctrinal Appeal for the free Colonies of America. If we can carry this out, we shall have erected a barrier of immense moral strength against Privy Council latitudinarianism. My view is that God gives us the opportunity, as at home latitudinarianism must spread, of encircling the Home Church with a band of far more dogmatic truth-holding communions who will act most strongly in favour of truth here. I was in great measure the framer of the "Pan-Anglican" for this purpose, and the result has abundantly satisfied me. The American Bishops won golden opinions."

And so this modest effort in the direction of "Life and Liberty," which had begun amid obloquy and ridicule, gained strength with each succeeding year. The Conference was repeated, with vastly increased numbers and general recognition, in 1878, 1888, 1898, and 1908. The war makes the date of the next assemblage, as it makes all things, doubtful; but already Churchmen, including some who have hitherto shrunk in horror from the prospect of Disestablishment, are beginning to look forward to the next Conference of Bishops as to something which may be a decisive step in the march of the English Church towards freedom and self-government. Men who have been reared in a system of ecclesiastical endowments are apt to cherish the very unapostolic belief that money is a sacred thing; but even they are coming, though by slow degrees, to realize that the Faith may be still more sacred. For the rest of us, the issue was formulated by Gladstone sixty years ago: "You have our decision: take your own; choose between the mess of pottage and the birthright of the Bride of Christ."

IV

LIFE AND LIBERTY

The title is glorious; and, so far as I know, the credit of inventing it belongs to my friend the Rev. H. R. L. Sheppard, the enterprising Vicar of St. Martin's-in-the-Fields. Mr. Sheppard has what in newspapers we call a "magnetic personality," and no one has more thoroughly laid to heart the sagacious saying that "Sweet are the uses of advertisement." Whatever cause he adopts, the world must know that he has adopted it; and it shall obtain a hearing, or he will know the reason why. The cause to which (outside his pastoral work) he is just now devoted is that which is summarized in the phrase, "Life and Liberty for the Church of England." It is a fine ideal, and Mr. Sheppard and his friends have been expounding it at the Queen's Hall.

It was no common achievement to fill that hall on a hot summer evening in the middle of the war, and with very little' assistance from the Press. Yet Mr. Sheppard did it, and he filled an "over-flow meeting" as well. The chair was taken by the Rev. William Temple, who tempered what might have been the too fervid spirit of the gathering with the austerity which belongs to a writer on philosophy, an ex-Head Master, and a prospective Bishop. The hall was densely crowded with clergy, old and young—old ones who had more or less missed their mark, and young ones keen to take warning by these examples. There were plenty of laymen, too, quite proud to realize that, though they are not in Holy Orders, they too are "in the Church"; and a brilliant star, if only he had appeared, would have been a Second-Lieutenant in khaki, who unfortunately was detained at the front by military duties. A naval and a military chaplain did the "breezy" business, as befitted their cloth; and, beaming on the scene with a paternal smile, was the most popular of Canons, who by a vehement effort kept silence even from good words, though it must have been pain and grief to him.[*]

[Footnote *: Alas! we have lost him since.]

The oratorical honours of the evening were by common consent adjudged to a lady, who has since been appointed "Pulpit Assistant" to the City Temple. May an old-fashioned Churchman suggest that, if this is a sample of Mr. Sheppard's new movement, the "Life" of the Church of England is likely to be a little too lively, and its "Liberty" to verge on licence? A ministry of undenominational feminism is "a thing imagination boggles at." Here it is to be remarked that the leaders of the movement are male and female after their kind. Dr. and Mrs. Dingo sit in council side by side, and much regret is expressed that Archdeacon Buckemup is still a celibate. But let us be of good cheer. Earnest-minded spinsters, undeterred by the example of Korah (who, as they truly say, was only a man), are clamouring for the priesthood as well as the vote; and in the near future the "Venerable Archdeaconess" will be a common object of the ecclesiastical sea-shore. Miss Jenkyns, in *Cranford*, would have made a capital Dean.

So much for the setting of the scene. The "business" must be now considered, and we will take the programme of "Life and Liberty" point by point, as set forth in a pamphlet by Mr. Temple. In the first place, its leaders are very clear that they wish to keep their endowments; but it must not be supposed that they dread reform. Their policy is "Redistribution." Those great episcopal incomes are again threatened; the Bishops are to be delivered from that burden of wealth which presses so hardly on them; and the slum parson is to have a living wage. But the incumbent, though his income may thus be increased, is by no means to have it all his own way. His freehold in his benefice is to be abolished; and, even while he retains his position, he is to have his duties assigned to him, and his work arranged, by a "Parochial Church Council," in which the "Pulpit Assistant" at Bethesda or Bethel may have her place. Life and Liberty indeed! But further boons are in store for us. We have at present two Archbishops, and, I hope, are thankful for them. Under the new scheme we are promised eight, or even nine. "Showers of blessing," as the hymn says! I presume that the six (or seven) new Archbishops are to be paid out of the "redistributed" incomes of the existing two. The believers in "Life and Liberty" humanely propose to compensate the Archbishop of Canterbury for the diminution of his £15,000 a year by letting him call himself a "Patriarch," but I can hardly fancy a Scotsman regarding this as a satisfactory bargain.

But how are these and similar boons to be attained? The promoters of Life and Liberty (not, I fancy, without a secret hope of frightening the Bishops into compliance with their schemes) affirm their readiness to accept Disestablishment "if no other way to self-government seems feasible"; but they, themselves, prefer a less heroic method. While retaining the dignity of Establishment and the opulence of Endowment, they propose that the Church should have "power to legislate on all matters affecting the Church, subject to Parliamentary veto.... This proposal has the immense practical advantage that, whereas it is now necessary to secure time for the passage of any measure through Parliament, if this scheme were adopted it would become necessary for the opponent or obstructor to find time to prevent its passage. The difference which this would make in practice is enormous." It is indeed; and the proposal is interesting as a choice specimen of what the world knows (and dislikes) as Ecclesiastical Statesmanship.

"Life and Liberty"—there is music in the very words; and, ever since I was old enough to have an opinion on serious matters, I have cherished them as the ideals for the Church to which I belong. From the oratory of Queen's Hall and the "slim" statesmanship which proposes to steal a march on the House of Commons I turn to that great evangelist, Arthur Stanton, who wrote as follows when Welsh Disestablishment was agitating the clerical mind.

"Nothing will ever reconcile me to the Establishment of Christ's Church on earth by Sovereigns or Parliaments. It is established by God on Faith and the Sacraments, and so endowed, and all other pretended establishment and endowment to me is profane." And again:

"Taking away endowments doesn't affect me; but what does try me is the inheriting them, and denying the faith of the donors—and then talking of sacrilege. The only endowment of Christ's Church comes from the Father and the Son, and is the Holy Ghost, Which no man can give and no man can take away.'"

Here, if you like, is the authentic voice of Life and Liberty.

V

LOVE AND PUNISHMENT

Lord Hugh Cecil is, I think, one of the most interesting figures in the public life of the time. Ten years ago I regarded him as the future leader of the Tory party and a predestined Prime Minister. Of late years he has seemed to turn away from the strifes and intrigues of ordinary politics, and to have resigned official ambition to his elder brother; but his figure has not lost—rather has gained—in interest by the change. Almost alone among our public men, he seems to have "his eyes fixed on higher lodestars" than those which guide Parliamentary majorities. He avows his allegiance to those moral laws of political action of which John Bright so memorably said that "though they were not given amid the thunders of Sinai, they are not less the commandments of God."

Now, the fearless utterance of this ethical creed does not tend to popularity. Englishmen will bear a good deal of preaching, so long as it is delivered from the pulpit; but when it is uttered by the lips of laymen, and deals with public problems, it arouses a curious irritation. That jovial old heathen, Palmerston, once alluded to Bright as "the Honourable and Reverend Member"; Gladstone's splendid appeals to faith and conscience were pronounced "d——d copy-book-y"; and Lord Houghton, who knew the world as well as most men, said, "Does it ever strike you that nothing shocks people so much as any immediate and practical application of the character and life of Christ?"

Lord Hugh Cecil need not mind the slings and arrows of outrageous partisanship, so long as he shares them with Bright and Gladstone. Just lately, his pronouncement that we ought to love the Germans, as our fellow-citizens in the Kingdom of God on earth, has provoked very acrid criticism from some who generally share his political beliefs; and in a Tory paper I noticed the singularly inept gibe that this doctrine was "medieval." For my own part I should scarcely have thought that an undue tendency to love one's enemies was a characteristic trait of the Middle Age, or that Englishmen and Frenchmen, Guelphs and Ghibellines, were inclined to sink their racial differences in the unity of Christian citizenship. Lord Hugh's doctrine might be called by some modern and by others primitive; but medieval it can only be called on the principle that, in invective, a long word, is better than a short one.

Having thus repelled what I think a ridiculous criticism, I will admit that Lord Hugh's doctrine raises some interesting, and even disputable, points.

In the first place, there is the theory of the Universal Church as the Divine Kingdom on earth, and of the citizenship in which all its members are united. I grant the theory; but I ask myself if I am really bound by it to love all these my fellow-citizens, whatever their conduct and character may be. Love is an elastic word; and, if I am to love the Germans, I must love them in some very different sense from that in which I love my country and my race. It really is, in another form, the old controversy between cosmopolitanism and patriotism. The "Enthusiasm of Humanity" is a noble sentiment; but the action of our fellow-members of the human family may be such as to render it, at least for the moment, impossible of realization. Under the pressure of injury from without, cosmopolitanism must contract itself into patriotism. We may wish devoutly that the whole human family were one in heart and mind—that all the citizens of the kingdom of God obeyed one law of right and wrong; but when some members of the family, some citizens of the kingdom, have "given themselves over to a reprobate mind," our love must be reserved for those who still own the claim of righteousness. If our own country stood as a solitary champion of right against a world in unrighteous arms, patriotism would be a synonym for religion, and cosmopolitanism for sin.

And then again I ask myself this question: Even assuming that Lord Hugh is right, and that it is our bounden duty to love the Germans, is love inconsistent with punishment? We postulate the love of God towards mankind, and we rightly regard it as the highest manifestation of what love means; but is it inconsistent with punishment for unrighteous action? Neither Revelation, nor Nature, nor History, knows anything of the conception which has been embodied in the words, "a good-natured God." Of Revelation I will not speak at length, for this is not the place for theological discussion; I only remark in passing that the idea of punishment for wrong-doing is not, as some sciolists imagine, confined to the Old Testament, though there it is seen in its most startling form; in the New Testament it is exhibited, alike by St. Paul and by St. Paul's Master, as a manifestation of love—not vindictive, but remedial. The disciplining love of a human father is used to illustrate the Divine dealings with insubordinate mankind. About Nature we need scarcely argue. "In the physical world there is no forgiveness of sins," and rebellion against the laws of righteous living brings penal consequences which no one can mistake. And yet again, has History any more unmistakable lesson than that "for every false word or unrighteous deed, for cruelty and oppression, for lust or vanity, the price has to be paid at last"? Froude was right. "Injustice and falsehood may be long-lived, but doomsday comes at last to them, in French Revolutions and other terrible ways."

What we believe of the Divine Love, thus dealing with human transgression, we may well believe of human love, when it is called by duty to chastise unrighteousness. I do not suppose that John Stuart Mill was actuated by hatred of Palmer or Pritchard or any other famous malefactor of his time when he said that there are some people so bad that they "ought to be blotted out of the catalogue of living men." It was the dispassionate judgment of philosophy on crime. When the convicted murderer exclaimed, "Don't condemn me to death; I am not fit to die!" a great Judge replied, "I know nothing about that; I only know that you are not fit to live"; but I do not suppose that he hated the wretch in the dock. Even so, though it may be our duty to love our enemies as our fellow-citizens in the kingdom of God, we need not shrink, when the time comes, from being the ministers of that righteous vengeance which, according to the immutable order of the world, is prepared for impenitent wrong-doing.

VI

HATRED AND LOVE

I lately saw the following sentence quoted from Sir Arthur Conan Doyle: "Hatred steels the mind and sets the resolution as no other emotion can do." The enlightened conscience of humanity (to say nothing of Christianity) repudiates this sentiment as ethically unsound and historically untrue; and yet, erroneous as it is, it is worth pondering for the sake of a truth which it overstates.

However little we may like to make the confession in the twentieth century of the Christian era, hatred is a very real power, and there is more of it at work in civilized society than we always recognize. It is, in truth, an abiding element of human nature, and is one of those instincts which we share with the lower animals. "The great cur showed his teeth; and the devilish instincts of his old wolf-ancestry looked out from his eyes, and yawned in his wide mouth and deep red gullet." Oliver Wendell Holmes was describing a dog's savagery; but he would have been the first to admit that an exactly similar spirit may be concealed—and not always concealed—in a human frame. We have lived so long, if not under the domination, still in the profession, of the Christian ethic, that people generally are ashamed to avow a glaringly anti-Christian feeling. Hence the poignancy of the bitter saying: "I forgive him as a Christian—which means that I don't forgive him at all." Under a decent, though hypocritical, veil of religious commonplace, men go on hating one another very much as they hated in Patriarchal Palestine or Imperial Rome.

Hatred generally has a personal root. An injury or an insult received in youth may colour the feelings and actions of a whole lifetime. "Revenge is a dish which can be eaten cold"; and there are unhappy natures which know no enjoyment so keen as the satisfaction of a long-cherished grudge. There is an even deeper depravity which hates just in proportion to benefits received; which hates because it is enraged by a high example; which hates even more virulently because the object of its hatred is meek or weak or pitiable. "I have read of a woman who said that she never saw a cripple without longing to throw a stone at him. Do you comprehend what she meant? No? Well, I do." It was a woman who wrote the words.

The less abhorrent sort of hatred (if one can discriminate where all is abominable) is the hatred which has no personal root, but is roused by invincible dislike of a principle or a cause. To this type belong controversial hatreds, political hatreds, international hatreds. Jael is the supreme instance of this hatred in action, and it is only fair to assume that Sir Arthur Conan Doyle had this kind of hatred in his mind when he wrote the sentence which I quoted above. But hatred, which begins impersonally, has a dangerous habit of becoming personal as it warms to its work; and an emotion which started by merely wishing to check a wrong deed may develop before long into a strong desire to torture the wrong-doer. Whatever be the source from which it springs, hatred is a powerful and an energetic principle. It is capable, as we all know, of enormous crimes; but it does not despise the pettiest methods by which it can injure its victim. "Hatred," said George Eliot, "is like fire—it makes even light rubbish deadly."

Sir Arthur Conan Doyle is perfectly right when he says that hatred "steels the mind and sets the resolution." If he had stopped there, I should not have questioned his theory. Again and again one has seen indolent, flabby, and irresolute natures stimulated to activity and "steeled" into hardness by the deep, though perhaps unuttered, desire to repay an insult or avenge an injury. It is in his superlative that Sir Arthur goes astray. When he affirms that hatred "steels the mind and sets the resolution as no other emotion can do," his psychology is curiously at fault. There is another emotion quite as powerful as hatred to "steel the mind and set the resolution"—and the name of this other emotion is love. It required some resolution and a "steeled" mind for Father Damien to give himself in early manhood to the service of a leper-struck island, living amid, and dying of, the foul disease which he set out to tend. It was love that steeled John Coleridge Patteson to encounter death at the hands of "savage men whom he loved, and for whose sake he gave up home and country and friends dearer than his life." There was "steel" in the resolve which drew Henry Martyn from the highest honours of Cambridge to preach and die in the fever-stricken solitude of Tokat; and "steel" in an earlier and even more memorable decision when Francis Xavier consecrated rank, learning, eloquence, wit, fascinating manners, and a mirthful heart, to the task of evangelizing India.

But it is not only in the missionary field, or in any other form of ecclesiastical activity, that the steeling effect of love on the human will is manifested. John Howard devoted the comforts and advantages which pertain to a position in the opulent Middle Class to the purely philanthropic work of Prison Reform; and Lord Shaftesbury used the richer boons of rank and eloquence and political opportunity for the deliverance of tortured lunatics, and climbing boys and factory slaves. If ever I knew a man whose resolution was "steeled," it was this honoured friend of my early manhood, and the steeling power was simply love. A humbler illustration of the same spirit may be supplied by the instance of one whom worldly people ridiculed and who "for fifty years seized every chance of doing kindness to a man who had tormented him at school"; and this though a boy's nature is "wax to receive, and marble to retain." The name of E. C. Hawtrey is little remembered now even by Eton men, but this tribute to the power of love ought not to be withheld.

I am only too painfully aware that we live just now in conditions in which love must take the aspect of severity; in which the mind must be "steeled" and the resolution "set" for a solemn work of international justice. But hatred will not help us; for hatred is fundamentally at variance with that moral law which we daily and hourly invoke as the sanction of our enterprise. Hatred is natural enough, and at least as old as the Fall of Man; but its doom was pronounced by a Teacher Who said to His disciples: "A new commandment I give unto you, that ye love one another." Twelve men heard and heeded that new commandment, and they changed the face of the world. Are we to abjure the doctrine which wrought this change, and give heed to the blind guides who would lure us straight back to barbarism?

"What though they come with scroll and pen,
  And grave as a shaven clerk,
By this sign shall ye know them,
  That they ruin and make dark;

"By thought a crawling ruin,
  By life a leaping mire,
By a broken heart in the breast of the world,
  And the end of the world's desire;

"By God and man dishonoured,
  By death and life made vain,
Know ye the old Barbarian,
  The Barbarian come again."[*]

[Footnote *: G. K. Chesterton.]

VII

THE TRIUMPHS OF ENDURANCE

"By your endurance ye shall make your souls your own." If the origin of this saying were unknown, one could fancy much ingenious conjecture about it; but no one, I think, would attribute it to an English source. An Englishman's idea of self-realization is action. If he is to be truly himself he must be doing something; life for him means energy. To be laid on one side, and to exist only as a spectator or a sufferer, is the last method of making his soul his own which would occur to him. *Dolce far niente* is a phrase which could never have originated on English soil. The greater the difficulties by which he is confronted, the more gnawing becomes the Englishman's, hunger for action. "Something must be done!" is his instinctive cry when dangers or perplexities arise, and he is feverishly eager to do it. What exactly "it" should be, and how it may be most wisely done, are secondary, and even tertiary, considerations. "Wisdom is profitable to direct"; but the need for wisdom is not so generally recognized in England as the need for courage or promptitude or vigour.

Some of the shallower natures find a substitute for action in speech. If only they talk loud enough and long enough, they feel that they are doing something valuable towards the desired end, and they find others, still weaker than themselves, who take their words at their own valuation. Who does not recall moments of the present war when the man-in-the-street has exclaimed, "That was a splendid speech of Blower's! I feel now that we are on the right line"; or, "After what Bellowell said last night, there can be no going back to the discredited policy"? The man-in-the-street did not realize that Blower's words are only articulated air, or that Bellowell could speak with equal effect whether his brief were to defend Belgium or to annex her. But alike the Englishman who acts and the Englishman who talks look askance on the people who think. Our national history is a history of action, in religion, in politics, in war, in discovery. It is only now and then that an Englishman can allow himself a moment for contemplation, for the endeavour to "see into the life of things," for contact with those spiritual realities of which phenomena are only the shadows. Burke did it, but then he was an Irishman. Lord Beaconsfield did it, but then he was a Jew. Gladstone did it, but then he was a Scotsman. May I add that the present Prime Minister does it, but then he is a Welshman? Englishmen, as a rule, are absorbed in action; it is to them a religion, and it takes the place of a philosophy.

At this moment all England is acting, from the King and the War Cabinet to the children who play at soldiers in the gutter. There is no distinction of class, or sex, or temperament. All alike feel that they must be doing something to win the war, and that they would die or go mad if they were restrained from action. Limitations, physical or mental, incapacities for effort, restrictions of opportunity, gall as they never galled before. To compare great things with small, the whole nation pulsates with the spirit of the fiercely contested cricket-match:

> "Oh, good lads in the field they were,
> Laboured and ran and threw;
> But we that sat on the benches there
> Had the hardest work to do!"

Action, then, is the creed and the consolation of the English race, and God forbid that we should disparage that on which national salvation depends. The war must be won by action; but in the strain and stress of these tremendous days we are tempted to forget that there is something to be won or lost besides the war. It is possible to conquer on the Western front, and at the same time to be defeated on the not less important field of moral being. The promise which heads this paper was uttered in full view of an impending agony which should crush religion and civilization into powder. We can realize the consternation with which a patriotic audience heard those premonitions from the lips of a patriotic Teacher; but in the midst of all that was harrowing and heart-rending came the promise of triumph through endurance. "Ye shall make your souls your own." The gloomy and the cheerful prediction were alike made good.

> "The East bow'd low before the blast
> In patient, deep disdain;
> She let the legions thunder past,
> And plunged in thought again.

> "So well she mused, a morning broke
> Across her spirit grey;
> A conquering, new-born joy awoke,
> And fill'd her life with day."

The Roman Eagles led a momentary triumph, but they fled before the newly discovered Cross. Endurance won.

And so it has been from that time to this. The triumphs of endurance have no end. The barbarism of the Cæsars, the barbarism of Islam, the barbarism of Odin and Thor, all in turn did their uttermost to destroy the new religion. Persecution fell, not on armed men strong to resist, but on slaves and women and boys and girls. "We could tell of those who fought with savage beasts, yea, of maidens who stept to face them as coolly as a modern bully steps into the ring. We could tell of those who drank molten lead as cheerfully as we would the juice of the grape, and played with the red fire and the bickering flames as gaily as with golden curls." These were the people who by endurance made their souls their own; and, by carrying endurance even unto death, propagated the faith for which they gave their lives. It did not take Rome long to discover that "the blood of Christians is seed."

The victorious power of endurance is not yet exhausted; but, on the other hand, the peril of moral defeat must never be ignored. It was a strange coincidence that the most trying phase of a four-years' war should have occurred in the week which, for Western Christendom, commemorates the supreme example of endurance. As far as action is concerned, the national will is not in the slightest danger of collapse. The British nation will plan, and work and fight for ever, if need be. Our only danger is in the moral field. Though our power of action is undiminished, our power of endurance may ebb. We may begin to cry, in our impatience, "Lord, how long?"; to repine against the fate which condemns us to this protracted agony; to question within ourselves whether the cause which we profess to serve is really worth the sacrifices which it entails. It is just by mastering these rebellious tendencies that we can make our souls our own. If we went into the war believing in the sacredness of Freedom, Brotherhood, and Right against Might, it would be a moral collapse to emerge from it believers in tyranny, imperialism, and the rule of the strong. "He that endureth to the end shall be saved." On that "end" we must keep heart and eye unflinchingly fixed; and strive to add one more to the age-long triumphs of endurance.

VIII

A SOLEMN FARCE

Sweet to the antiquarian palate are the fragments of Norman French which still survive in the formularies of the Constitution. In Norman French the King acknowledges the inconceivable sums which from time to time his faithful Commons place at his disposal for the prosecution of the war. In Norman French the Peers of the Realm are summoned to their seats in Parliament which they adorn. In Norman French, the Royal Assent has just been given to a Bill which doubles the electorate and admits over six million women to the franchise. All these things are dear to the antiquary, the historian, and (perhaps we should add) the pedant, as witnessing to the unbroken continuity of our constitutional forms, though the substance of our polity has been altered beyond all recognition.

Another instance of Norman French which has lately emerged into unusual prominence is the "Congé d'élire." We can trace this "Licence to Elect" from the days of the Great Charter downwards; but it will suffice for my present purpose to recall the unrepealed legislation of Henry VIII. "It was then enacted that, at every future avoidance of a bishopric, the King may send to the Dean and Chapter his usual licence (called his 'Congé d'Élire') to proceed to election; which is always, accompanied by a Letter Missive from the King containing the name of the person whom he would have them elect; and if the Dean and Chapter delay their election above twelve days the nomination shall devolve to the King, who may then by Letters Patent appoint such person as he pleases.... And, if such Dean and Chapter do not elect in the manner by their Act appointed they shall incur all the penalties of a præmunire—that is, the loss of all civil rights, with forfeiture of lands, goods, and chattels, and imprisonment, during the Royal pleasure."

Such are the singular conditions under which the Church of England now exercises that right of electing her chief pastors which has been from the beginning the heritage of Christendom. It would be difficult to imagine a more dexterous use of chicanery, preserving the semblance but carefully precluding the reality of a free choice. We all know something of Deans and Chapters—the well-endowed inhabitants of cathedral closes—and of those "greater Chapters" which consist of Honorary Canons, longing for more substantial preferment. It would indeed require a very bold flight of fancy to imagine those worthy and comfortable men exposing themselves to the "loss of civil rights, the forfeiture of goods and chattels, and imprisonment during the King's pleasure," for a scruple of conscience about the orthodoxy of a divine recommended by the Crown. Truly in a capitular election, if anywhere, the better part of valour is discretion, and the Dean and Chapter of Hereford have realized this saving truth. But my view is wholly independent of local or personal issues, and is best expressed by these words of Arthur Stanton, true Catholic and true Liberal: "I am strongly in favour of Disestablishment, and always have been. The connexion between Church and State has done harm to both—more, however, to the Church. Take our plan of electing Bishops. In the early centuries they were elected by the people—as they ought to be. Now they are chosen, sometimes by a Tory, sometimes by a Radical Government. The Dean and Chapter meet and ask the guidance of the Holy Ghost to enable them to choose, knowing all the while they have the 'Letter Missive' in their pockets. To me this comes perilously near blasphemy."

But let us suppose an extreme case. Let us imagine a Dean and Chapter so deeply impressed by the unsuitableness of the Crown's nominee that they refuse to elect him. Here, again, the law dodges us. Except as a protest their refusal would have not the slightest effect. The Crown has nothing to do but issue Letters Patent in favour of its nominee, and he would be as secure of his bishopric as if the Chapter had chosen him with one consent of heart and voice. True, he would not yet be a Bishop; for the episcopal character can only be conferred by consecration, and at this point the Archbishop becomes responsible. To him the King signifies the fact that Dr. Proudie has been elected to the See of Barchester, requiring him to "confirm, invest, and consecrate" that divine. Should the Archbishop refuse compliance with this command, he exposes himself to exactly the same penalties as would be inflicted on a recalcitrant Chapter, only with this aggravation—that he has more to lose. When my good friend the Bishop of Oxford addressed the Archbishop of Canterbury, imploring him to withhold consecration from Dr. Henson, he made a valiant and faithful protest against what he holds to be a flagitious action on the part of the Crown; but, knowing the respected occupant of Lambeth as well as he does, I think he must have anticipated the reply which, as a matter of fact, he received.

Such being the absurdities and unrealities which surround the Congé d'Élire, one naturally asks, Why not abolish it? This question was raised in a pointed form by the late Mr. C. J. Monk, for many years Liberal M.P. for the City of Gloucester, who, in 1880, introduced a Bill to abolish the Congé and to place the appointment of Bishops formally, as it is really, in the hands of the Prime Minister. He urged the painful sense of unreality which clings to the whole transaction, and the injury to religion which is involved in thus paltering in a double sense with sacred forms and words. It is amusing to those who can recall the two men to remember that Mr. Monk was opposed by Lord Randolph Churchill, who thought he perceived in the proposal some dark design hostile to the interests of the Established Church; but the important speech was made by Gladstone. That great man, always greatest in debate when his case was weakest, opposed the abolition of the Congé. He deprecated any legislation which would interfere with one of the most delicate functions of the Crown, and he insisted that the true path of reform lay, not in the abolition of the form of election, but in an attempt to re-invest it with some elements of reality. This was well enough, and eminently characteristic of his reverence for ancient forms of constitutional action; but what was more surprising was that, speaking from long and intimate experience of its practical working he maintained that the Congé d'Élire, even under the nullifying conditions now attached to it, was "a moral check upon the prerogatives of the Crown," which worked well rather than ill. "I am," he said, "by no means prepared to say that, from partial information or error, a Minister might not make an appointment to which this moral obstacle might be set up with very beneficial effect. It would tend to secure care in the selections, and its importance cannot be overstated."

I must confess, with the greatest respect for my old leader, that the "importance" of the Congé d'Élire as a restraint upon the actions of the Prime Minister can be very easily "overstated." Indeed, the Congé could only be important if the Capitular Body to which the "Letter Missive" is addressed have the courage of conscientious disobedience, and were prepared to face, for the sake of imperilled truth, the anger of the powers that be and the laughter of the world. Courage of that type is a plant of slow growth in Established Churches; and as long as my friends hug the yoke of Establishment, I cannot sympathize with them when they cry out against its galling pressure. To complainants of that class the final word was addressed by Gladstone, nearly seventy years ago: "You have our decision: take your own; choose between the mess of pottage and the birthright of the Bride of Christ."

IV
POLITICS

I

MIRAGE

"Operations had to be temporarily suspended owing to the mirage." This sentence from one of Sir Stanley Maude's despatches struck me as parabolic. There are other, and vaster, issues than a strategic victory on the Diala River which have been "suspended owing to the mirage." Let us apply the parable.

The parched caravan sees, half a mile ahead, the gleaming lake which is to quench its thirst. It toils along over the intervening distance, only to find that Nature has been playing a trick. The vision has vanished, and what seemed to be water is really sand. There can be no more expressive image of disillusionment.

To follow the "Mirage" of receding triumph through long years of hope deferred was the lot of Labour generally, and it was especially the lot of agricultural labour. The artisans gained their political enfranchisement in 1867, and, though they made remarkably little use of it, still they had the power, if they had the will, to better their condition. But the agricultural labourers remained inarticulate, unnoticed, unrepresented. A Tory orator, said—and many of his class agreed with him, though they were too prudent to say it—that the labourer was no fitter for the vote than the beasts he tended. But there were others who knew the labourers by personal contact, and by friendly intercourse had been able to penetrate their necessary reserve; and we (for I was one of these) knew that our friends in the furrow and the cow-shed were at least as capable of forming a solid judgment as their brethren in the tailor's shop and the printing-works. There was nothing of the new Radicalism in this—it was as old as English history. The toilers on the land had always been aspiring towards freedom, though social pressure made them wisely dumb. Cobbett and Cartwright, and all the old reformers who kept the lamp of Freedom alive in the dark days of Pitt and Liverpool and Wellington, bore witness to the "deep sighing" of the agricultural poor, and noted with indignation the successive invasions of their freedom by Enclosure Acts and press-gangs and trials for sedition, and all the other implements of tyranny.

> "The Good Old Code, like Argus, had a hundred watchful eyes,
> And each old English peasant had his Good Old English spies
> To tempt his starving discontent with Good Old English lies,
> Then call the British Yeomanry to hush his peevish cries."

To a race of peasants thus enthralled and disciplined the Mirage appeared in the guise of the first Reform Bill. If only that Bill could pass into law, the reign of injustice and oppression would cease, starvation and misery would flee away, and the poor would rejoice in a new heaven and a new earth. But no sooner was the Royal Assent given to the Bill than the Mirage—that deceitful image of joy and refreshment—receded into the dim distance, and men woke to the disheartening fact that, though power had been transferred from the aristocracy to the middle class, the poor were as badly off as ever. The visible effects of that disillusionment were Chartism, rioting, and agrarian crime, and there was a deep undercurrent of sullen anger which seldom found expression. As late as the General Election of 1868 an old man in the duke-ridden borough of Woodstock declined to vote for the Liberal candidate expressly on the ground of disappointed hopes. Before 1832, he said, arms had been stored in his father's cottage to be used if the Lords threw out the Bill. They had passed it, and the arms were not required; but no one that he knew of had ever been a ha'porth the better for it; and he had never since meddled with politics, and never would again. In this case the despondency of old age was added to the despondency of disappointment; but among younger men hope was beginning to dawn again, and the Mirage beckoned with its treacherous gleam. The Agricultural Labourers' Union, starting on its pilgrimage from the very heart of England, forced the labourer's wants and claims upon the attention of the land-owners, the farmers, and the clergy.

Those who had been brought by early association into touch with the agricultural population knew only too well how deep and just was the discontent of the villages, and how keen the yearning for better chances. To secure the vote for the agricultural labourer seemed to be the first step towards the improvement of his lot. The General Election of 1880 was, as nearly as our constitutional forms admit, a plébiscite on foreign policy; but to many a man who was then beginning public life the emancipation of the labourer was an object quite as dear as the dethronement of Lord Beaconsfield. It was not for nothing that we had read *Hodge and His Masters*, and we were resolved that henceforward "Hodge" should be not a serf or a cipher, but a free man and a self-governing citizen.

We carried our Bill in 1884, and as the General Election of 1885 drew on, it was touching to feel the labourer's gratitude to all who had helped him in the attainment of his rights. By that time Gladstone had lost a great deal of his popularity in the towns, where Chamberlain was the hero. But in the rural districts the people worshipped Gladstone, and neither knew nor cared for any other politician. His was the name to conjure with. His picture hung in every cottage. His speeches were studied and thumbed by hard hands till the paper was frayed into tatters. It was Gladstone who had won the vote for the labourer, and it was Gladstone who was to lead them into the Land of Promise. "Three Acres and a Cow," from being a joke, had passed into a watchword, though Gladstone had never given it the faintest sanction. And the labourers vaguely believed that the possession of the vote would bring them some material benefit. So they voted for Gladstone with solid enthusiasm, and placed their Mirage in his return to power. But alas! they only realized a new and a more tragical disappointment. In January, 1886, an amendment to the Address embodying the principle of "Three Acres and a Cow" was carried against the Tory Government; Gladstone became Prime Minister, and the disconsolate labourers found that the Mirage had cheated them once again. It is not easy to depict the sorrow and mortification which ensued on this discovery. The vote, after all, was only a Dead Sea apple. The energies which were to have been bestowed on the creation of better surroundings for English labourers were suddenly transferred to the creation of an Irish Parliament, and in wide areas of rural population the labourers sank back again into hopelessness and inactivity. Once bit, twice shy. They had braved the wrath of their employers and all the banded influences of the Hall and the Vicarage in order to vote Liberal in December, 1885. They had got nothing by their constancy; and in six months, when they were again incited to the poll, they shook their heads and abstained. The disillusionment of the labourers gave the victory of 1886 to the Tories, and kept the Liberals out of power for twenty years.

II

MIST

"Mistiness is the Mother of Wisdom." If this sarcastic dogma be true, we are living in a generation pre-eminently wise. A "season of mists" it unquestionably is; whether it is equally marked by "mellow fruitfulness" is perhaps more disputable.

My path in life is metaphorically very much what Wordsworth's was literally. "I wander, lonely as a cloud that floats on high, o'er vales and hills." I find hills and vales alike shrouded in mist. Everyone is befogged, and the guesses as to where exactly we are and whither we are tending are various and perplexing. While all are, in truth, equally bewildered, people take their bewilderment in different ways. Some honestly confess that they cannot see a yard in front of them; others profess a more penetrating vision, and affect to be quite sure of what lies ahead. It is a matter of temperament; but the professors of clear sight are certainly less numerous than they were three years ago.

We are like men standing on a mountain when the mist rolls up from the valley. At first we all are very cheerful, and assure one another that it will pass away in half an hour, leaving our path quite clear. Then by degrees we begin to say that it promises to be a more tedious business than we expected, and we must just wait in patience till the clouds roll by. At length we frankly confess to one another that we have completely lost our bearings, and that we dare not move a foot for fear we should tumble into the abyss. In this awkward plight our "strength is to sit still"; but, even while we so sit, we try to keep ourselves warm by remembering that the most persistent mists do not last for ever.

In one section of society I hear voices of melancholy vaticination. "I don't believe," said one lady in my hearing—"I don't believe that we shall ever again see six-feet footmen with powdered hair," and a silent gloom settled on the company, only deepened by another lady, also attached to the old order, who murmured: "Ah! and powdered footmen are not the only things that we shall never see again." Within twenty-four hours of this depressing dialogue I encounter my democratic friend, the Editor of the *Red Flag*. He glories in the fact that Labour has "come into its own," and is quite sure that, unless it can get more to eat, it will cease to make munitions, and so will secure an early, if not a satisfactory, peace. In vain I suggest to my friend that his vision is obscured by the mist, and that the apparition which thus strangely exhilarates him is the creation of his own brain.

Then I turn to the politicians, and of these it is to be remarked that, however much befogged they may be, they always are certain that they see much more clearly than the world at large. This circumstance would invest their opinions with a peculiar authority, if only they did not contradict one another flat. We are doubling the electorate: what result will the General Election produce? Politicians who belong to the family of Mr. Despondency and his daughter, Muchafraid, reply that Monarchy will be abolished, Capital "conscripted" (delightful verb), debt repudiated, and Anarchy enthroned. Strangely dissimilar results are predicted by the Party-hacks, who, being by lifelong habit trained to applaud whatever Government does, announce with smug satisfaction that the British workman loves property, and will use his new powers to conserve it; adores the Crown, and feels that the House of Lords is the true protector of his liberties.

Again, there are publicists who (like myself) have all their lives proclaimed their belief in universal suffrage as the one guarantee of freedom. If we are consistent, we ought to rejoice in the prospect now unfolding itself before us; but perhaps the mist has got into our eyes. Our forefathers abolished the tyranny of the Crown. Successive Reform Acts have abolished the tyranny of class. But what about the tyranny of capital? Is Democracy safe from it?

I do not pretend to be clearer-sighted than my neighbours; but in the mist each of us sees the form of some evil which he specially dislikes; and to my thinking Bureaucracy is just as grave a menace to Freedom as Militarism, and in some ways graver, as being more plausible. We used to call ourselves Collectivists, and we rejoiced in the prospect of the State doing for us what we ought to do for ourselves. We voted Political Economy a dismal science (which it is), and felt sure that, if only the Government would take in hand the regulation of supply and demand, the inequalities of life would be adjusted, everyone would be well fed, and everyone would be happy. As far as we can see through the blinding mist which now surrounds us, it looks as if the State were about as competent to control trade as to control the weather. Bureaucracy is having its fling, and when the mist clears off it will stand revealed as a well-meant (and well-paid) imposture.

Closely related to all these problems is the problem of the women's vote. Here the mist is very thick indeed. Those who have always favoured it are naturally sanguine of good results. Women will vote for peace; women will vote for temperance; women will vote for everything that guards the sanctity of the home. Those who have opposed the change see very different consequences. Women will vote for war; women will vote as the clergyman bids them; women will vote for Socialism. All this is sheer guess-work, and very misty guess-work too.

And yet once more. There are (though this may to some seem strange) people who consider the Church at least as important as the State, and even more so, inasmuch as its concernments relate to an eternal instead of a transitory order. What are the prospects of the Church? Here the mists are thicker than ever. Is the ideal of the Free Church in the Free State any nearer realization than it was three years ago? All sorts of discordant voices reach me through the layers of cloud. Some cry, "Our one hope for national religion is to rivet tighter than ever the chains which bind the Church to the chariot-wheels of the State." Others reply, "Break those chains, and let us go free—even without a roof over our heads or a pound in our pockets." And there is a third section—the party which, as Newman said, attempts to steer between the Scylla of Aye and the Charybdis of No through the channel of no meaning, and this section cries for some reform which shall abolish the cynical mockery of the Congé d'Élire, and secure to the Church, while still established and endowed, the self-governing rights of a Free Church. In ecclesiastical quarters the mist is always particularly thick.

Certainly at this moment, if ever in our national life, we must be content to "walk by faith and not by sight." This chapter began with imagery, and with imagery it shall end. "I have often stood on some mountain peak, some Cumbrian or Alpine hill, over which the dim mists rolled; and suddenly, through one mighty rent in that cloudy curtain, I have seen the blue heaven in all its beauty, and, far below my feet, the rivers and cities and cornfields of the plain sparkled in the heavenly sunlight."

That is, in a figure, the vision for which we must hope and pray.

III

"DISSOLVING THROES"

I borrow my title from a poet.

> "He grew old in an age he condemned;
> He looked on the rushing decay
> Of the times which had sheltered his youth;
> Felt the dissolving throes
> Of a social order he loved."

It seems odd that Matthew Arnold should have spoken thus about Wordsworth; for one would have expected that the man who wrote so gloriously of the French Revolution, "as it appeared to enthusiasts at its commencement," would have rejoiced in the new order which it established for all Europe. But the younger poet knew the elder with an intimacy which defies contradiction; and one must, I suppose, number Wordsworth among those who, in each succeeding age, have shed tears of useless regret over the unreturning past. Talleyrand said that, to know what an enjoyable thing life was capable of being, one must have been a member of the *ancienne noblesse* before the Revolution. It was the cynical and characteristic utterance of a nature singularly base; but even the divine Burke (though he had no personal or selfish interests in the matter) was convinced that the Revolution had not only destroyed political freedom, but also social welfare, and had "crushed everything respectable and virtuous in the nation." What, in the view of Burke and Talleyrand, the Revolution did for France, that, by a curious irony of fate, our attempt to defeat the Revolution did for England. Burke forced us into the Revolutionary War, and that war (as Gladstone once said in a letter to the present writer) "almost unmade the liberties, the Constitution, even the material interests and prosperity, of our country." Patriots like William Cobbett and Sydney Smith, though absolutely convinced that the war was just and necessary, doubted if England could ever rally from the immense strain which it had imposed on her resources, or regain the freedom which, in order to beat France, she had so lightly surrendered.

At a time when Manchester was unrepresented and Gatton sent two Members to Parliament, it was steadily maintained by lovers of the established order that the proposed enlargement of the electorate was "incompatible with a just equality of civil rights, or with the necessary restraints of social obligation." If it were carried, religion, morality, and property would perish together, and our venerable Constitution would topple down in ruins. "A thousand years have scarce sufficed to make England what she is: one hour may lay her in the dust." In 1861 J. W. Croker wrote to his patron, the great borough-monger Lord Hertford: "There can be no doubt that the Reform Bill is a stepping-stone in England to a republic, and in Ireland to separation. Both *may* happen without the Bill, but with it they are inevitable." Next year the Bill became law. Lord Bathurst cut off his pigtail, exclaiming: "Ichabod, for the glory is departed"—an exquisitely significant combination of act and word—and the Duke of Wellington announced that England had accomplished "a revolution by due course of law." In some sense the words were true. Political power had passed from the aristocracy to the middle class. The English equivalents of Talleyrand—the men who directly or in their ancestors had ruled England since 1688, had enjoyed power without responsibility, and privilege which alike Kings and mobs had questioned in vain—were filled with the wildest alarms. Emotional orators saw visions of the guillotine; calmer spirits anticipated the ballot-box; and the one implement of anarchy was scarcely more dreaded than the other.

Sixteen years passed. Property and freedom seemed pretty secure. Even privilege, though shaken, had not been overthrown; and a generation had grown up to which the fears of revolution seemed fantastic. Then suddenly came the uprising of the nations in '48; and once again "dissolving throes" were felt, with pain or joy according to the temperament of those who felt them. "We have seen," said Charles Greville, "such a stirring-up of all the elements of society as nobody ever dreamt of; we have seen a general saturnalia—ignorance, vanity, insolence, poverty, ambition, escaping from every kind of restraint, ranging over the world, and turning it topsy-turvy as it pleased. All Europe exhibits the result—a mass of ruin, terror, and despair." Matthew Arnold, young and ardent, and in some ways democratic, wrote in a different vein: "The hour of the hereditary peerage, and eldest sonship, and immense properties, has, I am convinced, as Lamartine would say, struck." Seventy years ago! And that "hour" has not struck yet!

The "dissolving throes" were lulled again, and I scarcely made themselves felt till 1866, when a mild attempt to admit the pick of the artisans to the electoral privileges of the middle class woke the panic-stricken vehemence of Robert Lowe. "If," he asked, "you want venality, ignorance, drunkenness, and the means of intimidation; if you want impulsive, unreflecting, and violent people, where will you go to look for them—to the top or to the bottom?" Well might Bishop Wilberforce report to a friend, "It was enough to make the flesh creep to hear Bob Lowe's prognostications for the future of England."

Next year the artisans got the vote, though the great Lord Shaftesbury, who knew more than most of his peers about working-men, plainly told the

House of Lords that "a large proportion of the working classes have a deep and solemn conviction that property is not distributed as property ought to be; that some checks ought to be kept upon the accumulation of property in single hands; and that to take away by legislation that which is in excess with a view to bestowing it on those who have less, is not a breach of any law, human or Divine."

Yet once more. When in 1885 the agricultural labourers (of whom a Tory M.P. said that they were no fitter for a vote than the beasts they tended), were admitted to the franchise, the same terrors shook the squirearchy. We were warned that the land would soon be broken up into small holdings; that sport would become impossible; and that "the stately homes of England" must all be closed, for lack of money to keep them open. The country, we were told, had seen its best days, and "Merry England" had vanished for ever.

I only recall these "dissolving throes," real or imaginary, because I fancy that just now they are again making themselves felt, and perhaps with better reason than ever before in our history. People who venture to look ahead are asking themselves this question: If this war goes on much longer, what sort of England will emerge? Some are looking forward with rapture to a new heaven and a new earth; others dread the impending destruction "of a social order they loved." Can we not trace something of this dread in Lord Lansdowne's much-canvassed letter? He is one of the most patriotic and most experienced men in public life; he "looks on the rushing decay of the times which sheltered his youth"; and it may well be that he is striving to avert what seems to him a social catastrophe.

IV

INSTITUTIONS AND CHARACTER

As a rule, I call a spade a spade. When I mean *The Times*, I say *The Times*, and I condemn the old-fashioned twaddle of talking about "a morning contemporary." But to-day I depart from my rule and content myself with saying that I lately read in an important newspaper a letter dealing with Mr. Asquith's distinction between "Prussian Militarism" and "German Democracy." For my own part, I did not think that distinction very sound. The experience of the last three years has led me to the conclusion that the German democracy is to the full as bellicose as the military caste, and that it has in no way dissociated itself from the abominable crimes against decency and humanity which the military caste has committed. I hold that the German people, as we know it to-day, is brutalized; but when one thus frames an indictment against a whole nation, one is bound to ask oneself what it is that has produced so calamitous a result. How can a whole nation go wrong? Has any race a "double dose of original sin"? I do not believe it. Human nature as it leaves the Creator's hand is pretty much the same everywhere; and when we see it deformed and degraded, we must look for the influence which has been its bane. In dealing with individuals the enquiry is comparatively simple, and the answer not far to seek. But when we deal with nations we cannot, as a rule; point to a single figure, or even a group of figures, and say, "He, or they, did the mischief." We are forced to look wider and deeper, and we shall be well advised if we learn from Burke to realize "the mastery of laws, institutions, and government over the character and happiness of man." Let me apply Burke's teaching to the case before us.

The writer of the letter which I am discussing has a whole-hearted dislike of the Germans, and especially of the Prussians; charges them with "cruelty, brutal arrogance, deceit, cunning, manners and customs below those of savages"; includes in the indictment professors, commercial men, and women; recites the hideous list of crimes committed during the present war; and roundly says that, however you label him, "the Prussian will always remain a beast."

I dispute none of these propositions. I believe them to be sadly and bitterly true; but if I am to follow Burke's counsel, I must enquire into the "laws, institutions, and government" which have prevailed in Germany, and which have exercised so disastrous a "mastery over the character and happiness of man." In this enquiry it would be obvious to touch military ascendency, despotic monarchy, representative institutions deprived of effective power, administration made omnipotent, and bureaucratic interference with every detail of human life. Sydney Smith's words about unreformed England apply perfectly to modern Germany. "Of all ingenious instruments of despotism I most commend a popular assembly where the majority are paid and hired, and a few bold and able men, by their brave speeches, make the people believe they are free."

But for our present purpose I must concentrate attention on another institution which has had an even more direct and practical bearing on the character of the German people—and this is the enforcement of military service. This, like every other institution, must be judged by its effects on the character of those who are subject to it. The writer of the letter holds that "the only good thing about the German nation" is the "national service through which all men pass, and which makes soldiers of all not physically unfit, and which inculcates patriotism, loyalty, obedience, courage, discipline, duty." Now, these words, read in connexion with the description of the German people quoted above, suggest a puzzling problem. The Germans are cruel, brutally arrogant, deceitful, and cunning, and "the Prussian will always remain a beast." Yet these same people have all passed through a discipline "which inculcates patriotism, loyalty, obedience, courage, discipline, duty." Doth a fountain send forth at the same place sweet water and bitter? Does the same system make men patriotic and cruel, loyal and arrogant, obedient and deceitful, courageous and cunning, dutiful and beastly?

Perhaps it does. I can conceive some of these pairs of qualities united in a single character. A man might be a zealous patriot, and yet horribly cruel; loyal to his Sovereign, but arrogant to his inferiors; obedient to authority, yet deceitful among coequals; courageous in danger, yet cunning in avoiding it; dutiful according to his own standard of duty, and yet as "beastly" as the torturers of Belgium. But a system which produces such a very chequered type of character is scarcely to be commended.

Now, the writer might reply, "I only said that the military system *inculcated* certain virtues. I did not say that it ensured them." Then it fails. If it has produced only the "vile German race" which the writer so justly dislikes, unredeemed by any of the virtues which it "inculcates," then it has nothing to say for itself. It stands confessed as an unmixed evil.

It is right to expose a logical fallacy, but I am not fond of the attempt to obscure by logic-chopping what is a writer's real meaning. I will therefore say that, as far as I can make out, what this particular writer really believes is that the German people, through some innate and incurable frowardness of disposition, have turned the inestimable blessings of compulsory soldiership to their own moral undoing, and have made themselves wholly bad and beastly, in spite of a beneficent institution which would have made them good and even pleasant.

Here I take leave to differ, and to range myself on the side of Burke. Great, indeed—nay, incalculable—is "the mastery of laws, institutions, and government over the character and happiness of man." The system is known by its fruits. We may think as badly as we like of the Germans—as badly as they deserve—but we must remember the "laws, institutions, and government" that have dominated their national development. And this is not only a matter of just and rational thinking, but is also a counsel of safety for ourselves. If, as a result of this war, we allow our personal and social liberties (rightly suspended for the moment) to be permanently abolished or restricted; and, above all, if we bend our necks to the yoke of a military despotism; we shall be inviting a profound degradation of our national character. It would indeed be a tragical consummation of our great fight for Freedom if, when it is over, the other nations could point to us and say: "England has sunk to the moral level of Germany."

V

REVOLUTION—AND RATIONS

"A revolution by due course of law." This, as we have seen, was the Duke of Wellington's description of the Reform Act of 1832, which transferred the government of England from the aristocracy to the middle class. Though eventually accomplished by law, it did not pass without bloodshed and conflagration; and timid people satisfied themselves that not only the downfall of England, but the end of the world, must be close at hand.

Twenty years passed, and nothing in particular happened. National wealth increased, all established institutions seemed secure, and people began to forget that they had passed through a revolution. Then arose John Bright, reminding the working-men of the Midlands that their fathers "had shaken the citadel of Privilege to its base," and inciting them to give the tottering structure another push. A second revolution seemed to be drawing near. Dickens put on record, in chapter xxvi. of *Little Dorrit*, the alarms which agitated respectable and reactionary circles. The one point, as Dickens remarked, on which everyone agreed, was that the country was in very imminent danger, and wanted all the preserving it could get. Presently, but not till 1867, the second revolution arrived. Some of the finest oratory ever heard in England was lavished on the question whether the power, formerly exercised by the aristocracy and more recently by the middle class, was to be extended to the artisans. The great Lord Shaftesbury predicted "the destruction of the Empire," and Bishop Wilberforce "did not see how we were to escape fundamental changes in Church and State." "History," exclaimed Lowe, "may record other catastrophes as signal and as disastrous, but none so wanton and so disgraceful." However, the artisans made a singularly moderate use of their newly acquired power; voted Conservative as often as they voted Liberal; and so again belied the apprehensions of the alarmists.

When the workman of the town had been enfranchised, it was impossible to keep his brother who worked on the land permanently in the position of a serf or a cipher. So we began to agitate for the "County Franchise"; and once again the cry of "Revolution" was heard—perhaps in its most typical form from the lips of a Tory M.P., who, as I said before, affirmed that the labourer was no fitter for the suffrage than the beasts he tended. Even ten years later, Lord Goschen, who was by nature distrustful of popular movements, prognosticated that, if ever the Union with Ireland were lost, it would be lost through the votes of the agricultural labourers. To those who, like myself, were brought up in agricultural districts, the notion that the labourer was a revolutionary seemed strangely unreal; but it was a haunting obsession in the minds of clubmen and town-dwellers.

So, in each succeeding decade, the next extension of constitutional freedom has been acclaimed by its supporters as an instalment of the millennium, and denounced by its opponents as the destruction of social order. So it had been, time out of mind; and so it would have been to the end had not the European war burst upon us, and shaken us out of all our habitual concernments. Now "the oracles are dumb." The voices, of lugubrious prophecy are silent. The Reform Act which has become law this year is beyond doubt the greatest revolution which has as yet been effected "by due course of law." It has doubled the electorate; it has enfranchised the women; it has practically established universal suffrage; it has placed all property, as well as all policy, under the control of a class, if only that class chooses to vote and act together. All these effects of the Act (except one) are objects which I have desired to see attained ever since I was a boy at Harrow, supporting the present Bishop of Oxford and the late Lord Grey in the School Debating Society; so it is not for me to express even the faintest apprehension of evil results. But I am deliberately of opinion that the change now effected in our electoral arrangements is of farther-reaching significance than the substitution of a republic for a monarchy; and the amazing part of the business is that no one has protested at any stage of it. We were told at the beginning of the war that there was to be no controversial legislation till it was over. That engagement was broken; no one protested. A vitally important transaction was removed from the purview of Parliament to a secret conference; no one protested. If we suggested that the House of Commons was morally and constitutionally dead, and that it ought to renew its life by an appeal to the constituencies before it enforced a revolution, we were told that it was impossible to hold a General Election with the soldiers all out of the country; but now it seems that this is to be the next step, and no one protests against it.

But these may be dismissed as constitutional pedantries. So be it. The Whigs, who made the Constitution, may be pardoned if they have a sneaking regard for their handiwork. Much more astonishing is the fact that no resistance was offered on behalf of wealth and privilege by the classes who have most of both to lose. The men of £100,000 a year—not numerous, according to the Chancellor of the Exchequer, but influential—have been as meekly acquiescent as clerks or curates. Men who own half a county have smiled on an Act which will destroy territorial domination. What is the explanation? Was their silence due to patriotism or to fear? Did they laudably decline the responsibility of opposing a Government which is conducting a great war? Or did they, less laudably, shrink from the prospect of appearing as the inveterate enemies of a social and economic revolution which they saw to be inevitable? Let us charitably incline to the former hypothesis.

But there is something about this, our most recent revolution, which is even more astonishing than the absence of opposition and panic. It is that no one, whether friend or foe, has paid the least attention to the subject. In ordinary society it has been impossible to turn the conversation that way. Any topic in the world—but pre-eminently Rations,—seemed more vital and more pressing. "The Reform Bill? What Bill is that? Tell me, do you find it very difficult to get sugar?" "The Speaker's Conference? Haven't heard about it. I'm sure James Lowther won't allow them to do anything very silly—but I really cannot imagine how we are to get on without meat." Or yet again: A triumphant Suffragist said to a Belgravian sister: "So we've got the vote at last!" "What vote?" replied the sister. "Surely we've had a vote for ever so long? I'm sure I have, though I never used it."

When the real history of this wonderful war is written, methinks the historian will reckon among its most amazing features the fact that it so absorbed the mind of the nation as to make possible a 'silent revolution.'

VI

"THE INCOMPATIBLES"

My title is borrowed from one of the few Englishmen who have ever written wisely about Ireland. Our ways of trying to pacify our Sister Kingdom have been many and various—Disestablishment Acts, Land Acts, Arrears Acts, Coercion Acts, Crimes Acts, and every other variety of legislative experiment; but through them all Ireland remained unpacified. She showed no gratitude for boons which she had not asked, and seemed to crave for something which, with the best intentions in the world, England was unable to supply. This failure on the part of England may have been due to the fact that Gladstone, who, of all English statesmen, most concerned himself with Irish affairs, knew nothing of Ireland by personal contact. It is startling to read, in Lord Morley's *Life* this casual record of his former chief: "In October, 1878, Gladstone paid his first and only visit to Ireland. It lasted little more than three weeks, and did not extend beyond a very decidedly English pale.... Of the multitude of strange things distinctly Irish, he had little chance of seeing much."

One of the "strange things" which he did not see was the resolve of Ireland to be recognized as a nation; and that recognition was the "something" which, as I said just now, England was unable or unwilling to supply. Late in life Gladstone discovered that Ireland was a nation, and ought to be treated as such. As regards his own share in the matter, the change came too late, and he went to the grave leaving Ireland (in spite of two Home Rule Bills) still unpacified; but his influence has lived and wrought, not only in the Liberal party. The principle of Irish nationality has been recognized in legislative form, and the most law-abiding citizen in Great Britain might drink that toast of "Ireland a Nation" which aforetime was considered seditious, if not treasonable.

It was certainly a very odd prejudice of English Philistinism which prevented us, for so many centuries, from recognizing a fact so palpable as Irish nationality. If ever a race of men had characteristics of its own, marking it out from its nearest neighbours, that race is the Irish, and among the best of those characteristics are chastity, courtesy, hospitality, humour, and fine manners. The intense Catholicism of Ireland may be difficult for Protestants to applaud; yet most certainly those who fail to take it into account are hopelessly handicapped in the attempt to deal with Irish problems. The Irish are born fighters. One of the most splendid passages which even Irish oratory ever produced was that in which Sheill protested against the insolence of stigmatizing the countrymen of Wellington as "aliens" from England, and no policy could be more suicidal than that which deflects the soldiership of Ireland from the British cause.

Charles James Fox shares with Edmund Burke the praise of having brought the ideas which we call Liberal to bear on Irish government, and his words are at least as true to-day as when they were written: "We ought not to presume to legislate for a nation in whose feelings and affections, wants and interests, opinions and prejudices, we have no sympathy." Are "The Incompatibles" to be always incompatible, or can we now, even at the eleventh hour, make some effort to understand the working of the Irish temperament?

The incompatibility, as Matthew Arnold read it, is not between the two nations which Providence has so closely knit together, but between insolence, dulness, rigidity, on the one hand, and sensibility, quickness, flexibility, on the other. What Arnold lamented was that England has too often been represented in Ireland, and here also when Irish questions were discussed, by "the genuine, unmitigated Murdstone—the common middle-class Englishman, who has come forth from Salem House—and Mr. Creakle. He is seen in full force, of course, in the Protestant North; but throughout Ireland he is a prominent figure of the English garrison. Him the Irish see, see him only too much and too often"—and to see him is to dislike him, and the country which sent him forth.

Is there not a touch of Murdstone and Creakle in the present dealings of Parliament with Ireland? Forces greater than that of Salem House have decreed that Ireland is to have self-government, and have converted—for the astonishment of after-ages—Mr. Balfour and Lord Curzon into Home Rulers. Surely, if there is one question which, more conspicuously than another, a nation is entitled to settle for itself it is the question whether military service shall be compulsory. True, the legislative machinery of Home Rule is not yet in action; but legislative machinery is not the only method by which national sentiment can be ascertained. To introduce conscription into Ireland by an Act of the Imperial Parliament, after you have conceded to the Irish their claim to have a Parliament of their own, may not indeed be a breach of faith, but it surely is a breach of manners and good sense.

VII

FREEDOM'S NEW FRIENDS

Many, said the Greek proverb, are they who bear the mystic reed, but few are the true bacchanals. Many, in the present day, are they who make an outward display of devotion to Liberty, but few, methinks, are her real worshippers. "We are fighting for Freedom" is a cry which rises from the most unexpected quarters; and, though 'twere ungracious to question its sincerity, we must admit that this generous enthusiasm is of very recent growth.

Liberty has always had her friends in England; but where she could count one, Authority could count two.[*] Five years ago, how many Englishmen really cared for Liberty, not rendering her mere lip-service, but honestly devoting themselves to her sacred cause? If you polled the nation from top to bottom, how many liberty-lovers would you find? At one election their number, as disclosed by the polls, would rise, at another it would sink. At the best of times, if you divide the nation into strata, you would find large sections in which Liberty had no worshippers and very few friends. It had long been one of the bad signs of the times that the love of Liberty had almost ceased to animate what are called, in the odious language of social convention, "the upper classes." For generations the despised and calumniated Whigs had maintained the cause of Freedom in their peculiarly dogged though unemotional fashion, and had established the political liberties of England on a strong foundation. But their day was done, their work was accomplished, and their descendants had made common cause with their hereditary opponents.

[Footnote *: I am speaking here of England only—not of Scotland, Ireland, or Wales.]

After the great split of 1886 a genuine lover of Freedom in the upper strata of society was so rare a character that people encountering him instinctively asked, "Is he insincere? Or only mad?" Deserted by the aristocracy, Liberty turned for her followers to the great Middle Class; but there also the process of apostasy had begun; and substantial people, whose fathers had fought and suffered for Freedom, waxed reactionary as the claims of Labour became more audible, and betook themselves to the side of Authority as being the natural guardian of property. If you make the division geographically, you may say, in the broadest terms, that the North stood firm for Freedom; but that London and the South were always unfriendly to it, and, after 1886, the Midlands joined the enemy.

If we apply a test which, though often illusory, cannot be regarded as wholly misleading, the Metropolitan Press was, in a remarkable degree, hostile to Freedom, and reflected, as one must suppose, the sentiments of the huge constituency for whom it catered. How many friends could Irish Nationalism count? How many could Greece, in her struggle with Turkey? How many the Balkan States? How many Armenia? How many, even in the ranks of professed Liberalism, opposed the annexation of the South African Republics? At each extension of the suffrage; at each tussle with the Lords; at each attempt to place the burden of taxation on the shoulders best able to bear it, few indeed were the friends of Freedom in the upper classes of society; in the opulent Middle Class; in London and the Midlands and the South; in the Church, alas!; in the Universities, the Professions, and the Press.

And yet, at the present moment, from these unlikely quarters there rises a diapason of liberty-loving eloquence which contrasts very discordantly with the habitual language of five years ago. To-day the friends of Freedom are strangely numerous and admirably vocal. Our Lady of Liberty, one thinks, must marvel at the number and the energy of her new worshippers. Lapses from grace are not unknown in the after-history of revivals, but we must, in charity, assume the conversion to be genuine until experience has proved it insincere. And to what are we to attribute it? Various answers are possible. Perhaps, as long as it was only other people's liberty which was imperilled, we could look on without concern. Perhaps we never realized the value of Freedom, as the chief good of temporal life, till the prospect of losing it, under a world-wide reign of force, first dawned on our imagination. Perhaps—and this is the happiest supposition—we have learnt our lesson by contemplating the effects of a doglike submission to Authority in corrupting the morals and wrecking the civilization of a powerful and once friendly people.

But, theorize as we may about the cause, the effect is unmistakable, and, at least on the surface, satisfactory. To-day we all are the friends and lovers of Liberty—and yet the very multitude of our new comrades gives us, the veterans in the cause, some ground for perplexity and even for concern. "He who really loves Liberty must walk alone." In spite of all that has come and gone, I believe that this stern dogma still holds good; and I seem to see it illustrated afresh in the career, so lately closed amid universal respect and regret, of Leonard, Lord Courtney.[*]

[Footnote *: Leonard, Henry Courtney (Lord Courtney of Penwith), died May 11, 1918, in his eighty-sixth year.]

V

EDUCATION

I

EDUCATION AND THE JUDGE

Not long ago a Judge of the High Court (who was also a Liberal) made what struck me as an eminently wise observation. While trying a couple of Elementary School-teachers whose obscenity was too gross for even an Old Bailey audience, and who themselves were products of Elementary Schools, the Judge said: "It almost makes one hesitate to think that elementary education is the blessing which we had hoped it was." Of course, all the prigs of the educational world, and they are not few, were aghast at this robust declaration of common sense; and the Judge thought it well to explain (not, I am thankful to say, to explain away) a remark which had been sedulously misconstrued.

Long years ago Queen Victoria recording the conversation at her dinner-table, said: "Lord Melbourne made us laugh very much with his opinions about Schools and Public Education; the latter he don't like, and when I asked him if he did he said, 'I daren't say in these times that I'm against it—but I *am* against it.'"

There is a pleasantly human touch in that confession of a Whig Prime Minister, that he was afraid to avow his mistrust of a great social policy to which the Liberal party was committing itself. The arch-charlatan, Lord Brougham, was raging up and down the kingdom extolling the unmixed blessings of education. The University of London, which was to make all things new, had just been set up. "The school-master was abroad." Lord John Russell was making some tentative steps towards a system of national education. Societies, Congresses, and Institutes were springing up like mushrooms; and all enlightened people agreed that extension of knowledge was the one and all-sufficient remedy for the obvious disorders of the body politic. The Victorian Age was, in brief, the age of Education; and the one dogma which no one ventured to question was that the extension of knowledge was necessarily, and in itself, a blessing.

When I say "no one" I should perhaps say "hardly anyone"; for the wisest and wittiest man of the time saw the crack in the foundation on which his friends were laboriously erecting the temple of their new divinity. "Reading and writing," said Sydney Smith, "are mere increase of power. They may be turned, I admit, to a good or a bad purpose; but for several years of his life the child is in your hands, and you may give to that power what bias you please. I believe the arm of the assassin may be often stayed by the lessons of his early life. When I see the village school, and the tattered scholars, and the aged master or mistress teaching the mechanical art of reading or writing, and thinking that they are teaching that alone, I feel that the aged instructor is protecting life, insuring property, fencing the Altar, guarding the Throne, giving space and liberty to all the fine powers of man, and lifting him up to his own place in the order of Creation."

That first sentence contain? the pith of the whole matter. "Reading and writing are mere increase of power," and they may be turned to a good or a bad purpose. Here enters the ethical consideration which the zealots of sheer knowledge so persistently ignored. The language about fencing the Altar and guarding the Throne might, no doubt, strike the Judge who tried the school-teachers as unduly idealistic; but the sentiment is sound, and knowledge is either a blessing or a curse, according as it is used.

Sydney Smith was speaking of the Elementary School, and, indeed, was urging the claims of the working classes to better education. But his doctrine applies with at least equal force to the higher and wider ranges of knowledge. During the Victorian Age physical science came into its own, and a good deal more than its own. Any discovery in mechanics or chemistry was hailed as a fresh boon, and the discoverer was ranged, with Wilberforce and Shaftesbury, among our national heroes. As long ago as 1865 a scientific soldier perceived the possibilities of aerial navigation. His vision has been translated into fact; but Count Zeppelin has shown us quite clearly that the discovery is not an unmixed blessing. Chemistry is, to some minds, the most interesting of studies, just because it is, as Lord Salisbury once said of it, the science of things as they are. Yet aconitine, strychnine, and antimony have played their part in murders, and chloroform has been used for destruction as well as for salvation. Dr. Lardner was one of the most conspicuous figures in that March of Mind which Brougham and his congeners led; and his researches into chemistry resulted in the production of an effluvium which was calculated to destroy all human life within five miles of the spot where it was discharged. This was an enlargement of knowledge; but if there had been Nihilists in the reign of William IV. they would have found in Dr. Lardner's discovery a weapon ready to their hand. Someone must have discovered alcohol; and my teetotal friends would probably say, invented it, for they cannot attribute so diabolical an agency to the action of purely natural causes. But even those who least sympathize with "the lean and sallow abstinence" would scarcely maintain that alcohol has been an unmixed blessing to the race.

To turn from material to mental discoveries, I hold that a great many additions which have been made to our philosophical knowledge have diminished alike the happiness and the usefulness of those who made them. "To live a life of the deepest pessimism tempered only by the highest mathematics" is a sad result of sheer knowledge. An historian, toiling terribly in the muniment-rooms of colleges or country houses, makes definite additions to our knowledge of Henry VIII. or Charles I.; learns cruelty from the one and perfidy from the other, and emerges with a theory of government as odious as Carlyle's or Froude's. A young student of religion diligently adds to his stock of learning, and plunges into the complicated errors of Manicheans, and Sabellians, and Pelagians, with the result that he absorbs the heresies and forgets the Gospel. In each of these cases knowledge has been increased, but mankind has not been benefited. We come back to what Sydney Smith said. Increase of knowledge is merely increase of power. Whether it is to be a boon or a curse to humanity depends absolutely on the spirit in which it is applied. Just now we find ourselves engaged in a desperate conflict between materialism and morality—between consummate knowledge organized for evil ends, and the sublime ideal of public right. Education has done for Germany all that Education, divorced from Morality, can do; and the result has been a defeat of civilization and a destruction of human happiness such as Europe has not seen since the Middle Age closed in blood. What shall it profit a nation if it "gain the whole world" and lose its own soul?

II

THE GOLDEN LADDER

Education is an excellent thing, but the word has a deterrent sound. It breathes pedantry and dogmatism, and "all that is at enmity with joy." To people of my age it recalls the dread spirits of Pinnock and Colenso and Hamblin Smith, and that even more terrible Smith who edited Dictionaries of everything. So, though this chapter is to be concerned with the substance, I eschew the word, and choose for my title a figurative phrase. I might, with perfect justice, have chosen another figure, and have headed my paper "The Peg and the Hole"; for, after nearly a century of patient expectation, we have at last got a Square Peg in the Square Hole of Public Instruction. In simpler speech, England has at length got a Minister of Education who has a genuine enthusiasm for knowledge, and will do his appointed work with a single eye to the intellectual advancement of the country, neither giving heed to the pribbles and prabbles of theological disputants, nor modifying his plans to suit the convenience of the manufacturer or the squire. He is, in my judgment, exactly the right man for the office which he fills; and is therefore strikingly differentiated not only from some Ministers of Education whom we have known, but also from the swarm of Controllers and Directors and salaried busybodies who have so long been misdirecting us and contradicting one another.

When I say that Mr. Fisher will not give heed to theological disputants, I by no means ignore the grievance under which some of those disputants have suffered. The ever-memorable majority of 1906 was won, not wholly by Tariff Reform or Chinese Labour, but to a great extent by the righteous indignation of Nonconformity at the injury which had been inflicted on it by the Tory Education Acts. There were Passive Resisters in those days, as there are Conscientious Objectors now; and they made their grievance felt when the time for voting came. The Liberal Government, in spite of its immense victory at the polls, scored a fourfold failure in its attempts to redress that grievance, and it remains unredressed to this hour. Not that I admired the Liberal Education Bills. My own doctrine on the matter was expressed by my friend Arthur Stanton, who said in 1906: "I think National and Compulsory Education must be secular, and with facilities for the denominations to add their particular tenets. My objection to this Bill" (Mr. Birrell's Bill) "is that it subsidizes undenominationalism." And again in 1909, when another of our Liberal practitioners was handling the subject: "I object altogether to the State teaching religion. I would have it teach secular matters only, and leave the religious teaching entirely to the clergy, who should undertake it at their own expense. This is the only fair plan—fair to all. The State gives, and pays for, religious teaching which I do not regard as being worth anything at all. It is worse than useless. Real religious teaching can only be given by the Church, and when Christ told us to go and teach, He did not mean mathematics and geography."

That was, and is, my doctrine on religious education; but in politics we must take things as they are, and must not postpone practicable reforms because we cannot as yet attain an ideal system. So Mr. Fisher, wisely as I think, has left the religious question on one side, and has proposed a series of reforms which will fit equally well the one-sided system which still oppresses Nonconformists and the simply equitable plan to which I, as a lover of religious freedom, aspire.

I see that some of Mr. Fisher's critics say: "This is not a great Bill." Perhaps not, but it is a good Bill; and, as Lord Morley observes, "that fatal French saying about small reforms being the worst enemies of great reforms is, in the sense in which it is commonly used, a formula of social ruin." Enlarging on this theme, Lord Morley points out that the essential virtue of a small reform—the quality which makes it not an evil, but a good—is that it should be made "on the lines and in the direction" of the greater reform which is desiderated.

Now, this condition Mr. Fisher's Bill exactly fulfils. I suppose that the "greater reform" of education which we all wish to see—the ideal of national instruction—is that the State should provide for every boy and girl the opportunity of cultivating his or her natural gifts to the highest perfection which they are capable of attaining. When I speak of "natural gifts" I refer not only to the intellect, but also to the other parts of our nature, the body and the moral sense. This ideal involves a system which, by a natural and orderly development, should conduct the capable child from the Elementary School, through all the intermediate stages, to the highest honours of the Universities.

The word "capable" occurs in Mr. Fisher's Bill, and rightly, because our mental and physical capacities are infinitely varied. A good many children may be unable to profit by any instruction higher than that provided by the Elementary School. A good many more will be able to profit by intermediate education. Comparatively few—the best—will make their way to really high attainment, and will become, at and through the Universities, great philosophers, or scholars, or scientists, or historians, or mathematicians.

At that point—and it ought to be reached at a much earlier age than is now usual—the State's, concern in the matter ends. The child has become, a man, and henceforth must work out his own intellectual salvation; but in the earlier stages the State can and must exercise a potent influence. The earliest stage must be compulsory—that was secured by the Act of 1870. In the succeeding stages, the State, while it does not compel, must stimulate and encourage; and above all must ensure that no supposed exigencies of money-making, no selfish tyranny of the employing classes, shall be allowed to interfere with mental or physical development, or to divert the boy or the girl from any course of instruction by which he or she is capable of profiting. This ideal Mr. Fisher's Bill, with its plain enactment that education shall be free; with its precaution against "half-time"; with its ample provision for Continuation Schools, goes far to realize. Even if it is a "small" reform—and I should dispute the epithet—it is certainly "on the lines and in the direction" of that larger reform which the enthusiasts of education have symbolized by the title of "The Golden Ladder."[*]

[Footnote *: Happily for Education, Mr. Fisher's Bill is now an Act.]

III

My title is figurative, but figures are sometimes useful. Murray's Dictionary defines an oasis as "a fertile spot in the midst of a desert"; and no combination of words could better describe the ideal which I wish to set before my readers.

The suggestion of this article came to me from a correspondent in Northumberland—"an old miner, who went to work down a mine before he was eight years old, and is working yet at seventy-two." My friend tells me that he has "spent about forty years of his spare time in trying to promote popular education among his fellow working-men." His notice was attracted by a paper which I recently wrote on "The Golden Ladder" of Education, and that paper led him to offer some suggestions which I think too valuable to be lost.

My friend does not despise the Golden Ladder. Quite the contrary. He sees its usefulness for such as are able to climb it, but he holds that they are, and must be, the few, while he is concerned for the many. I agree. When (following Matthew Arnold at a respectful distance) I have urged the formation of a national system by which a poor man's son may be enabled to climb from the Elementary School to a Fellowship or a Professorship at Oxford or Cambridge, I have always realized that I was planning a course for the exceptionally gifted boy. That boy has often emerged in real life, and the Universities have profited by his emergence; but he is, and always must be, exceptional. What can be done for the mass of intelligent, but not exceptional, boys, who, to quote my Northumbrian friend, "must be drilled into a calling of some kind, so as to be able to provide for themselves when they grow up to manhood"? When once their schooling, in the narrow sense, is over, must their minds be left to lie fallow or run wild? Can nothing be done to supplement their elementary knowledge, to stimulate and discipline their mental powers?

The University Extension Movement was an attempt to answer these questions in a practical fashion, and my friend does full justice to the spirit which initiated that movement, and to the men—such as the late Lord Grey—who led it. But I suppose he speaks from experience when he says: "University Extension, as it is, will never become established in working-class villages. Forty-five to fifty pounds is too big a sum to be raised in three months, and is also considered too much to be paid for a man coming to lecture once a week for twelve weeks, and then disappear for ever like a comet." My friend uses an astronomical figure, I a geographical one; but we mean the same thing. The idea is to establish Oases—"fertile spots in the midst of deserts"—permanent centres of light and culture in manufacturing districts. "The Universities teach and train ministers of religion, and they go and live in their parishes among their flocks all the year round. Why not send lecturers and teachers of secular subjects in the same way? A system something similar to the Wesleyan or Primitive Methodists' ministerial system would answer the purpose. The country might be divided into circuits of four or five centres each, and a University man stationed in each circuit, to organize Students' Associations, give lectures, hold classes, and superintend scientific experiments, as the case may be."

This is a good illustration. The Church professes to place in each parish an official teacher of religion and morality, and most of the Nonconformist communities do the same. To place an official teacher of culture (in its widest sense) in every parish is perhaps a task beyond our national powers as at present developed; but to place one in every industrial district is not conceivable only, but, I believe, practicable. The lecturer who comes from Oxford or Cambridge, delivers his course, and departs, has no doubt his uses. He is like the "Hot Gospeller" of an earlier age, or the "Missioner" of to-day. He delivers an awakening message, and many are the better for it; but if culture is to get hold of the average lads and young men of an industrial district, its exponent must be more like the resident minister, the endowed and established priest. That he should live among the people whom he is to instruct, know them personally, understand their ways of thinking and speaking, is at least as important as that he should be a competent historian or mathematician or man of letters. If the State, or voluntary effort, or a combination of the two, could secure the permanent presence of such a teacher in every district where men work hard, and yet have leisure enough to cultivate their intellects, a yawning gap in our educational system would be filled.

It would not be polite to mention actual names; but take by way of example such a district as Dickens's "Coketown," or Disraeli's "Wodgate," or George Eliot's "Milby," or any of those towns which Cobbett expressively called "Hell-Holes." Let the State establish in each of those places a qualified and accredited teacher for adult students. The teacher may, if necessary, be paid in part by voluntary subscription; but it is, in my view, all-important that he should have the sanction and authority of the State to give him a definite place among local administrators, and to the State he should be responsible for the due discharge of his functions. In Coketown or Wodgate or Milby his lecture-room would be a real Oasis—"a fertile spot in the midst of a desert." Even if it has not been our lot to dwell in those deserts, we all have had, as travellers, some taste of their quality. We know the hideousness of all that meets the eye; the necessary absorption in the struggle for subsistence; the resulting tendency to regard money as the one subject worth serious consideration; the inadequate means of intellectual recreation; the almost irresistible atmosphere of materialism in which life and thought are involved. The "Oasis" would provide a remedy for all this. It would offer to all who cared to seek them "the fairy-tale of science," the pregnant lessons of history, the infinitely various joys of literature, the moral principles of personal and social action which have been thought out "by larger minds in calmer ages."

That there may be practical difficulties in the way of such a scheme I do not dispute. The object of this chapter is not to elaborate a plan, but to exhibit an idea. That the amount of definite knowledge acquired in this way might be small, and what Archbishop Benson oddly called "unexaminable," is, I think, quite likely. A man cannot learn in the leisure-hours left over by exhausting work as he would learn if he had nothing to think of except his studies and his examination. But Education has a larger function than the mere communication of knowledge. It opens the windows of the mind; it shows vistas which before were unsuspected; and so, as Wordsworth said, "is efficacious in making men wiser, better, and happier."

IV

LIFE, LIBERTY, AND JUSTICE

When an article in a newspaper produces a reply, the modest writer is gratified; for he knows that he has had at any rate one reader. If the reply comes to him privately, he is even better pleased, for then he feels that his reader thinks the matter worthy of personal discussion and of freely exchanged opinion. I have lately written an article on "Life and Liberty" as proposed by some earnest clergymen for the English Church, and an article on Mr. Fisher's Education Bill, in which I avowed my dislike to all attempts on the part of the State to teach religion. Both these articles have brought me a good deal of correspondence, both friendly and hostile. The term allotted to human life does not allow one to enter into private controversy with every correspondent, so I take this method of making a general reply. "Life and Liberty" are glorious ideals, but, to make the combination, perfect, we must add Justice. Hence my title.

The State consists of persons who profess all sorts of religion, and none. If the State compels its citizens to pay for religious teaching in which they do not believe, it commits, in my opinion, a palpable injustice. This is not merely a question between one sect and another sect. It is, indeed, unjust to make a Quaker pay for teaching the doctrine of the Sacraments, or a Unitarian for teaching the Deity of Christ; but it is equally unjust to make an Atheist pay for teaching the existence of God, or a Churchman for teaching that curious kind of implied Socinianism which is called "undenominational religion."

The only way out of these inequities is what is commonly called "Secularism." The word has some unfortunate associations. It has been connected in the past with a blatant form of negation, and also with a social doctrine which all decent people repudiate. But, strictly considered, it means no more than "temporal" or "worldly"; and when I say that I recommend the "Secular" system of education, I mean that the State should confine itself to the temporal or worldly work with which alone it is competent to deal, and should leave religion (which it cannot touch without inflicting injustice on someone) to those whose proper function is to instil it.

Who are they? Speaking generally, parents, ministers of religion, and teachers who are themselves convinced of what they teach; but I must narrow my ground. To-day I am writing as a Churchman for those Churchmen whom my previous articles disturbed; and I have only space to set forth some of the grounds on which we Churchmen should support the "secular solution."

A Churchman is bound by his baptismal vows to "believe all the articles of the Christian Faith." These, according to his catechism, are summed up in the Apostles' Creed. He cannot, therefore, be satisfied with any religious instruction which is not based on that formula; and yet such instruction cannot rightly be enforced in schools which belong as much to unbelievers as to Christians. A Churchman's religious faith is not derived primarily from the Bible, but from the teaching of the Christian Church, who is older than the oldest of her documents. There was a Church before the New Testament was written, and that Church transmitted the faith by oral tradition. "From the very first the rule has been, as a matter of fact, that the Church should teach the truth, and then should appeal to Scripture in vindication of its own teaching." For a Churchman, religious instruction must be the teaching of the Church, tested by the Bible. The two cannot be separated. Hence it follows that, while the State is bound to respect the convictions of those who adhere to all manner of beliefs and disbeliefs, the Churchman cannot recognize religious teaching imparted under such conditions as being that which his own conscience demands.

And, further, supposing that some contrivance could be discovered whereby the State might authorize the teaching of the Church's doctrine, the Churchman could not conscientiously be a party to it; for, according to his theory, there is only one Body divinely commissioned to decide what is to be taught—and that Body is not the State, but the Church; and there is only one set of persons qualified to teach it—viz., those who are duly authorized by the Church, and are fully persuaded as to the truth of what they teach.

It is sometimes asked how the Church is to fulfil this obligation without being subsidized in some way by the State. The principal requisite is greater faith in its Divine mission. If the Bishops and clergy had a stronger conviction that what they are divinely commissioned to undertake they will be divinely assisted to fulfil, this question need not be suggested. The first teachers of the Christian religion performed their task without either "Rate-aid" or "State-aid" and the result of their labour is still to be seen; whereas now the object of leaders of religion seems to be to get done for them what they ought to do for themselves. It may be well to quote an utterance of the Bishop of Oxford at the time when the Liberal Government was dealing with education. "We are now, more or less, in the middle of a crisis. We are always in the middle of a crisis. This crisis is about the religious question in our day-schools. I would ask you, then, to get at the root of our difficulty. What is it? The heart of our difficulty is partly that we have *shifted on to the wrong shoulders* the central function of teaching children; secondly, that we have so lost the idea of what the teaching of the Church is, and *the meaning of religious education*, that we are considered by the public to be unreasonable and uncompromising people if we are not disposed to admit that the County Councils can settle the standard of sufficient religious knowledge for everybody."

The difficulty as to means might be overcome if the Church would mind its own business, and leave to the State what the State can do so much more effectively. Let me quote the words of a great Christian and a great Churchman—Mr. Gladstone—written in 1894: "Foul fall the day when the persons of this world shall, on whatever pretext, take into their uncommissioned hands the manipulation of the religion of our Lord and Saviour."

Surely Churchmen will best serve the religion which they profess by joining with other "men of goodwill," though of different faiths, who desire the secular solution. In that way only, as far as I can see, can the interests of Education be reconciled with the higher interests of Justice.

V

THE STATE AND THE BOY

When Mr. A. J. Balfour was a very young man he published *A Defence of Philosophic Doubt*. Nobody read it, but a great many talked about it; and serious people went about with long faces, murmuring, "How sad that Lord Salisbury's nephew should be an Agnostic!" When Mr. Balfour had become a conspicuous figure in politics, the serious people began to read the book which, so far, they had only denounced, and then they found, to their surprise and joy, that it was an essay in orthodox apologetic. Thenceforward Mr. Balfour ranked in their eyes as a "Defender of the Faith" second only to Henry VIII.

To compare small things with great, I have had a similar experience. Not long ago I wrote a paper designed to set forth the pretty obvious truth that increase in knowledge is not in itself a good. It evoked much criticism, and the critics once again exemplified our truly English habit of denouncing what we have not read. If these quaint people were to be believed, I was an enemy of education in general and of elementary education in particular. I hope that they will be as much relieved as were Mr. Balfour's critics when they discover that I am, and all my life have been, a zealous supporter of education, and, to some extent, an expert in it.

If the world could be exhaustively divided into two classes-the Educated and the Uneducated—I suppose that I should be included in the former, though I anticipate an inevitable sarcasm by allowing that I should find myself perilously near the dividing-line. It is more to the purpose to say that, whatever my own educational deficiencies, I have always been keenly interested in the education of other people, and have preached incessantly that the State has a sacred duty to its boys. If I leave the education of girls on one side, I do so, not because I consider it unimportant, but because I know nothing about it.

Information, as the great Butler said, is the least part of education. The greatest is the development of the child's natural power to its utmost extent and capacity; and the duty of so developing it must be admitted by everyone who ponders our Lord's teaching about the Buried Talent and the Pound laid up in the Napkin. Unless we enable and encourage every boy in England to bring whatever mental gifts he has to the highest point of their possible perfection, we are shamefully and culpably squandering the treasure which God has given us to be traded with and accounted for. We shall have no one but ourselves to blame if, as a Nemesis on our neglect, we lose our present standing among the educated peoples of the world. I always get back to the ideal of the "Golden Ladder," reaching from the Elementary Schools, by Scholarships or "free places," to the Secondary Schools, and from them again to the Universities. This ideal is, unlike some ideals, attainable, and has in repeated instances been attained. Again and again the highest mathematical honours of Cambridge have been won by Elementary Schoolboys, and what is true of mathematics might also be true of every branch of knowledge. I say advisedly that it "might" be true: whether or not it will be depends on our handling of quite young boys.

The pedagogic notion under which people of my time were reared was that every boy must learn exactly the same things as every other boy, and must go on learning them till his last day at school, whether that day arrived when he was fourteen or eighteen. "We must catch up every man, whether he is to be a clergyman or a duke, begin with him at six years of age, and never quit him till he is twenty; making him conjugate and decline for life and death; and so teaching him to estimate his progress in real wisdom as he can scan the verses of the Greek tragedians." So said Sydney Smith, and with perfect truth. "The grand, old, fortifying, classical curriculum" was enforced on the boy whose whole heart was in the engineer's shed, while his friend, to whom literature was a passion, was constrained to simulate an interest in the blue lights and bad smells of a chemical lecture. "Let it be granted" (as the odious Euclid, now happily dethroned, used to say) that there is a certain amount that all alike must learn but this amount will prove, when scrutinized, to be very small. I suppose we must all learn to read and write, and it is useful to be able to do a sum in simple addition; though very eminent people have often written very illegible hands, and Dean Stanley—one of the most accomplished men of his day—could never be persuaded that eighteen pence was not the equivalent of 1s. 8d. Zealots for various "knowledges" (to use the curious plural sanctioned by Matthew Arnold) will urge the indispensability of their respective hobbies. One will say let everybody learn that the earth is round; another, that James I. was not the son of Queen Elizabeth. But let us leave, these pribbles and prabbles. Let every boy be coerced into learning what is absolutely necessary for the daily work of life; but let him, at a very early age, have his powers concentrated on the subject which really interests him.

One of the highest gifts which a teacher can possess is the power of "discerning the spirits"—of discovering what a boy's mind really is; what it is made of; what can be made of it. This power is a natural gift, and can by no means be acquired. Many teachers entirely lack it; but those who possess it are among the most valuable servants of the State. This power may be brought to bear on every boy when he is, say, from fourteen to sixteen years old—perhaps in some cases even earlier; and, when once the teacher has made the all-important discovery, then let everything be done to stimulate, and at the same time to discipline, the boy's natural inclination, his inborn aptitude. Fifty years ago, every boy at every Public School, though he might be as unpoetical as Blackstone who wrote the Commentaries, or Bradshaw who compiled the Railway Guide, was forced to produce a weekly tale of Latin and Greek verses which would have made Horace laugh and Sophocles cry. The Rev. Esau Hittall's "Longs and Shorts about the Calydonian Boar," commemorated in *Friendship's Garland*, may stand for a sample of the absurdities which I have in mind; and the supporters of this amazing abuse assured the world that Greek and Latin versification was an essential element of a liberal education. It took a good many generations to deliver England from this absurdity, and there are others like unto it which still hold their own in the scholastic world. To sweep these away should be the first object of the educational reformer; and, when that preliminary step has been taken, the State will be able to say to every boy who is not mentally deficient: "This, or this, is the path which Nature intended you to tread. Follow it with all your heart. We will back you, and help you, and applaud you, and will not forsake you till the goal is won."

VI

A PLEA FOR THE INNOCENTS

My "spiritual home" is not Berlin, nor even Rome, but Jerusalem. In heart and mind I am there to-day, and have been there ever since the eternally memorable day on which our army entered it. What I am writing will see the light on the Feast of the Holy Innocents;[*] and my thoughts have been running on a prophetic verse which unites the place and the festival in a picturesque accord:

"Thus saith the Lord, I am returned unto Zion, and will dwell in the midst of Jerusalem:... and the streets of the city shall be full of boys and girls playing in the streets thereof."

The most brilliant Israelite of our times, Lord Beaconsfield, said of a brilliant Englishman, Dean Stanley, that his leading feature was his "picturesque sensibility," and that sensibility was never more happily expressed than when he instituted the service for children in Westminster Abbey on Innocents' Day—"Childermas Day," as our forefathers called it, in the age when holidays were also holy days, and the Mass was the centre of social as well as of spiritual life. On this touching feast a vast congregation of boys and girls assembles in that Abbey Church which has been rightly called "the most lovable thing in Christendom"; and, as it moves in "solemn troops and sweet societies" through aisles grey with the memories of a thousand years, it seems a living prophecy of a brighter age already at the door.

[Footnote *: December 28, 1917.]

It seems—rather, it seemed. Who can pierce the "hues of earthquake and eclipse" which darken the aspect of the present world? Who can foresee, or even reasonably conjecture, the fate which is in store for the children who to-day are singing their carols in the church of the Confessor? Will it be their lot to be "playing in the streets" of a spiritual Jerusalem—the Holy City of a regenerated humanity? or are they destined to grow up in a reign of blood and iron which spurns the "Vision of Peace" as the most contemptible of dreams?

In some form or another these questions must force themselves on the mind of anyone who contemplates the boys and girls of to-day, and tries to forecast what may befall them in the next four or five years.

It is a gruesome thought that the children of to-day are growing up in an atmosphere of war. Bloodshed, slaughter, peril and privation, bereavement and sorrow and anxiety—all the evils from which happy childhood is most sedulously guarded have become the natural elements in which they live and move and have their being. For the moment the cloud rests lightly on them, for not "all that is at enmity with joy" can depress the Divine merriment of healthy childhood; but the cloud will become darker and heavier with each succeeding year of war; and every boy and girl is growing up into a fuller realization of miseries which four years ago would have been unimaginable.

But at Christmastide, if ever, we are bound to take the brightest view which circumstances allow. Let us then assume the best. Let us assume that before next Innocents' Day the war will have ended in a glorious peace. God grant it; but, even in that beatific event, what will become of the children? They cannot be exactly what they would have been if their lot had been cast in normal times. Unknown to themselves, their "subconscious intelligence" must have taken a colour and a tone from the circumstances in which they have been reared. As to the colour, our task will be to wipe out the tinge of blood; as to the tone, to restore the note which is associated with the Angels' Song.

This is my "Plea for the Innocents." What will the State offer them as they emerge from childhood into boyhood, and from boyhood into adolescence?

Perhaps it will offer Conscription; and, with no "perhaps" at all, some strident voices will pronounce that offer the finest boon ever conferred upon the youth of a nation. Then, if there is any manliness or fibre left in the adherents of freedom, they will answer that we adopted Conscription for a definite object, and, when once that object is attained, we renounce it for ever.

What will the State offer? Obviously it must offer education—but what sort of education? The curse of militarism may make itself felt even in the school-room. It would be deplorable indeed if, as a result of our present experience, children were to be taught what J. R. Green called a "drum-and-trumpet history," and were made to believe that the triumphs of war are the highest achievements of the human spirit.

As long as there is an Established Church, the State, in some sense, offers religion. Is the religion of the next few years to be what Ruskin commends: a "religion of pure mercy, which we must learn to defend by fulfilling"; or is it to be the sort of religion which Professor Cramb taught, and which Prussian Lutheranism has substituted for the Gospel?

And, finally, what of home? After all said and done, it is the home that, in the vast majority of cases, influences the soul and shapes the life. What will the homes of England be like when the war is over? Will they be homes in which the moral law reigns supreme; where social virtue is recognized as the sole foundation of national prosperity; where the "strange valour of goodwill towards men", is revered as the highest type of manly resolution?

It is easy enough to ask these questions: it is impossible to answer them. The Poet is the Prophet, and this is the Poet's vision:

> "The days are dark with storm;—
> The coming revolutions have to face
> Of peace and music, but of blood and fire;
> The strife of Races scarce consolidate,
> Succeeded by the far more bitter strife
> Of Classes—that which nineteen hundred years,
> Since Christ spake, have not yet availed to close,
> But rather brought to issue only now,
> When first the Peoples international
> Know their own strength, and know the world is theirs."[*]

Know their own strength, and know the world is theirs—a solemn line, which at this season we may profitably ponder.

[Footnote *: "The Disciples," by H. E. Hamilton King.]

VI

MISCELLANEA

I

THE "HUMOROUS STAGE"

I am not adventuring on the dangerous paths of dramatic criticism. When I write of the "humorous stage," I am using the phrase as Wordsworth used it, to signify a scene where new characters are suddenly assumed, and the old as suddenly discarded.

Long ago, Matthew Arnold, poking fun at the clamours of Secularism, asked in mockery, "Why is not Mr. Bradlaugh a Dean?" To-day I read, in a perfectly serious manifesto forwarded to me by a friendly correspondant, this searching question: "Why is not the Archbishop of Canterbury Censor of Plays?" It really is a great conception; and, if adopted in practice, might facilitate the solution of some perplexing problems. If any lover of the ancient ways should demur on the ground of incongruity, I reply that this objection might hold good in normal times, but that just now the "humorous stage" of public life so abounds in incongruities that one more or less would make no perceptible difference. Everyone is playing a part for which, three years ago, we should have thought him or her totally unqualified. Old habits, old prepossessions—even in some cases old principles—are cast aside with a levity which even Wordsworth's young actor could not have surpassed. We all are saying and doing things of which we should have thought ourselves incapable; and even our surprise at ourselves, great as it is, is less than our surprise at our friends.

To begin at the top. I have long held the present Prime Minister in high admiration. I can never forget—nor allow others to forget—that he fought for the cause of Justice and Freedom in South Africa almost single-handed, and at the risk of his life. An orator, a patriot, a lover of justice, a hater of privilege, I knew him to be. I did not see in him the makings of a Dictator directing the destinies of an Empire at war, and in his spare moments appointing Successors to the Apostles within the precincts of an Established Church. Certainly of Mr. Lloyd George, if of no one else, it is true that

> The little actor cons another part,"

and I heartily wish him success in it. But it is true of everyone, and true in every corner of the stage. Let me strike into the medley at random. The anti-feminists, where are they? They have changed their garb and their "lines" so thoroughly that it is difficult for even a practised eye to recognize them in their new parts. Lord Curzon is a member of a Cabinet which established the women's vote, and such stalwarts as Mr. Asquith and Lord Harcourt welcome with effusion the enfranchisement of the victorious suffragette.

And what of the Pacificists? Where are they? Some, I know, are in prison, but, if it had not been for the rapid change of parts which the war has brought, they would have had a good many more fellow-captives than they have. The writer of this article was, from his first entrance into public affairs, a Pacificist to the backbone. He believed that war was the greatest of preventible evils, and that no war which had occurred in his lifetime had been justified by the laws of right and wrong. To-day that Pacificist is heart and soul with his countrymen in their struggle; and, having lived to see England engaged in a righteous war, he has changed his motto from "Rub lightly" to "Mak sicker."

Not less remarkable is the transformation of the liberty-lovers (among whom also the present writer has always reckoned himself). Four years ago we were eagerly and rightly on the alert to detect the slightest attempt by Ministers or bureaucrats or public bodies to invade our glorious privilege of doing and saying exactly what we like. To-day the pressure of the war has turned us into the willing subjects of a despotism. We tumble over each other in our haste to throwaway the liberties which we used to consider vital to our being; and some of us have been not merely the victims, but the active agents, of an administrative system which we believe to be necessary for the safety of the State.

But is there not a remnant? Have all the lovers of Liberty changed their garb and conned new parts? Not all. A remnant there is, and it is to be found in the House of Lords. This is perhaps the most astonishing feature of the "humorous stage"; and if, among superlatives, a super-superlative is possible, I reserve that epithet for the fact that the most vigorous champion of personal freedom in the House of Lords has been an ecclesiastical lawyer. From Lord Stowell to Lord Parmoor is indeed a far cry. Who could have dreamt that, even amid the upheaval of a world, a spokesman of liberty and conscience would emerge from the iron-bound precincts of the Consistory Court and the Vicar-General's Office?

Bishops again—not even these most securely placed of all British officials can escape the tendency to change which pervades the whole stage of public life. The Bishop of Winchester, whom all good Progressives used to denounce as a dark conspirator against the rights of conscience; the Bishop of Oxford, whom we were taught to regard as a Hildebrand and a Torquemada rolled into one—these admirable prelates emerge from the safe seclusion of Castle and Palace to rebuke the persecution of the Conscientious Objector, even when his objection is "nearly intolerable."

That the Press should have had its share in this general readjustment of parts was only natural; but even in what is natural there may be points of special interest. There is a weekly journal of high repute which has earned a secure place in the regard of serious-minded people by its lifelong sobriety, moderation, and respect for the prunes and prisms. When this staid old print, this steady-going supporter of all established institutions, bursts out in a furious attack on the man who has to bear the chief responsibility of the war, I can only rub my eyes in amazement. If a sheep had suddenly gone mad, and begun to bark and bite, the transformation could not have been more astonishing.

But I reserve my most striking illustration of the "humorous stage" for the last. Fifteen years ago it was the fashion to point at Lord Hugh Cecil as a belated upholder of exploded superstitions; as an "ecclesiastical layman" (the phrase was meant to be sarcastic) who lived in a realm of speculative theology, out of touch with all practical life; as a zealot, a bigot, a would-be persecutor; an interesting survival of the Middle Age; a monk who had strayed into politics. To-day we salute him as the one Member of Parliament who has had the courage to affirm the supremacy of the moral law, and to assert the imperious claim which Christianity makes on the whole of man's being.

II

THE JEWISH REGIMENT

It was an old and a true allegation against John Bull that he had no tact in dealing with other races than his own. He did not mean to be unjust or unfair, but he trampled on the sensitiveness, which he could not understand. In Ireland he called the Roman Catholic faith "a lie and a heathenish superstition"; or, in a lighter mood, made imbecile jokes about pigs and potatoes. In Scotland, thriftiness and oatmeal were the themes of his pleasantry; in Wales, he found the language, the literature, and the local nomenclature equally comic, and reserved his loudest guffaw for the Eisteddfod. Abroad, "Foreigners don't wash" was the all-embracing formula. Nasality, Bloomerism, and Dollars epitomized his notion of American civilization; and he cheerfully echoed the sentiments

> "Of all who under Eastern skies
> Call Aryan man a blasted nigger."

Now, of late years, John has altered his course. Some faint conception of his previous foolishness has dawned on his mind; and, as he is a thoroughly good fellow at heart, he has tried to make amends. The present war has taught him a good deal that he did not know before, and he renders a homage, all the more enthusiastic because belated, to the principle of Nationality. His latest exploit in this direction has been to suggest the creation of a Jewish Regiment. The intention was excellent and the idea picturesque; but for the practical business of life we need something more than good intentions and picturesque ideas. "Wisdom," said Ecclesiastes, "is profitable to direct;" and Wisdom would have suggested that it was advisable to consult Jewish opinion before the formation of a Jewish Regiment was proclaimed to the world. There is probably no race of people about which John Bull has been so much mistaken as he has been about the Jews. Lord Beaconsfield's description of Mr. Buggins, with his comments on the Feast of Tabernacles in Houndsditch, is scarcely yet anachronistic.[*] But slowly our manners and our intelligence have improved in this as in other directions; and Lord Derby (who represents John Bull in his more refined development) thought that he would be paying his Jewish fellow-citizens a pretty compliment if he invited them to form a Jewish Regiment.

[Footnote *: See *Tancred*, Book V., chapter vi.]

Historically, Lord Derby and those who applauded his scheme had a great deal to say for themselves. The remote history of Judaism is a history of war. The Old Testament is full of "the battle of the warrior" and of "garments rolled in blood." Gideon, and Barak, and Samson, and Jephthah, and David are names that sound like trumpets; and the great Maccabean Princes of a later age played an equal part with Romans and Lacedæmonians. All this is historically true; but it never occurred to Lord Derby and his friends that the idea which underlay their scheme is the opposite of that which animates modern Judaism. Broadly speaking, the idea of modern Judaism is not Nationality, but Religion. Mr. Lucien Wolf has lately reminded us that, according to authoritative utterances, "The Jews are neither a nation within a nation, nor cosmopolitan," but an integral part of the nations among whom they live, claiming the same rights and acknowledging the same duties as are claimed and acknowledged by their fellow-citizens. It is worth noticing that Macaulay accepted this position as disposing of the last obstacle to the civil and political enfranchisement of the English Jews, and ridiculed the notion that they would regard England, "not as their country, but merely as their place of exile." Mr. Wolf thus formulates his faith: "In the purely religious communities of Western Jewry we have the spiritual heirs of the law-givers, prophets, and teachers who, from the dawn of history, have conceived Israel, not primarily as a political organism, but as a nation of priests, the chosen servants of the Eternal."

Mr. Claude Montefiore, who is second to none as an interpreter of modern Judaism, has lately been writing in a similar strain. The Jew is a Jew in respect of his religion; but, for the ordinary functions of patriotism, fighting included, he is a citizen of the country in which he dwells. A Jewish friend of mine said the other day to a Pacificist who tried to appeal to him on racial grounds: "*I would shoot a Jewish Prussian as readily as a Christian Prussian, if I found him fighting under the German flag.*" Thus, to enrol a regiment of Jews is about as wise as to enrol a regiment of Roman Catholics or of Wesleyan Methodists. Jews, Romans, and Wesleyans alike hold with laudable tenacity the religious faiths which they respectively profess; but they are well content to fight side by side with Anglicans, or Presbyterians, or Plymouth Brethren. They need no special standard, no differentiating motto. They are soldiers of the country to which they belong.

Here let me quote the exhilarating verses of a Jewish lady,[*] written at the time of the Boer War (March, 1900):

"Long ago and far away, O Mother England,
We were warriors brave and bold,
But a hundred nations rose in arms against us,
And the shades of exile closed o'er those heroic
        Days of old.

"Thou hast given us home and freedom, Mother England.
Thou hast let us live again
Free and fearless 'midst thy free and fearless children,
Sparing with them, as one people, grief and gladness,
    Joy and pain.

"Now we Jews, we English Jews, O Mother England,
Ask another boon of thee!
Let us share with them the danger and the glory;
Where thy best and bravest lead, there let us follow
    O'er the sea!

"For the Jew has heart and hand, our Mother England,
And they both are thine to-day—
Thine for life, and thine for death, yea, thine for ever!
Wilt thou take them as we give them, freely, gladly?
    England, say!"

[Footnote *: Mrs. Henry Lucas (reprinted in her *Talmudic Legends, Hymns and Paraphrases*. Chatto and Windus, 1908).]

I am well aware that in what I have written, though I have been careful to reinforce myself with Jewish authority, I may be running counter to that interesting movement which is called "Zionism." It is not for a Gentile to take part in the dissensions of the Jewish community; but I may be permitted to express my sympathy with a noble idea, and to do so in words written by a brilliant Israelite, Lord Beaconsfield: "I do not bow to the necessity of a visible head in a defined locality; but, were I to seek for such, it would not be at Rome. When Omnipotence deigned to be incarnate, the ineffable Word did not select a Roman frame. The prophets were not Romans; the Apostles were not Romans; she, who was blessed above all women—I never heard that she was a Roman maiden. No; I should look to a land more distant than Italy, to a city more sacred even than Rome."[*]

[Footnote *: *Sybil*, Book II., chapter xii.]

III

INDURATION

Though my heading is as old as Chaucer, it has, I must admit, a Johnsonian sound. Its sense is conveyed in the title of an excellent book on suffering called *Lest We Grow Hard*, and this is a very real peril against which it behoves everyone

> "Who makes his moral being his prime care"

to be sedulously on his guard. During the last four years we have been, in a very special way and degree, exposed to it; and we ought to be thankful that, as a nation, we seem to have escaped. The constant contemplation, even with the mental eye, of bloodshed and torture, has a strong tendency to harden the heart; and a peculiar grace was needed to keep alive in us that sympathy with suffering, that passion of mercy, which is the characteristic virtue of regenerate humanity. I speak not only of human suffering. Animals, it has been said, may have no rights, but they have many wrongs, and among those wrongs are the tortures which war inflicts. The suffering of all sentient nature appeals alike to humanitarian sympathy.

It has always seemed to me a signal instance of Wordsworth's penetrating thought "on Man, on Nature, and on Human Life," that he assigned to this virtue a dominant place in the Character of the Happy Warrior—

> "Who, doomed to go in company with Pain,
> And Fear, and Bloodshed, miserable train!
> Turns his necessity to glorious gain";

and who, "as more exposed" than others "to suffering and distress," is

> "Hence, also, more alive to tenderness."

This tribute to the moral nature of the Warrior, whether his warfare be on land or on sea or in the air, is as true to-day as when Wordsworth paid it. The brutal and senseless cry for "reprisals" which of late has risen from some tainted spots of the Body Politic will wake no response unless it be an exclamation of disgust from soldiers and sailors and airmen. Of course, everyone knows that there is a sense in which reprisals are a necessary part of warfare. Generation after generation our forefathers fought bow to bow and sword to sword and gun to gun against equally armed and well-matched foes; this was reprisal, or, if you prefer, retaliation. And when, in more recent times, the devilish ingenuity of science invented poisonous gas, there was nothing unmanly or unchivalrous in retorting on our German enemies with the hideous weapon which they had first employed.

But this is not the kind of reprisal which indurated orators demand. They contend that because the Germans kill innocent civilians, and women, and little children in English streets, Englishmen are to commit the same foul deeds in Germany. "It is hard," says the *Church Times*, "to say whether futility or immorality is the more striking characteristic of the present clamour for reprisals in the matter of air-raids.... Mr. Joynson Hicks would 'lay a German town in ashes after every raid on London,' and he is not much worse than others who scream in the same key." Nay, he is better than many of them. The people who use this language are not the men of action. They belong to a sedentary and neurotic class, who, lacking alike courage and mercy, gloat over the notion of torture inflicted on the innocent and the helpless.

A German baby is as innocent as an English baby, a German mother is as helpless as an English mother; and our stay-at-home heroes, safely ensconced in pulpits or editorial chairs, shrilly proclaim that they must be bombed by English airmen. What a function to impose on a band of fighters, peculiarly chivalrous and humane!

I refer to the pulpit because one gross and disgusting instance of clerical ferocity has lately been reported. A raving clergyman has been insolently parodying the Gospel which he has sworn to preach. Some of the newspapers commended his courage; and we do not know whether his congregation quitted the church or his Bishop rebuked him. Both results are possible, and I sincerely hope that the latter is true. The established and endowed teachers of religion have not always used their influence on the side of mercy; but on the question of reprisals I have observed with thankfulness that the Archbishop of Canterbury and the Bishop of London have spoken on the right side, and have spoken with energy and decision. They, at any rate, have escaped the peril of induration, and in that respect they are at one with the great mass of decent citizens.

I am no advocate of a mawkish lenity. When our soldiers and sailors and airmen meet our armed foes on equal terms, my prayers go with them; and the harder they strike, the better I am pleased. When a man or woman has committed a cold-blooded murder and has escaped the just penalty of the crime, I loathe the political intrigue which sets him or her free. Heavy punishment for savage deeds, remorseless fighting till victory is ours— these surely should be guiding principles in peace and war; and to hold them is no proof that one has suffered the process of induration.

Here I am not ashamed to make common cause with the stout old Puritan in *Peveril of the Peak:* "To forgive our human wrongs is Christian-like and commendable; but we have no commission to forgive those which have been done to the cause of religion and of liberty; we have no right to grant immunity or to shake hands with those who have poured forth the blood of our brethren."

But let us keep our vengeance for those who by their own actions have justly incurred it. The very intensity of our desire to punish the wrong-doer should be the measure of our unwillingness to inflict torture on the helpless and the innocent. "Lest we grow hard"—it should be our daily dread. "A black character, a womanish character, a stubborn character: bestial, childish, stupid, scurrilous, tyrannical." A pagan, who had observed such a character in its working, prayed to be preserved from it. Christians of the twentieth century must not sink below the moral level of Marcus Aurelius.

IV

FLACCIDITY

My discourse on "Induration" was intended to convey a warning which, as individuals, we all need. But Governments are beset by an even greater danger, which the learned might call "flaccidity" and the simple—"flabbiness."

The great Liddon, always excellent in the aptness of his scriptural allusions, once said with regard to a leader who had announced that he would "set his face" against a certain policy and then gave way, "Yes, the deer 'set his face,' but he did not 'set it as a flint'—rather *as a pudding*."

To set one's face as a pudding is the characteristic action of all weak Governments. Lord Randolph Churchill once attracted notice by enouncing the homely truth that "the business of an Opposition is to oppose." A truth even more primary is that the duty of a Government is to govern; to set its face, not as a pudding, but as a flint, against lawlessness and outrage; to protect the innocent and to punish the wrong-doer.

This is a duty from which all weak Governments shrink. If a Minister is not very sure of his position; if he is backed, not by a united party, but by a haphazard coalition; if he is unduly anxious about his own official future; if his eye is nervously fixed on the next move of the jumping cat, he always fails to govern. He neither protects the law-abiding citizen nor chastises the criminal and the rebel. In this particular, there is no distinction of party. Tories can show no better record than Whigs, nor Liberals than Conservatives. It is a question of the governing temper, which is as absolutely requisite to the character of the ruler as courage to the soldier or incorruptibility to the Judge.

It used to be held, and perhaps still is held, by what may be styled the toad-eating school of publicists, that this governing temper was an hereditary gift transmitted by a long line of ancestors, who in their successive generations had possessed it, and had used it on a large scale in the governance of England. "How natural," they exclaimed, "that Lord Nozoo, whose ancestors have ruled half Loamshire since the Conquest, should have more notion of governing men than that wretched Bagman, whose grandfather swept out the shop, and who has never had to rule anyone except a clerk and a parlourmaid!"

This sounded plausible enough, especially in the days when heredity was everything, and when ancestral habit was held to explain, and if necessary extenuate, all personal characteristics; but experience and observation proved it false. Pitt was, I suppose, the greatest Minister who ever ruled England; but his pedigree would have moved a genealogist to scorn. Peel was a Minister who governed so effectually that, according to Gladstone, who served under him, his direct authority was felt in every department, high or low, of the Administration over which he presided; and Peel was a very recent product of cotton. Abraham Lincoln was, perhaps, the greatest ruler of the modern world, and the quality of his ancestry is a topic fit only to be handled in a lecture on the Self-Made Men of History.

When we regard our own time, I should say that Joseph Chamberlain had, of all English statesmen I have ever known, both the most satisfactory ideal of government and the greatest faculty for exercising it. But the Cordwainers' Company was the school in which his forefathers had learnt the art of rule. Ancestral achievements, hereditary possessions, have nothing to do with the matter. What makes a man a ruler of men, and enables him to set his face as a flint against wrong-doing; is a faculty born in himself—"the soul that riseth with him, his life's star."

And it has no more to do with politics than with pedigree. Sydney Smith, though he was as whole-hearted a reformer as ever breathed, knew that sternness towards crime was an essential part of government, and after the Bristol Riots of 1831 he warned Lord Grey against flaccidity with great plainness of speech. "Pray do not be good-natured about Bristol. I must have ten people hanged, and twenty transported, and thirty imprisoned. You will save lives by it in the end."

It was a Tory Government which in the London Riots of 1866 made, as Matthew Arnold said, "an exhibition of mismanagement, imprudence, and weakness almost incredible." Next year the Fenians blew up Clerkenwell Prison, and the same acute critic observed: "A Government which dares not deal with a mob, of any nation or with any design, simply opens the floodgates to anarchy. Who can wonder at the Irish, who have cause to hate us, and who do not own their allegiance to us, making war on a State and society which has shown itself irresolute and feeble?"

But the head of that feeble State, the leader of that irresolute society, was the fourteenth Earl of Derby, whose ancestors had practised the arts of government for eight hundred years.

In Ireland the case is the same. Both parties have succeeded in governing it, and both have failed. Mr. Balfour has been justly praised for his vigour in protecting property and restoring order; but it was Lord Spencer and Sir George Trevelyan who, four years before, had caught and hanged the assassins of the Phœnix Park, and had abolished agrarian murder. It was, alas! a Liberal Government that tolerated the Ulster treason, and so prepared the way for the Dublin rebellion. Highly placed and highly paid flaccidity then reigned supreme, and produced its inevitable result. But last December we were assured that flaccidity had made way for firmness, and that the pudding had been replaced by the flint. But the transactions of the last few weeks—one transaction in particular[*]—seem worthy of our flabbiest days.

[Footnote *: A release for political objects.]

I turn my eyes homewards again, from Dublin to the House of Commons. The report of the Mesopotamia Commission has announced to the world a series of actions which every Briton feels as a national disgrace. Are the perpetrators of those actions to go unpunished? Are they to retain their honours and emoluments, the confidence of their Sovereign, and the approbation of his Ministers? If so, flaccidity will stand revealed as what in truth it has always been—the one quality which neutralizes all other gifts, and makes its possessor incapable of governing.

V

THE PROMISE OF MAY

This is the real season for a holiday, if holidays were still possible. It is a point of literary honour not to quote the line which shows that our forefathers, in the days of Chaucer, felt the holiday-making instinct of the spring, and that instinct has not been affected by the lapse of the centuries. It stirs us even in London, when the impetuous lilacs are bursting into bud, and the sooty sparrows chirrup love-songs, and "a livelier iris changes on the burnished dove"—or, to be more accurate, pigeon—which swells and straddles as if Piccadilly were all his own. The very wallflowers and daffodils which crown the costers' barrows help to weave the spell; and, though pleasure-jaunts are out of the question, we welcome a call of duty which takes us, even for twenty-four hours, into "the country places, which God made and not man."

For my own part, I am no victim of the "pathetic fallacy" by which people in all ages have persuaded themselves that Nature sympathized with their joys and sorrows. Even if that dream had not been dispelled, in prose by Walter Scott, and in verse by Matthew Arnold, one's own experience, would have proved it false.

"Alas! what are we, that the laws of Nature should correspond in their march with our ephemeral deeds or sufferings?" *The Heart of Midlothian.*

"Man must begin, know this, where Nature ends;
Nature and man can never be fast friends."[*]

[Footnote *: *In Harmony with Nature.*]

A funeral under the sapphire sky and blazing sun of June loses nothing of its sadness—perhaps is made more sad—by the unsympathetic aspect of the visible world. December does not suspend its habitual gloom because all men of goodwill are trying to rejoice in the Birthday of the Prince of Peace. We all can recall disasters and disappointments which have overcast the spring, and tidings of achievement or deliverance which have been happily out of keeping with the melancholy beauty of autumn.

In short, Nature cares nothing for the acts and sufferings of human kind; yet, with a strange sort of affectionate obstinacy, men insist on trying to sympathize with Nature, who declines to sympathize with them; and now, when she spreads before our enchanted eyes all the sweetness and promise of the land in spring, we try to bring our thoughts into harmony with the things we see, and to forget, though it be only for a moment, alike regrets and forebodings.

And surely the effort is salutary. With Tom Hughes, jovial yet thoughtful patriot, for our guide, we make our way to the summit of some well-remembered hill, which has perhaps already won a name in history, and find it "a place to open a man's soul and make him prophesy, as he looks down on the great vale spread out, as the Garden of the Lord, before him": wide tracts of woodland, and fat meadows and winding streams, and snug homesteads embowered in trees, and miles on miles of what will soon be cornfields. Far away in the distance, a thin cloud of smoke floats over some laborious town, and whichever way we look, church after church is dotted over the whole surface of the country, like knots in network.

Such, or something like it, is the traditional aspect of our fair English land; but to-day she wears her beauty with a difference. The saw is at work in the woodlands; and individual trees, which were not only the landmarks, but also the friends and companions of one's childhood, have disappeared for ever. The rich meadows by the tranquil streams, and the grazing cattle, which used to remind us only of Cuyp's peaceful landscapes, now suggest the sterner thought of rations and queues. The corn-fields, not yet "white to harvest," acquire new dignity from the thought of all that is involved in "the staff of life." The smoke-cloud over the manufacturing town is no longer a mere blur on the horizon, but tells of a prodigality of human effort, directed to the destruction of human life, such as the world has never known. Even from the towers of the village churches floats the Red Cross of St. George, recalling the war-song of an older patriotism—"In the name of our God we will set up our banners."[*]

[Footnote: Psalm xx. 5.]

Yes, this fair world of ours wears an altered face, and what this year is "the promise of May"? It is the promise of good and truth and fruitfulness forcing their way through "the rank vapours of this sin-worn mould." It is the promise of strong endurance, which will bear all and suffer all in a righteous cause, and never fail or murmur till the crown is won. It is the promise of a brighter day, when the skill of invention and of handicraft may be once more directed, not to the devices which destroy life, but to the sciences which prolong it, and the arts which beautify it. Above all, it is the promise of a return, through blood and fire, to the faith which made England great, and the law which yet may wrap the world in peace.

"For as the earth bringeth forth her bud, and as the garden causeth the things that are sown in it to spring forth; so the Lord God will cause righteousness and praise to spring forth before all the nations" (Isa. lxi. II).

VI

PAGEANTRY AND PATRIOTISM

Long years ago, when religious people excited themselves almost to frenzy about Ritualism, Mr. Gladstone surveyed the tumult with philosophic calm. He recommended his countrymen to look below the surface of controversy, and to regard the underlying principle. "In all the more solemn and stated public acts of man," he wrote, "we find employed that investiture of the acts themselves with an appropriate exterior, which is the essential idea of Ritual. The subject-matter is different, but the principle is the same: it is the use and adaptation of the outward for the expression of the inward." The word "ritual" is by common usage restricted to the ecclesiastical sphere, but in reality it has a far wider significance. It gives us the august rite of the Convocation, the ceremonial of Courts, the splendour of regiments, the formal usages of battleships, the silent but expressive language of heraldry and symbol; and, in its humbler developments, the paraphernalia of Masonry and Benefit Societies, and the pretty pageantry of Flag-days and Rose-days. Why should these things be? "Human nature itself, with a thousand tongues, utters the reply. The marriage of the outward and the inward pervades the universe."

The power of the outward reaches the inward chiefly through the eye and the ear. Colour, as Ruskin taught us, is not only delightful, but sacred. "Of all God's gifts to the sight of man, colour is the holiest, the most divine, the most solemn.... Consider what sort of a world it would be if all flowers were grey, all leaves black, and the sky *brown*." The perfection of form—the grace of outline, the harmony of flowing curves—appeals, perhaps, less generally than colour, because to appreciate it the eye requires some training, whereas to love colour one only needs feeling. Yet form has its own use and message, and so, again, has the solemnity of ordered movement; and when all these three elements of charm—colour and form and motion—are combined in a public ceremony, the effect is irresistible.

But the appeal of the inward reaches us not solely through the eye. The ear has an even higher function. Perhaps the composer of great music speaks, in the course of the ages, to a larger number of human hearts than are touched by any other form of genius. Thousands, listening enraptured to his strain, hear "the outpourings of eternal harmony in the medium of created sound." And yet again there are those, and they are not a few, to whom even music never speaks so convincingly as when it is wedded to suitable words; for then two emotions are combined in one appeal, and human speech helps to interpret the unspoken.

It is one of the deplorable effects of war that it so cruelly diminishes the beauty of our public and communal life. Khaki instead of scarlet, potatoes where geraniums should be, common and cheap and ugly things usurping the places aforetime assigned to beauty and splendour—these are our daily and hourly reminders of the "great tribulation" through which the nation is passing. Of course, one ought not to wish it otherwise. Not, indeed, "sweet," but eminently salutary, are these "uses of adversity," for they prevent us from forgetting, even if we were inclined to such base obliviousness, the grim realities of the strife in which we are engaged. And yet, and in spite of all this, beauty retains its sway over "the common heart of man." Even war cannot destroy, though it may temporarily obscure, the beauty of Nature; and the beauty of Art is only waiting for the opportunity of Peace to reassert itself.

To the prevailing uncomeliness of this war-stricken time a welcome exception has been made by the patriotic pageantry which, during the week now closed, has been enacted at Queen's Hall.[*] There were critics, neither malicious nor ill-informed, who contended that such pageantry was ill-timed. They advanced against it all sorts of objections which would have been quite appropriate if the public had been bidden to witness some colossal farce or burlesque; some raree-show of tasteless oddities, or some untimely pantomime of fairy-lore. What was really intended, and was performed, at a great cost of toil and organizing skill, was the opposite of all this. All the best elements of a great and glorious ceremonial were displayed—colour and form and ordered motion; noble music set to stirring words; and human voices lifted even above their ordinary beauty by the emotion of a high occasion. The climax, wisely ordered, was our tribute of gratitude to the United States, and never did the "Battle-hymn of the Republic" sound its trumpets more exultingly. For once, the word "Ritual" might with perfect propriety be separated from its controversial associations, and bestowed on this great act of patriotic pageantry. It was, in the truest sense, a religious service, fitly commemorating the entry of all the world's best powers into the crowning conflict of light with darkness.

[Footnote *: Under the direction of Madame Clara Butt (May, 1918).]

VII
FACT AND FICTION

N. B.—*These two stories are founded on fact; but the personal allusions are fictitious. As regards public events, they are historically accurate.*—G. W. E. R.

I

A FORGOTTEN PANIC

Friday, the 13th of September, 1867, was the last day of the Harrow holidays, and I was returning to the Hill from a visit to some friends in Scotland. During the first part of the journey I was alone in the carriage, occupied with an unlearnt holiday task; but at Carlisle I acquired a fellow-traveller. He jumped into the carriage just as the train was beginning to move, and to the porter who breathlessly enquired about his luggage he shouted, "This is all," and flung a small leathern case on to the seat. As he settled himself into his plate, his eye fell upon the pile of baggage which I had bribed the station-master to establish in my corner of the carriage—a portmanteau, a hat-box, a rug wrapped round an umbrella, and one or two smaller parcels—all legibly labelled

> G. W. E. RUSSELL,
>   Woodside,
>   Harrow-on-the-Hill.

After a glance at my property, the stranger turned to me and exclaimed: "When you have travelled as much as I have, young sir, you will know that, the less the luggage, the greater the ease." Youth, I think, as a rule resents overtures from strangers, but there was something in my fellow-traveller's address so pleasant as to disarm resentment. His voice, his smile, his appearance, were alike prepossessing. He drew from his pocket the *Daily News*, in those days a famous organ for foreign intelligence, and, as he composed himself to read, I had a full opportunity of studying his appearance. He seemed to be somewhere between thirty and forty, of the middle height, lean and sinewy, and, as his jump into the train had shown, as lissom as a cat. His skin was so much tanned that it was difficult to guess his natural complexion; but his closely cropped hair was jet-black, and his clean-shaven face showed the roots of a very dark beard. In those days it was fashionable to wear one's hair rather long, and to cultivate whiskers and a moustache. Priests and actors were the only people who shaved clean, and I decided in my mind that my friend was an actor. Presently he laid down his paper, and, turning to me with that grave courtesy which when one is very young one appreciates, he said: "I hope, sir, that my abrupt entry did not disturb you. I had a rush for it, and nearly lost my train as it was. And I hope what I said about luggage did not seem impertinent. I was only thinking that, if I had been obliged to look after portmanteaus, I should probably still be on the platform at Carlisle." I hastened to say, with my best air, that I had not been the least offended, and rather apologized for my own encumbrances by saying that I was going South for three months, and had to take all my possessions with me. I am not sure that I was pleased when my friend said: "Ah, yes; the end of the vacation. You are returning to college at Harrow, I see." It was humiliating to confess that Harrow was a school, and I a schoolboy; but my friend took it with great composure. Perfectly, he said; it was his error. He should have said "school," not "college." He had a great admiration for the English Public Schools. It was his misfortune to have been educated abroad. A French lycée, or a German gymnasium, was not such a pleasant place as Eton or Harrow. This was exactly the best way of starting a conversation, and, my schoolboy reserve being once broken, we chatted away merrily. Very soon I had told him everything about myself, my home, my kinsfolk, my amusements, my favourite authors, and all the rest of it; but presently it dawned upon me that, though I had disclosed everything to him, he had disclosed nothing to me, and that the actor, if I rightly deemed him so, was not very proud of his profession. His nationality, too, perplexed me. He spoke English as fluently as I did, but not quite idiomatically; and there was just a trace of an accent which was not English. Sometimes it sounded French, but then again there was a tinge of American. On the whole, I came to the conclusion that my friend was an Englishman who had lived a great deal abroad, or else an American who had lived in Paris. As the day advanced, the American theory gained upon me; for, though my friend told me nothing about himself, he told me a great deal about every place which we passed. He knew the industries of the various towns, and the events connected with them, and the names of the people who owned the castles and great country-houses. I had been told that this habit of endless exposition was characteristic of the cultured American. But, whatever was the nationality of my companion, I enjoyed his company very much. He talked to me, not as a man to a boy, but as an elder to a younger man; paid me the courtesy of asking my opinion and listening to my answers; and, by all the little arts of the practised converser, made me feel on good terms with myself and the world. Yankee or Frenchman, my actor was a very jolly fellow; and I only wished that he would tell me a little about himself.

When, late in the afternoon, we passed Bletchley Station, I bethought me that we should soon be separated, for the London and North-Western train, though an express, was to be stopped at Harrow in order to disgorge its load of returning boys. I began to collect my goods and to prepare myself for the stop, when my friend said, to my great joy, "I see you are alighting. I am going on to Euston. I shall be in London for the next few weeks. I should very much like to pay a visit to Harrow one day, and see your 'lions.'" This was exactly what I wished, but had been too modest to suggest; so I joyfully acceded to his proposal, only venturing to add that, though we had been travelling together all day, I did not know my friend's name. He tore a leaf out of a pocket-book, scrawled on it, in a backward-sloping hand, "H. Aulif," and handed it to me, saying, "I do not add an address, for I shall be moving about. But I will write you a line very soon, and fix a day for my visit." Just then the train stopped at the foot of the Hill, and, as I was fighting my way through the welter of boys and luggage on the platform, I caught sight of a smiling face and a waved hand at the window of the carriage which I had just quitted.

The beginning of a new school-quarter, the crowd of fresh faces, the greetings of old friends, and a remove into a much more difficult Form, rather distracted my mind from the incidents of my journey, to which it was recalled by the receipt of a note from Mr. Aulif, saying that he would be at Harrow by 2.30 on Saturday afternoon, the 21st of September. I met him at the station, and found him even pleasanter than I expected. He extolled Public Schools to the skies, and was sure that our English virtues were in great part due to them. Of Harrow he spoke with peculiar admiration as the School of Sheridan, of Peel, of Palmerston. What was our course of study? What our system of discipline? What were our amusements? The last question I was able to answer by showing him both the end of cricket and the beginning of football, for both were being played; and, as we mounted the Hill towards the School and the Spire, he asked me if we had any other amusements. Fives or racquets he did not seem to count. Did we run races? Had we any gymnastics? (In those days we had not.) Did we practise rifle-shooting? Every boy ought to learn to use a rifle. The Volunteer movement was a national glory. Had we any part in it?

The last question touched me on the point of honour. In those days Harrow was the best School in England for rifle-shooting. In the Public Schools contest at Wimbledon we carried off the Ashburton Challenge Shield five times in succession, and in 1865 and 1866 we added to it Lord Spencer's Cup for the best marksman in the school-teams. All this, and a good deal more to the same effect, I told Mr. Aulif with becoming spirit, and proudly led the way to our "Armoury." This grandly named apartment was in truth a dingy cellar under the Old Schools, and held only a scanty store of rifles (for the corps, though keen, was not numerous). Boyhood is sensitive to sarcasm, and I felt an uncomfortable twinge as Mr. Aulif glanced round our place of arms and said, "A gallant corps, I am sure, if not numerically strong. But this is your School corps only. Doubtless the citizens of the place also have their corps?" Rather wishing to get my friend away from a scene where he obviously was not impressed, and fearing that perhaps he might speak lightly of the Fourth Form Room, even though its panels bear the carved name of BYRON, I seized the opening afforded by the mention of the local corps, and proposed a walk towards the drill-shed.

This was a barn, very roughly adapted to military purposes, and standing, remote from houses, in a field at Roxeth, a hamlet of Harrow on the way to Northolt. It served both for drill-shed and for armoury, and, as the local corps (the 18th Middlesex) was a large one, it contained a good supply of arms and ammunition. The custodian, who lived in a cottage at Roxeth, was a Crimean veteran, who kept everything in apple-pie order, and on this Saturday afternoon was just putting the finishing touches of tidiness to the properties in his charge. Mr. Aulif made friends with him at once, spoke enthusiastically of the Crimea, talked of improvements in guns and gunnery since those days, praised the Anglo-French alliance, and said how sad it was that England now had to be on her guard against her former allies across the Channel. As the discourse proceeded, I began to question my theory that Aulif was an actor. Perhaps he was a soldier. Could he be a Jesuit in disguise? Jesuits were clean-shaved and well-informed. Or was it only his faculty of general agreeableness that enabled him to attract the old caretaker at the drill-shed as he had attracted the schoolboy in the train? As we walked back to the station, my desire to know what my friend really was increased momentarily, but I no more dared to ask him than I should have dared to shake hands with Queen Victoria; for, to say the truth, Mr. Aulif, while he fascinated, awed me. He told me that he was just going abroad, and we parted at the station with mutual regrets.

The year 1867 was conspicuously a year of Fenian activity. The termination of the Civil War in America had thrown out of employment a great many seasoned soldiers of various nationalities, who had served for five years in the American armies. Among these were General Cluseret, educated at Saint-Cyr, trained by Garibaldi, and by some good critics esteemed "the most consummate soldier of the day." The Fenians now began to dream not merely of isolated outrages, but of an armed rising in Ireland; and, after consultation with the Fenian leaders in New York, Cluseret came to England with a view to organizing the insurrection. What then befell can be read in Lathair, where Cluseret is thinly disguised as "Captain Bruges," and also in his own narrative, published in *Fraser's Magazine* for 1872. He arrived in London in January, 1867, and startling events began to happen in quick succession. On the 11th of February an armed party of Fenians attacked Chester Castle, and were not repulsed without some difficulty. There was an armed rising at Killarney. The police-barracks at Tallaght were besieged, and at Glencullen the insurgents captured the police-force and their weapons. At Kilmallock there was an encounter between the Fenians and the constabulary, and life was lost on both sides. There was a design of concentrating all the Fenian forces on Mallow Junction, but the rapid movement of the Queen's troops frustrated the design, and the general rising was postponed. Presently two vagrants were arrested on suspicion at Liverpool, and proved to be two of the most notorious of the Fenian leaders, "Colonel" Kelly and "Captain" Deasy. It was when these prisoners, remanded for further enquiry, were being driven under a strong escort to gaol that the prison-van was attacked by a rescue-party, and Sergeant Brett, who was in charge of the prisoners, was shot. The rescuers, Allen, Larkin, and Gould, were executed on the 2nd of November, and on the 1st of December Clerkenwell Prison was blown up, in an ineffectual attempt to liberate the Fenian prisoners confined in it. On the 20th of December Matthew Arnold wrote to his mother, "We are in a strange uneasy state in London, and the profound sense I have long had of the hollowness and insufficiency of our whole system of administration does not inspire me with much confidence." The "strange uneasy state" was not confined to London, but prevailed everywhere. Obviously England was threatened by a mysterious and desperate enemy, and no one seemed to know that enemy's headquarters or base of operations. The Secret Societies were actively at work in England, Ireland, France, and Italy. It was suspected then—it is known now, and chiefly through Cluseret's revelations—that the isolated attacks on barracks and police-stations were designed for the purpose of securing arms and ammunition; and, if only there had been a competent General to command the rebel forces, Ireland would have risen in open war. But a competent General was exactly what the insurgents lacked; for Cluseret, having surveyed the whole situation with eyes trained by a lifelong experience of war, decided that the scheme was hopeless, and returned to Paris.

Such were some—for I have only mentioned a few—of the incidents which made 1867 a memorable year. On my own memory it is stamped with a peculiar clearness.

On Wednesday morning, the 2nd of October, 1867, as we were going up to First School at Harrow, a rumour flew from mouth to mouth that the drill-shed had been attacked by Fenians. Sure enough it had. The caretaker (as I said before) lived some way from the building, and when he went to open it in the morning he found that the door had been forced and the place swept clean of arms and ammunition. Here was a real sensation, and we felt for a few hours "the joy of eventful living"; but later in the day the evening papers, coming down from London, quenched our excitement with a greater. It appeared that during the night of the 1st of October, drill-sheds and armouries belonging to the Volunteer regiments had been simultaneously raided north, south, east, and west of London, and all munitions of war spirited away, for a purpose which was not hard to guess. Commenting on this startling occurrence, the papers said: "We have reason to believe that one of the ablest of the Fenian agents has been for some time operating secretly in the United Kingdom. He has been traced to Liverpool, Glasgow, Edinburgh, and London. It is believed at Scotland Yard that he organized these attacks on Volunteer headquarters, arranged for the arms and ammunition to be transferred by a sure hand to Ireland, and has himself returned to Paris." A friend of mine who had gone up to London to see a dentist brought back a *Globe* with him, and, as he handed it to me, he pointed out the passage which I have just cited. As I read it, my heart gave a jump—a sudden thrill of delicious excitement. My friend Mr. Aulif must be the Fenian agent who had organized these raids, and I, who had always dreamed romance, had now been brought into actual contact with it. The idea of communicating my suspicions to anyone never crossed my mind. I felt instinctively that this was a case where silence was golden. Fortunately, none of my school-fellows had seen Mr. Aulif or heard of his visit; and the old caretaker of the drill-shed had been too much gratified by talk and tip to entertain an unworthy thought of "that pleasant-spoken gentleman."

Soon the story of these raids had been forgotten in the far more exhilarating occurrences at Manchester and Clerkenwell which closed the year; and the execution of Michael Barrett on the 26th of May, 1868 (the last public execution, by the way), brought the history of Fenianism in England to an end.

As I looked back on my journey from Scotland, and my walk round Harrow with Mr. Aulif, I thought that the reason why he did not arrange for our School-armoury to be attacked was that he would not abuse the confidence of a boy who had trusted him. Perhaps it really was that the rifles were too few and the risks too many.

The year 1870 found me still a Harrow boy, though a tall one; and I spent the Easter holidays with my cousins, the Brentfords, in Paris. They were a remarkable couple, and if I were to mention their real name, they would be immediately recognized. They had social position and abundant means and hosts of friends; but, acting under irresistible impulse, they had severed themselves from their natural surroundings, and had plunged into democratic politics. It was commonly believed that Brentford would not have committed himself so deeply if it had not been for his wife's influence; and, indeed, she was one of those women whom it is difficult to withstand. Her enthusiasm was contagious; and when one was in her company one felt that "the Cause," as she always called it without qualifying epithet, was the one thing worth thinking of and living for. As a girl, she had caught from Mrs. Browning, and Swinburne, and Jessie White-Mario, and the authoress of *Aspromonte*, a passionate zeal for Italian unity and freedom; and, when she married, her enthusiasm fired her husband. They became sworn allies both of Garibaldi and of Mazzini, and through them were brought into close, though mysterious, relations with the revolutionary party in Italy and also in France. They witnessed the last great act of the Papacy at the Vatican Council; and then, early in 1870, they established themselves in Paris. French society was at that moment in a strange state of tension and unrest. The impending calamity of the Franco-German War was not foreseen; but everyone knew that the Imperial throne was rocking; that the soil was primed by Secret Societies; and that all the elements of revolution were at hand, and needed only some sudden concussion to stir them into activity. This was a condition which exactly suited my cousin Evelyn Brentford. She was "at the height of the circumstances," and she gathered round her, at her villa on the outskirts of Paris, a society partly political, partly Bohemian, and wholly Red. "Do come," she wrote, "and stay with us at Easter. I can't promise you a Revolution; but it's quite on the cards that you may come in for one. Anyhow, you will see some fun." I had some difficulty in inducing my parents (sound Whigs) to give the necessary permission; but they admitted that at seventeen a son must be trusted, and I went off rejoicing to join the Brentfords at Paris. Those three weeks, from the 12th of April to the 4th of May, 1870, gave me, as the boys now say, "the time of my life." I met a great many people whose names I already knew, and some more of whom we heard next year in the history of the Commune. The air was full of the most sensational rumours, and those who hoped "to see the last King strangled in the bowels of the last priest" enjoyed themselves thoroughly.

My cousin Evelyn was always at home to her friends on Sunday and Wednesday evenings, and her rooms were thronged by a miscellaneous crowd in which the Parisian accent mingled with the tongues of America and Italy, and the French of the southern provinces. At one of these parties I was talking to a delightful lady who lived only in the hope of seeing "the Devil come for that dog" (indicating by this term an Imperial malefactor), and who, when exhausted by regicidal eloquence, demanded coffee. As we approached the buffet, a man who had just put down his cup turned round and met my companion and me face to face. Two years and a half had made no difference in him. He was Mr. Aulif, as active and fresh as ever, and, before I had time to reflect on my course, I had impulsively seized him by the hand. "Don't you remember me?" I cried. He only stared. "My name is George Russell, and you visited me at Harrow." "I fear, sir, you have made a mistake," said Aulif, bowed rather stiffly to my companion, and hurried back into the drawing-room. My companion looked surprised. "The General seems put out—I wonder why. He and I are the greatest allies. Let me tell you, my friend, that he is the man that the Revolution will have to rely on when the time comes for rising. Ask them at Saint-Cyr. Ask

Garibaldi. Ask McClellan. Ask General Grant. He is the greatest General in the world, and has sacrificed his career for Freedom." "Is his name Aulif?" "No; his name is Cluseret."

Next day at *déjuner* I was full of my evening's adventure; but my host and hostess received it with mortifying composure. "Nothing could be more likely," said my cousin Evelyn. "General Cluseret was here, though he did not stay long. Perhaps he really did not remember you. When he saw you before, you were a boy, and now you look like a young man. Or perhaps he did not wish to be cross-examined. He is pretty busy here just now, but in 1867 he was constantly backwards and forwards between Paris and London trying to organize that Irish insurrection which never came off. England is not the only country he has visited on business of that kind, and he has many travelling names. He thinks it safer, for obvious reasons, to travel without luggage. If you had been able to open that leather case in the train you would probably have found nothing in it except some maps, a toothbrush, and a spare revolver. Certainly that Irish affair was a *fiasco*; but depend upon it you will hear of General Cluseret again."

And so indeed I did, and so did the whole civilized world, and that within twelve months of the time of speaking; but there is no need to rewrite in this place the history of the Commune.

II

A CRIMEAN EPISODE

It was eight o'clock in the evening of the 5th of April, 1880, and the Travellers' Club was full to overflowing. Men who were just sitting down to dinner got up from their tables, and joined the excited concourse in the hall. The General Election which terminated Lord Beaconsfield's reign was nearing its close, and the issue was scarcely in doubt; but at this moment the decisive event of the campaign was announced. Members, as they eagerly scanned the tape, saw that Gladstone was returned for Midlothian; and, as they passed, the news to the expectant crowd behind them, there arose a tumult of excited voices.

"I told you how it would be!" "Well, I've lost my money." "I could not have believed that Scotsmen would be such fools." "I'm awfully sorry for Dalkeith." "Why couldn't that old windbag have stuck to Greenwich?" "I blame Rosebery for getting him down." "Well, I suppose we're in for another Gladstone Premiership." "Oh, no fear. The Queen won't speak to him." "No, Hartington's the man, and, as an old Whig, I'm glad of it." "Perhaps Gladstone will take the Exchequer." "What! serve under Hartington? You don't know the old gentleman's pride if you expect that;" and so on and so forth, a chorus of excited and bewildering exclamations. Amid all the hurly-burly, one figure in the throng seemed quite unmoved, and its immobility attracted the notice of the throng. "Well, really, Vaughan, I should have thought that even you would have felt excited about this. I know you don't care much about politics in a general way, but this is something out of the common. The Duke of Buccleuch beaten on his own ground, and Gladstone heading straight for the Premiership! Isn't that enough to quicken your pulse?"

But the man whom they saluted as Vaughan still looked undisturbed. "Well, I don't think I ever was quite as much in love with Dizzy as you were; and as to the Premiership, we are not quite at the end yet, and *Alors comme alors.*"

Philip Vaughan was a man just over fifty: tall, pale, distinguished-looking, with something in his figure and bearing that reminded one of the statue of Sidney Herbert, which in 1880 still stood before the War Office in Pall Mall. He looked both delicate and melancholy. His face was curiously devoid of animation; but his most marked characteristic was an habitual look of meditative abstraction from the things which immediately surrounded him. As he walked down the steps of the club towards a brougham which was waiting for him, the man who had tried in vain to interest him in the Midlothian Election turned to his nearest neighbour, and said: "Vaughan is really the most extraordinary fellow I know. There is nothing on earth that interests him in the faintest degree. Politics, books, sport, society, foreign affairs—he I never seems to care a rap about any of them; and yet he knows something about them all, and, if only you can get him to talk, he can talk extremely well. It is particularly curious about politics, for generally, if a man has once been in political life, he feels the fascination of it to the end." "But was Vaughan ever in political life?" "Oh yes I suppose you are too young to remember. He got into Parliament just after he left Oxford. He was put in by an old uncle for a Family Borough— Bilton—one of those snug little seats, not exactly 'Pocket Boroughs,' but very like them, which survived until the Reform Act of 1867." "How long did he sit?" "Only for one Parliament—from 1852 to 1857. No one ever knew why he gave up. He put it on health, but I believe it was just freakishness. He always was an odd chap, and of course he grows odder as he grows older." But just at that moment another exciting result came, trickling down the tape, and the hubbub was renewed.

Philip Vaughan was, as he put it in his languid way, "rather fond of clubs," so long as they were not political, and he spent a good deal of his time at the Travellers', the Athenæum, and the United Universities, and was a member of some more modern institutions. He had plenty of acquaintances, but no friends—at least of his own age. The Argus-eyed surveyors of club-life noticed that the only people to whom he seemed to talk freely and cheerfully were the youngest members; and he was notoriously good-natured in helping young fellows who wished to join his clubs, and did his utmost to stay the hand of the blackballer.

He had a very numerous cousinship, but did not much cultivate it. Sometimes, yielding to pressure, he would dine with cousins in London; or pay a flying visit to them in the country; but in order, as it was supposed to avoid these family entanglements, he lived at Wimbledon, where he enjoyed, in a quiet way, his garden and his library, and spent most of the day in solitary rides among the Surrey hills. When winter set in he generally vanished towards the South of Europe, but by Easter he was back again at Wimbledon, and was to be found pretty often at one or other of his clubs.

This was Philip Vaughan, as people knew him in 1880. Some liked him; some pitied him; some rather despised him; but no one took the trouble to understand him; and indeed, if anyone had thought it worth while to do so, the attempt would probably have been unsuccessful; for Vaughan never talked of the past, and to understand him in 1880 one must have known him as he had been thirty years before.

In 1850 two of the best known of the young men in society were Arthur Grey and Philip Vaughan. They were, and had been ever since their schooldays at Harrow, inseparable friends. The people to whom friendship is a sealed and hopeless mystery were puzzled by the alliance. "What have those two fellows in common?" was the constant question, "and yet you never see them apart." They shared lodgings in Mount Street, frequented the same clubs, and went, night after night, to the same diners and balls. They belonged, in short, to the same set: "went everywhere," as the phrase is, and both were extremely popular; but their pursuits and careers were different. Grey was essentially a sportsman and an athlete. He was one of those men to whom all bodily exercises come naturally, and who attain perfection in them with no apparent effort. From his earliest days he had set his heart on being a soldier, and by 1850 had obtained a commission in the Guards. Vaughan had neither gifts nor inclinations in the way of sport or games. At Harrow he lived the life of the intellect and the spirit, and was unpopular accordingly. He was constantly to be found "mooning," as his schoolfellows said, in the green lanes and meadow-paths which lie between Harrow and Uxbridge, or gazing, as Byron had loved to gaze, at the sunset from the Churchyard Terrace. It was even whispered that he wrote poetry.

Arthur Grey, with his good looks, his frank bearing, and his facile supremacy on the cricket-ground and in the racquet-court, was a popular hero; and of all his schoolfellows none paid him a more whole-hearted worship than the totally dissimilar Philip Vaughan. Their close and intimate affection was a standing puzzle to hard and dull and superficial natures; but a poet could interpret it.

> "We trifled, toiled, and feasted, far apart
> From churls, who, wondered what our friendship meant;
> And in that coy retirement heart to heart
> Drew closer, and our natures were content."[*]

[Footnote *: William Cory.]

Vaughan and Grey left Harrow, as they had entered it, on the same day, and in the following October both went up to Christ Church. Neither contemplated a long stay at Oxford, for each had his career cut out. Grey was to join the Guards at the earliest opportunity, and Vaughan was destined for Parliament. Bilton was a borough which the "Schedule A" of 1832 had spared. It numbered some 900 voters; and, even as the electors of Liskeard "were commonly of the same opinion as Mr. Eliot," so the electors of Bilton were commonly of the same opinion as Lord Liscombe.

The eighth Lord Liscombe was the last male member of his family. The peerage must die with him; but his property, including the "Borough influence," was at his own disposal. His only sister had married a Mr.

Vaughan, and Lord Liscombe, having carefully watched the character and career of his nephew Philip Vaughan, determined to make him his heir. This was all very well; no one had a word to say against it, for no more obvious heir could be suggested. But when it became known that Lord Liscombe meant to bring Philip Vaughan into Parliament for Bilton there was great dissatisfaction. "What a shame," people said, "to disturb old Mr. Cobley, who has sat so long and voted so steadily! To be sure, he is very tiresome, and can't make himself heard a yard off, and is very stingy about subscriptions; and, if there was some rising young man to put into his seat, as the Duke of Newcastle put Gladstone, it might be all very well. But, really, Philip Vaughan is such a moody, dreamy creature, and so wrapped up in books and poetry, that he can never make a decent Member of Parliament. Politics are quite out of his line, and I shouldn't wonder if Lord Liscombe contrived to lose the seat. But he's as obstinate as a mule; and he has persuaded himself that young Vaughan is a genius. Was there ever such folly?"

Lord Liscombe had his own way—as he commonly had. Mr. Cobley received a polite intimation that at the next election he would not be able to rely on the Liscombe interest, and retired with a very bad grace, but not without his reward; for before long he received the offer of a baronetcy (which he accepted, as he said, to please his wife), and died honourably as Sir Thomas Cobley. Meanwhile Lord Liscombe, who, when he had framed a plan, never let the grass grow under his feet, induced Philip Vaughan to quit Oxford without waiting for a degree, made him address "Market Ordinaries" and political meetings at Bilton, presented him at the Levee, proposed him at his favourite clubs, gave him an ample allowance, and launched him, with a vigorous push, into society. In all this Lord Liscombe did well, and showed his knowledge of human nature. The air of politics stirred young Vaughan's pulses as they had never been stirred before. What casual observers had regarded as idle reveries turned out to have been serious studies. With the theory of English politics, as it shaped itself in 1852 when Lord Derby and Disraeli were trying to restore Protection, Vaughan showed himself thoroughly acquainted; and, as often happens when a contemplative and romantic nature is first brought into contact with eager humanity, he developed a faculty of public speaking which astonished his uncle as much as it astonished anyone, though that astute nobleman concealed his surprise. Meanwhile, Grey had got his commission. In those days officers of the Guards lived in lodgings, so it was obvious for Grey and Vaughan to live together; and every now and then Grey would slip down to Bilton, and by making himself pleasant to the shop-keepers, and talking appropriately to the farmers, would act as his friend's most effective election-agent. The Dissolution came in July, 1852, and Philip

Vaughan was returned unopposed for the Free and Independent Borough of Bilton.

Then followed a halcyon time. The two friends had long known that they had only one heart between them; and now, living under the same roof and going into the same society, they lived practically one life. There was just enough separation to make reunion more delightful—a dull debate at the House for Vaughan, or a dusty field-day at Aldershot for Grey; but for both there was the early gallop in Rotten Row, the breakfast which no third person ever shared, the evening of social amusement, and the long, deep, intimate talk over the last cigar, when the doings of the day were reviewed and the programme for to-morrow was sketched.

Grey had always been popular and always lighthearted. Vaughan, as a schoolboy and an undergraduate, had been unpopular and grave. But now people who knew them both observed that, at any rate as far as outward characteristics showed, the two natures were becoming harmonized. Vaughan was a visibly lighter, brighter, and more companionable fellow; and Grey began to manifest something of that manly seriousness which was wanted to complete his character. It is pleasant to contemplate "one entire and perfect chrysolite" of happiness, and that, during these bright years of opening manhood, was the rare and fragile possession of Philip Vaughan and Arthur Grey.

John Bright was once walking with one of his sons, then a schoolboy, past the Guards' Memorial in Waterloo Place. The boy asked the meaning of the single word inscribed on the base, CRIMEA. Bright's answer was as emphatic as the inscription: "A crime." There is no need to recapitulate in this place the series of blunders through which this country, in Lord Clarendon's phrase, "drifted towards war." Month by month things shaped themselves in a way which left no reasonable doubt about the issue. The two friends said little. Deep in the heart of each there lay the conviction that an event was at hand which would "pierce even to the dividing asunder of soul and spirit, and of the joints and marrow." But each held the conviction with a difference. To Grey it meant the approach of that to which, from the days of his chivalrous boyhood, he had looked forward, as the supreme good of life—the chance of a soldier's glory and a soldier's death. To Vaughan it meant simply the extinction of all that made life worth living. Each foresaw an agony, but the one foresaw it with a joy which no affection could subdue; the other with a despair which even religion seemed powerless to relieve. Before long silence became impossible. The decision of the Cabinet was made known. Two strong and ardent natures, which since boyhood had lived in and on one another, were forced to admit that a separation, which might be eternal, "was nigh, even at the doors." But there was this vital difference between the two cases— the one had to act; the other only to endure.

On the 22nd of February, 1854, the Guards sailed from Southampton, and on the 27th of March war between England and Russia was formally declared.

The events of the next two years must be compressed into a few lines. To the inseparable evils of war—bloodshed and sickness—were added the horrors of a peculiarly cruel winter. Five-sixths of the soldiers whom England lost died from preventable diseases, and the want of proper food, clothing, and shelter. Bullets and cholera and frost-bite did their deadly work unchecked. The officers had at least their full share of the hardships and the fatalities. What the Guards lost can be read on the walls of the Chapel at Wellington Barracks and in the pedigrees of Burke's Peerage. For all England it was a time of piercing trial, and of that hope deferred which maketh the heart sick. No one ever knew what Vaughan endured, for he as too proud to bare his soul. For two years he never looked at a gazette, or opened a newspaper, or heard a Ministerial announcement in the House of Commons, or listened to a conversation at his club, without the sickening apprehension that the next moment he would know that Arthur Grey was dead. Letters from Grey reached him from time to time, but their brave cheerfulness did nothing to soothe his apprehensions. For they were few and far between; postal communication was slow and broken, and by the time a letter reached him the hand which had penned it might be cold in death. Yet, in spite of an apprehensive dread which had become a second nature to Philip Vaughan, the fatal news lingered. Weeks lengthened into months, and months into two years, and yet the blow had not fallen. It was not in Philip's nature to "cheer up," or "expect the best," or "hope against hope," or to adopt any of the cheap remedies which shallow souls enjoy and prescribe. Nothing but certainty could give him ease, and certainty was in this case impossible. Nervousness, restlessness, fidgetiness, increased upon him day by day. The gossip and bustle of the House of Commons became intolerable to him. Society he had never entered since Grey sailed for the Crimea. As in boyhood, so again now, he felt that Nature was the only true consoler, and for weeks at a time he tried to bury himself in the wilds of Scotland or Cumberland or Cornwall, spending his whole day in solitary walks, with Wordsworth or the *Imitatio* for a companion, and sleeping only from physical exhaustion.

In the early part of 1856 the newspapers began to talk of peace. Sebastopol had fallen, and Russia was said to be exhausted. The Emperor of the French had his own reasons for withdrawing from the contest, and everything seemed to turn on the decision of Lord Palmerston. This tantalizing vision of a swift fulfilment of his prayers seemed to Philip Vaughan even less endurable than his previous apprehensions. To hear from hour to hour the contradictory chatter of irresponsible clubmen and M.P.'s was an insupportable affliction; so, at the beginning of the Session, he "paired" till Easter, and departed on one of his solitary rambles. Desiring to cut himself off as completely as possible from his usual environment, he left no address at his lodgings, but told his servant that when he wanted his letters he would telegraph for them from the place, whatever it might be, where he was halting. He kept steadily to his plan, wandering over hill and dale, by lake and river, and steeping his soul in "the cheerful silence of the fells." When he lighted on a spot which particularly took his fancy, he would halt there for two or three days, and would send what in those day was called "a telegraphic despatch" from the nearest town. In response to the despatch he would receive from his servant in Mount Street a package containing all the letters which had been accumulating during the fortnight or three weeks since he last telegraphed. One day in April, when he opened the customary package, he found in it a letter from Arthur Grey.

"The General has just told us that peace is practically settled. If this proves true, you will not get another letter from me. I presume we shall be sent home directly, and I shall make straight for London and Mount Street, where I expect I shall find you. Dear old chap, I can guess what you have been going through; but it looks as if we should meet again in this world after all."

What this letter meant to Philip Vaughan they only know who have been through a similar experience; and words are powerless to express it

After the first bewilderment of joy had subsided, Philip began to study the practical bearings of the letter. By a comparison of the date within and the post-mark outside, the letter appeared to have been a long time on the way, and another delay had occurred since it had arrived at Mount Street. It was possible that peace might have been actually concluded. News in those days took long to travel through Scottish glens, and Vaughan had never looked at a paper since he left England. It was conceivable that the Guards were already on their homeward voyage—nay, it might even be that they were just arriving, or had arrived, in London. The one clear point was that Vaughan must get home. Twenty miles on his landlord's pony brought him to a telegraph-office, whence he telegraphed to his servant, "Returning immediately," and then, setting his face southward, he travelled as fast as steamers and express trains would take him. As he travelled, he picked up the news. Peace had been concluded on the 30th of March, and some of our troops were homeward bound; some had actually arrived. The journey seemed unnaturally long, and it was dark when the train rattled into Euston Station.... In a bewildered mood of uncertainty and joy, he rang the bell in Mount Street. His servant opened the door. "You're just in time, sir. You will find him in the drawing-room."

The drawing-room of the lodging-house had always been Grey's sitting-room, and during his absence Vaughan had studiously kept it in it accustomed order. There were some stags' heads on the walls, and a fox's brush with a label; a coloured print of Harrow, and engravings of one or two Generals whom Grey had specially honoured as masters of the art of war; the book-case, the writing-desk, the rather stiff furniture, were just as he had left them. Philip flung open the door with a passionate cry of "Arthur! Arthur! At last! Thank God——" But the words died on his lips.

In the middle of the room, just under the central chandelier, there was a coffin supported by trestles, with its foot towards the door. On the white pillow there lay the still whiter face of a corpse, and it was the corpse of Arthur Grey.

What happened immediately after no one ever precisely knew. Not even the waiting servant had heard the street-door shut.

Next morning the park-keepers found a young man lying on the grass in Hyde Park, drenched to the skin with the night's heavy rain, unconscious, and apparently dying. The papers in his pockets proved that he was Philip Vaughan. A long and desperate illness followed, and for months both life and reason trembled in the balance. Lord Liscombe hurried up to London, and Vaughan's servant explained everything. Arthur Grey had been taken ill on the homeward voyage. The symptoms would now be recognized as typhoid, but the disease had not then been diagnosed, and the ship's surgeon pronounced it "low fever." He landed at Southampton, pushed his way to London, arrived at his lodgings more dead than alive, and almost immediately sank into the coma from which he never recovered. It was impossible to communicate with Vaughan, whose address was unknown; and when his telegram arrived, announcing his instant return, the servant and the landlady agreed that he must have heard the news from some other source, and was hurrying back to see his friend before he became invisible for ever. "You're just in time" meant just in time to see the body, for the coffin was to be closed that evening.

The struggle was long and desperate, but Vaughan had on his side youth and a constitution, not strong indeed, but unweakened by profligacy. By slow degrees his nervous system rallied from the shock, and after a long period of foreign travel he returned, in great part, to his former habits. Only he could not and would not re-enter the House of Commons, but announced his retirement, on the score of health, at the next Election. Soon afterwards he inherited Lord Liscombe's fortune, made over Liscombe Abbey and its responsibilities to a distant cousin, and insensibly glided into the way of living which I described at the outset. Two years after the Election of 1880 he died at Rome, where he had been spending the winter. The attack of fever to which he succumbed was not peculiarly severe, but the doctor said that he made no effort to live, and was in fact worn out, though not by years.

Nobody missed him. Nobody lamented him. Few even said a kind word about him. His will expressed only one personal wish—that he might be buried by the side of Arthur Grey. But his executors thought that this arrangement would cause them a great deal of trouble, and he rests in the English cemetery at Rome.